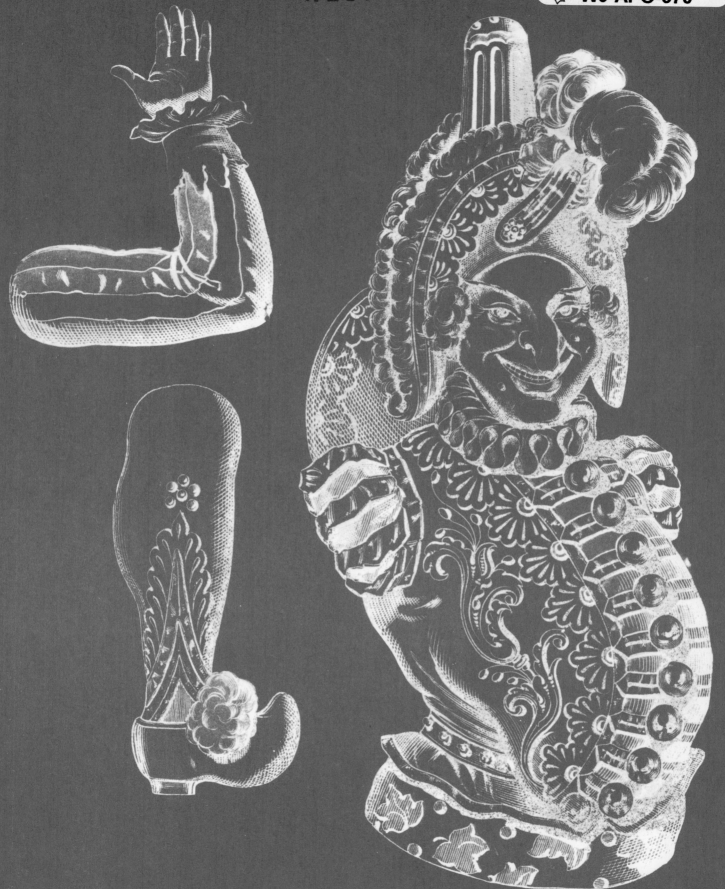

To Rose Winter

MISS CARR as ARIEL.

London Pub.d by C.Hodgson, N.o 22. Macclesfield Street, City Road.

Marian Hannah Winter

THE THEATRE OF MARVELS

Preface by

MARCEL MARCEAU

BENJAMIN BLOM, INC.

New York

Original Copyright © 1962 by Olivier Perrin, Paris

English translation by Charles Meldon,

© 1964 by OLIVIER PERRIN, INC.

L.C. Catalog No.: 64-18759

French edition designed by Brigitte Chabrol.
American edition designed by Fred Streitfeld.

PRINTED IN THE UNITED STATES OF AMERICA

Table of Contents

Acknowledgments

Many kind people have helped me at various stages of my work. Mr. Lincoln Kirstein, Director of the New York City Ballet, and Mr. George Balanchine, encouraged the publication of my first article on the *Theatre of Marvels* in *Dance Index*. Mrs. Marian Eames, the Editor, could not have been more cooperative. Olivier Perrin had the courage to publish my second article on the *Theatre of Marvels* and later this book in its original French edition.

The late Dr. William B. Van Lennep, the Curator of the Harvard Theatre Collection, followed and aided my research from its inception. With unfailing intuition he searched out key documents. His successor, Miss Helen D. Willard, has continued to extend both the courtesies and friendship which have always made the Harvard Theatre Collection one of my preferred research libraries.

In France, the good fortune of having the *Theatre of Marvels* accepted by the Sorbonne as subject for my doctoral thesis was equalled by obtaining Monsieur Pierre Lavedan as mentor in its preparation. Monsieur Etienne Souriau, Professor at the Sorbonne, also gave me expert advice.

I should never have been able to carry through my work in Paris without the help of Madame Madeline Horn-Monval, former Curator of the Rondel Collection at the *Bibliothèque de l'Arsenal*, and her successor, Monsieur André Veinstein; of Monsieur Jean Adhémar, Curator of the Print Collection at the *Bibliothèque Nationale*; of Mademoiselle Boschot, Assistant Curator, *Bibliothèque de l'Opéra*; of Monsieur Jacques Wilhelm, Director of the *Musée Carnavalet*; and of the regretted Pierre Michaut, President of the Society of Dance Critics of Paris.

I have always been able to count on friends such as Monsieur Paul Prouté, Monsieur Jacques Fort and Mr. George Chaffee, whose portfolios were put at my disposal. My thanks also to Monsieur Léon Chancerel, President of the Society for Theatre History, and my friends and colleagues of the *Club du Cirque*, particularly Monsieur Henry Thétard and Mademoiselle Marthe Vesque. Monsieur Pierre-Louis Duchartre sustained me with his encouragement and aided me in the pursuit of documents.

Dr. Carlo Ravelli of the *Biblioteca Civica* of Turin, placed exceptional unpublished material at my disposal. The personnel of the *Biblioteca Theatrale Livia Simoni* at La Scala, and that of the Bertarelli Print Collection of the *Castello Sforzesco* in Milan, uncovered some of my most fascinating documents.

Mrs. Genevieve Oswald, Curator of the Dance Collection, New York Public Library, kindly searched out some of the American documents. Mr. George Nash, Curator of the Enthoven Collection, Victoria and Albert Museum, and his assistant, Miss Johnson, extended the courtesies of that collection.

Brigitte Chabrol was responsible for everything from editorial chores to layout designs in the French edition; Margery White did much the same indispensable work for the English version.

All the foregoing still cannot make me forget that my mother, Rose Winter, first introduced me to the world of the Marvelous. She is no longer here to see this book in print, but without her it would never have existed.

PREFACE

The Theatre of Marvels is the theatre peopled by shadows and lights in which wicked genies, fairies, heroes and gods mingle; where angels and demons link hands and, with beating wings and tossing manes, pass through dream clouds in a shower of stardust. Hannah Winter, in a superb study, brings its history to life again. Let us slip silently into our place beside her and close our eyes. . . .

When Man sought to explain the mysteries of life, he created myth, reviving the essence of theatre by his symbols. At great moments in his history, through the elements—skies and seas, winds and tempests, objects and beasts—he rediscovered the shape of the legends. Thus was born the splendor of the miracle, the cradle of Marvels.

A phantasmagorical vision which takes hold of us when a world is born; transports the heart with astonishment and plunges it to depths beyond reason . . . overwhelms it by the unexpected . . . such is the Theatre Of Marvels. Thus events are situated between reality and fiction. The fantastic is beyond its own boundaries, now relying not on its vision but on its knowledge, with that Cyclops eye making the abstract visual and enlarging the concrete by bringing it face to face with the illimitable realms of imagination.

Starting with the mundane object, subjugated and concrete, Man—that eternal wanderer, dominated and dominating—projects his nature out of space into time, irradiating shapes and volumes with a poetic aureole, presenting to the eye undreamt of possibilities. Thus passions are matched by tempests, the natural becomes fantastic, and dreams rediscover their mystery. Ancient theatres, fairground theatres, shadow theatres, magic lanterns, deus ex machina, trapdoors to Hell, temples through which winged Mercury passes, or Jupiter, as a centaur, trampling Oedipus and his mystery underfoot, the Riddle of the Sphinx divined, signs of the Zodiac, visions of enchantment, diabolical plots—how you gratify the vision of Man seeking relief in the Age of Anxiety!

This world of the Marvelous, with a thousand aspects of vistas and colors in which Man reaches out to space, strikes sparks from the drama, and gathers into his hand the shifting sands of dreams— thus the eye becomes the crucible for fantastic shapes and the imagination surrenders itself to the soothing ministrations of the Graces. Children's cardboard theatres give birth to the multiple worlds of Jules Verne, linking the Thousand and One Nights to English and Chinese gardens, and, beneath the underseas tempests, the card houses collapse and are rebuilt to a wave of applause in which stalls and gallery share the same imagery.

When the man in the street forgets his dream, the theatre becomes a myth and a dispenser of signs: on the Boulevard du Crime, "velvet hands and horny hands" make the heart beat.

Two centuries ago, Molière at Versailles projected the fairy play between two Commedia dell'Arte intrigues, but the accents of high comedy were already knocking at Man's door like Fate. Shakespeare's fools and witches, amid their forests, overturned the forms of classical tragedy; men's souls turned faint, the mind escaped like vapor . . . the centuries sigh.

The Theatre of Marvels transports the spectator and overwhelms him with the wonderment of miracle. This phantasmagoric crowd moves across the wormeaten boards lit by wavering footlights, garbing itself in different styles from the Exotic to the Supernatural.

Fairs spring up amid palaces, Chinese shadow plays haunt our grandfathers' nights, performing wild animals become the companions of the Man-god, the "monster" who has turned actor. Time passes, but the struggle remains a noble one. The Seventh Art, which expected to dethrone the cardboard theatre, becomes a rival; the clans form, the clown is master after God under the Big Top, the dancer finds inspiration and glides in space, the mime arms himself with silence and takes a kick at the imaginary adversary, the magicians are wedded to their mystic boxes: the Opera and the Opera-Comique vie with one another—"Their music and singing are full of silences, as the silences are full of music."

The Theatre of Marvels remains watchful. Starting from one style, it rediscovers the miracle which links the effrontery of illusion with the baseless fragility of the dramatic instant. It knows that this feast for the eye is evanescent yet terribly actual, a moment suspended in space like the sword of Damocles. With a reminiscent heart it relives its memories.

Ye gods and planets who fly over the Theatre of Marvels, add your heavenly movements to those of the machines consigned to the flies. Jupiter, raise the dead; Saturn, God of Hunting; Mercury, God of Commerce; and Mars, God of War, and you Bulls, Fishes and Capricorns, linked by the Scales to the fields or the sea; near heavens, silvery moons, glowing suns, Saturn by Lead, Jupiter by fire and sword, signs and symbols linked by countless ages—open men's eyes to the apocalyptic world brought forth from the depths of volcanos which submerged the earth beneath its wars. Man created the theatre which broke the chains of his own limitations, anticipating the future, enlarging the poetical to epic proportions, turning song into light and action into silence. From the mundane object to the mysterious object, from Nature to Science, the Cyclops image turns into cinemascope.

Evanescent shadows of Méliès, Eisenstein and Robert Houdin, elves of the Douanier Rousseau, Charlie Chaplin's magic wand, Pierrot's smock, pantomime theatre masks, buffooneries, ballet and spangles, burn brightly under the circus tents; and you too, music-hall lights, unreal perukes lying in magic chests, Columbines, Harlequins, Macchiavelian worlds, Don Juan leaving Hell and greeting Faust, Don Quixote dreaming of the moon, Mephistopheles astride interplanetary missiles, giant universes—you all emerge from beneath the same cloak.

In this world in which thought sows the action and walks with giant's strides, Man ponders; he re-creates form through his need for stability, sets bounds to the temporal, makes the spiritual concrete and engenders the style that is the mark of his genius. Everything starts from what is within reach of his hand: here are the gardens of Allah, Aladdin's lamp, the flying carpet, the giant balloon, mysteries transformed into passions. Every object links man to the love of his profession, material things enable him to set off in quest of his dream, to fathom the impenetrable. Classical, Romantic, fairy and acrobatic pantomime, with its Bengal lights, places Man at the center of the action, holding him by Love, but also by gesture, to the heart of space, setting in motion the image-makers or heroes who—serving as models for marionettes—await the three echoing knocks that signal to Harlequin to doff his cloak. Thus the actor of Marvels creates the happening and assembles the picture in a moment, for he holds the universe in the hollow of his hand. Time stops for him, and his whisper projects the fantastic.

Everything that takes possesion of our hearts and minds, everything that sets the Last Judgment in motion, everything that is born and dies, everything that places the man from the gutter onto the Palace steps, he owes to his own creation. Everything miraculous that destiny has composed is due to this artifice of the Marvelous. As well as these volleys of sound and light, there are other actors of the Marvelous who project their silence. These themselves on the arena of the stage and display pictures of the universe which remain in every spectator's heart, because—to the mimes—action supplements the dream, the invisible becomes visible and the abstract concrete, the poetic illusion brings in harvests, the blades of wheat bend under the storm, dream is confounded with reality, and in the winged weight of silence, the laws of space overtime time. . . . The vision of the impossible stretches forth its hand to Love the Sorcerer, and Icarus in his fall joins Prometheus.

Man's genius, transitory and fragile, will be eternal so long as an angel from Heaven remains in the Theatre of Marvels, a veritable "seeing" brother guiding his blind brother toward the summits of a world on the march and eager for light. And Time who halts his progress, forgetting that everything is transient and mortal, will remain fixed in the soul's memory so long as the Theatre of Marvels endures.

MARCEL MARCEAU

Foreword

THE Theatre of Marvels is the realm of the realized fantastic. It is a classically essential pure escapism, a swinging door marked *Entrance* on one side and *Exit* on the other. One side opens on other-world, supernatural or exotic habitats, which man attempts to reproduce literally in tangible, visual form, defying time, space and natural forces. On the other side man plays the part of supernatural power, and attempts to create human attributes in such unlikely subjects as dogs, elephants, fleas, horses and machinery called automata; or vies with the supernatural by means of magic, legerdemain, juggling and the defiance of gravity. Acrobats, ballet dancers, equestrians and animal trainers, stage designers and magicians are the ideal initiators and interpreters of the Theatre of Marvels, which is a theatre not only of the fantastic but of the impossible.

It defies time by going back into the past or projecting a Wellsian future. It defies space and plunges into Vernesian ocean depths or volcano hearts. It is always spectacular and "popular." It achieves Karma through well-oiled machinery instead of mystic introspection.

This book will relate the history of the Theatre of Marvels and re-illumine its transient fantastic world as it was at its creation: the three literary and iconographic categories—Exotic, Troubadour and Supernatural—which characterize its development; miming, production, and the direction of masses of "supers," which are its essential elements; the climates in which it thrives; typical productions as revealed by scenarios, literary notices and contemporary illustrations, as well as the difficulties and triumphs of its creators. In particular, this book will reveal the part played by France in the evolution of a theatre, freed from the shackles imposed by the spoken word [which long delighted the Western world, and still does, in its vestigial manifestations.]

11

THE PANTOMIME QUADRILLE

PERFORMED NIGHTLY, AMIDST ROARS OF LAUGHTER, AT JULLIEN'S PROMENADE CONCERTS.

(Courtesy A & B Booksellers)

A simple line-up of the basic characters in English pantomime: Pantaloon, Columbine, Harlequin, the Good Fairy and Clown. Illustrated music title.

One of the earliest American theatrical prints published by Elton whose stationery shop is sometimes called "The Theatrical Print Depository." Elton himself signed this etching of William Myers, a circus clown of the 1840's—1850's, who is shown performing at Blanchard's Amphitheatre.

Mr. MYERS as CLOWN.

Blanchards Amphitheatre

Harvard Theatre Collection

Drawn in the Gardens, on the night of August the 19th 1833 by Robert Cruikshank Esqr

C. H. SIMPSON, ESQ. M.C.R.G.V.

For upwards of 36 Years — with a distant view of his Colossal Likeness in Variegated Lamps.

C. H. SIMPSON, ESQ., Master of Ceremonies at Vauxhall for 36 years. Without benefit of electric lights, this larger-than-life likeness was composed of variegated lamps hung on the branches of trees. Simpson engaged many of the greatest fairground performers for the Vauxhall programs.

"Drawn in the gardens on the night of August the 19th, 1833, by Robert Cruikshank."

THE ORRINS.

GEORGE.   EDWARD.

PERFORMED AS REPRESENTED WITHOUT THE ASSISTANCE OF CAPS

W. Uma

ACROBATIC MARVELS.

HABANA-CUBA   MARZO 1874.

A EDUAR...   A JORJE W. ORRIN
Po...   Por efectuar
EL MILA...   EL MILAGRO DEL SIGLO XIX
PR...   PRESENTADA
JOSE...   JOSE ALBISU·

CHAPTER I

In America: 1790-1860

FRENCH influence on ballet was sovereign in America until 1860. The language of dance, like that of the circus, is understood everywhere (*"les pieds n'ont pas d'accent"*), so that there is nothing astonishing in the number of French dancers, acrobats and ballet-masters who emigrated to America, especially around 1790. However, it is surprising how many famous names from the French and other European fairgrounds appear on American programs between 1790 and 1800.

The name of Alexandre Placide, a famous tightrope dancer, mime and pantomime writer, is prominent in American dance annals. He arrived in North America toward the end of 1791, via Santo Domingo, with his companion *"Le Petit Diable,"* a clown-animal trainer of the fairground tribe of the Spinacutas, a "Madame Placide" aged 14 (a dancer), and a few assistants. (1)

"The first people to raise rope dancing to a fine art," said the *Chroniqueur désoeuvré* of Placide and the first "Petit Diable." "But much as these two vagabonds are in demand with their talent, they are nevertheless universally shunned. Were they not known to be rope dancers from Nicolet's, you would think when meeting them on the boulevards that you were in a forest, surrounded by cut-throats. Insulting everyone, cheating those to whom they are indebted, rioting in all the ramparts dramshops, where they get drunk with the scum of the earth—that's how they carry on."

However, it was such vagabonds, and especially their director Placide, who were to establish French spectacle in America so successfully that the English dancing mimes were reduced to secondary roles and had to seek employment from the French performers. The first performances of the Placide troupe, given in circuses and theatres, were based upon feats of strength and skill, rope dancing and tumbling. They were so successful that New World theatre managers called upon Placide as soon as their takings started to dwindle.

Placide's "wife," Suzanne Vaillande, ran off with the handsome Louis Douvillier. A singer and actor, who danced sufficiently well to figure regularly in ballets and pantomimes, he had arrived in the United States early in 1793. After a spectacular duel with Douvillier, the indefatigable Placide made a new conquest. In 1794 the theatrical world rejoiced at a most romantic elopement when Placide, then about fifty, married a young miss of sixteen, Catherine Wrighten, daughter of a famous English singer, who considered herself a member of the aristocracy of the theatre and was indignant at having a rope-dancing son-in-law. Placide, nothing daunted, started a course of training which carried his wife to the top rank of women dancers and actresses in America.

Placide offered his adopted country its finest patriotic masque (Charleston, Feb. 9, 1798)—*Americania and Elutheria*. The anonymous libretto survives in a pamphlet; the cast of characters and "program" seem to indicate that Placide had seen either the published text of Jacques-Louis David's great pageant-like celebrations of the French Revolution, or more likely those of pantomimes inspired by them.

AMERICANIA AND ELUTHERIA

Jelemmo and Arianthus, great winged spirits attendant on Americania
           Mr. Cleveland & Mr. Jones
Offa, chief of the Alleganian Satyrs   Mr. Jones
Musidorus, the Alleganian Hermit, the only mortal in the piece
                Mr. Whitlock
Horbla, chief of the dancing spirits   Mr. Placide
Damonello, Lucifero, Horrendum, Zulpho, Dancing Satyrs
      Messrs. Hughes, Tubbs, J. Jones, M'Kenzie
Americania, Genius of America, residing since the Creation on the
  summit of the Allegani   Mrs. Cleveland
Hybla, chief of the Hemmadriads, or wood nymphs, and Principal
  Dancer   Mrs. Placide
Tintoretto, Luciabella, Juberaia, Ariella and Tempe, dancing nymphs
       Mrs. Hughes, Mrs. Edgar, Mrs. Arnold, etc.
Elutheria, Goddess of Liberty, who flies to the arms of Americania
  for Protection   Mrs. Whitlock

"Hybla, a mountain nymph, desirous to see a mortal, implores Offa, a satyr, to procure that pleasure. Offa deludes an old hermit up to the summit of the Allegani Mts. to a great rock, inhabited by Genii, or aerial spirits, the chief of whom, called Americania, understanding that the old hermit is ignorant of the American Revolution, commands her domestics to perform an allegorical masque for his information.

In Act First . . . A Grand Dance of nymphs and satyrs, who will form a group of the most whimsical kind.

In Act Second . . . A meeting taking place between Elutheria, the Goddess of Liberty, and Americania, who descend on clouds on opposite sides.

A pas de deux, between the satyr Horbla and the nymph Hybla, the whole to conclude with a general dance of the nymphs and satyrs, a pas de deux by a young master and lady; and a pas de trois, by Mrs. Placide, Mr. Placide, and Mr. Tubbs."

The masque within the masque referred to in the above program portrayed the defeat of Typhon, Genius of Tyranny, and Fastidio, Genius of Pride, by Eltherius, Commander-in-Chief of the American forces, assisted by Galiana, Genius of France, and Fulmenifer, a scientific spirit apotheosizing Benjamin Franklin. Fulmenifer, with his electric rod, vanquishes Typhon and Fastidio, after

Nº 80   THE BLOOD RED KNIGHT

London Pub. by J. REDINGTON. 208 Hoxton Old Town.

"The Blood Red Knight" (first produced at Astley's in 1810) embodied the English "troubadour style." London enjoyed chivalric pomp as greatly as Paris; even in the 1850s (period of the Redington "tuppence coloured" above) the "knights" were still featured.

which an incense "brewed from fragments of their clipped wings" is offered up as a restorative to Elutheria. These characters are not listed in the program, but are in the published libretto.

The ballets, pantomimes and operettas put on by Placide, and the music of Grétry, Philidor, Dalayrac, Monsigny and Duni that he introduced to America, do him honor. Out of sheer vanity he gave tightrope performances until 1802. He was manager of a theatre in Charleston and became owner of the Variétés in New Orleans. Founder of a theatrical dynasty, he became both respectable and respected, sometimes even giving interviews to the press. His son Henry, an elegant "gentleman actor," starred in England and America; of his daughters, Jane was a gifted actress and Caroline married a banker.

The Francisquis, Vals, Dumoulins (or Dumoulains), Douvilliers, Corbys and Légés also played a part in this triumph, as did Charles Cicéri, a French scene painter and designer of Italian origin, like his famous younger cousin, P.-L. Cicéri, in Paris.

French influence did not decline subsequently, despite the importance assumed by the English pantomime or "harlequinade." The latter, given the impetus of Grimaldi's genius, revolved increasingly around the clown, with a strong tendency to include comic scenes demanding considerable knowledge of contemporary life in London. French pantomime, which conversely relied on local color and developed the visual aspects of the art, became increasingly popular. The chronologies of spectacular entertainments of all types became almost identical in France and America. Thus, in 1794, a Philadelphia Theatre bill [2] announces: *"The Grand French Pantomime 'La Fôret Noire,' by Mr. Arnold."* The date is of some interest, because *La Fôret Noire* is a pantomime that tends toward melodrama. Now, according to the French scripts, it was first performed in Paris at the Ambigu-Comique in 1801, and its author, Arnould-Mussot (Audinot's co-manager at the Ambigu-Comique) had been dead since 1795. It seems unlikely that the French production of his play would be staged

only after his death, or that an American performance preceded the Paris one. The inference is that the French players arrived in America around 1790, their pockets crammed with scripts of Parisian successes. Similarly, Audinot's pantomime *Dorothée,* first performed at the Foire Saint-Laurent in 1782 and revived at the Ambigu-Comique in 1790, appears on the American stage about 1792. *La Belle Dorothée or Maternal Affection* [sic], and some fifty pantomimes from the same source, were still being played in Philadelphia in 1797.

A new word, "Melodrama," appears on the bills in 1800, and the name of Guilbert de Pixérécourt becomes synonymous with a new theatrical form, a melange of scenery, music, ballet, combats and processions, accompanied by improbable but highly moral plots: *Victor or the Child of the Forest, Coelina, The Daughter of the Exile,* and many more, were translated and played in America immediately after their first performances in Paris.

Two Paris theatres appear as special attractions in American advertising: "The Theatre of the Porte-Saint-Martin" and "The Grand Opera of Paris." They enjoyed a reputation in American publicity comparable to that of the "Great Haymarket Theatre" (the London Opera) and the two "patent theatres," Covent Garden and Drury Lane.

If the French could not act in English, they could and did extend their monopoly to all branches of wordless theatre—music, dancing and the circus. Newspaper advertisements, programs and music-shop advertisements between 1800 and 1850 inform us that one of the five most popular composers in America at that time was D. F. Aumer. Moreover, French dancers continued to pour in: Labottière from Bordeaux, the Fleurys, Duports, Manfredis (French fairground performers of Piedmontese origin settled in France since 1750), the Roussets, the Petipas, etc. Céline Céleste, the dancer and mime who was to become the darling of the American public for some twenty years, arrived in 1827. The Ravel troupe, which toured America for thirty years with Mazurier's pantomime-ballets and with acrobatic ballets, tumbling and rope dancing, influenced two generations of American artists. Fairy plays like *Les Sept Châteaux du Diable* and the countless creations of the Cogniard brothers, such as *La Biche aux Bois,* maintained their place on the American stage until around 1855.

The circus, always and everywhere the most international entertainment, was from the outset a melange of English, French, Spanish, Italian, German, Dutch and American artists. In America, Pépin and Breschard's circus was already renowned in 1803, while from 1840 on the great circuses and Boulevard theatres in France welcomed the acrobatic rider Levi North, the animal tamer Van Amburgh, and the acrobatic Risleys.

Thus in 19th-century America ballet was not limited to simple ballet or to pantomime-ballet, but joined forces with melodrama and its offshoot, the fairy play; it was anticipated by the public and formed an integral part of the entertainment. In Van Bellen's words it was indeed the "kernal of dramatic art and its promordial strength." It was the essential Theatre of Marvels, from which ballet, combined with the other elements of pure spectacle, could not be separated.

American posters, mid-19th century. As in France, they were usually printed in some large city, without any text, and taken on the road by the travelling companies who filled in place names and dates of performance as appropriate.

The "Underseas Kingdom" in "La Biche au Bois, féerie" by the Cogniard brothers. (Porte-Saint-Martin, 1845) It was from a Paris revival of this "spectacular" that Jarrett and Palmer bought the scenery and costumes which were used for "The Black Crook," and pre-determined certain of its scenes.

SPALDING & ROGERS' CIRCUS FLEET

FLOATING PALACE

INTERIOR VIEW OF

FLOATING PALACE

SPALDING & ROGERS' NEW RAIL ROAD CIRCUS.

Les Artistes des Cirques Americains a leurs freres, les Artistes de l'Europe, Salut:

Le Cirque est le divertissement populaire de l'Amérique puisque c'est naturellement celui des pays nouveaux colonisés parmi les travaux et les périls.

Les premiers colons Américains s'appuyèrent sur la fortitude, l'activité, la patience, le courage, qualités qui se trouvent au fondement du Cirque. Supporter un climat rigoureux, soutenir les fatigues prolongées de la chasse, tenir tête au fiéroce sauvage, tout ceci demande la même force et la même agilité qui sont indispensables à l'écuyer et au gymnaste. Jusqu'à nos jours les pionniers intrépides de l'Ouest font à leur tour les expériences de la generation précédente et nourrissent de la sorte indirectement le goût pour les jeux du Cirque. Même dans les États plus vieux, ou l'opulence permet une culture et une élégance plus considérable, le Cirque tient encore aux affections du peuple, comme il arrivera toujours dans les communautés ou l'on sait apprécier l'adresse et la bravoure. Les Jeux Olympiques et les luttes de Gladiateurs fleurissaient aux jours les plus glorieux de la Grèce et de Rome; a Paris même, ce siège des arts et des sciences le Cirque tient un rang distingué. Le robuste chasseur de nos prairies doit être encore bien plus sensible aux traits qu'il reconnait comme essentiels de son existence.

Il y a dans les États-Unis vingt deux Cirques, divers dans leur grandeur et leurs prétentions, mais tous emploient de grands capitaux et exigent de grandes dépenses courantes. Les statistiques nous font voir que plus de trois millions de piastres sont placés sur cette profession, que les dépenses s'en approchent près de deux millions de piastres par an, et que les recus en gros se montent à peu près à un million cinq cent mille piastres. La direction des Cirques Américains s'accommode aux exigences du climat, à l'étendue du pays, et au caractère du peuple. Sinon pendant l'hiver on ne l'établit pas dans les villes. L'été ils parcourent le pays; ils passent d'une ville principale à l'autre et voyagent plus ou moins par vingt milles, ayant une cavalcade royale qui compte quelquefois deux cents personnes et chevaux, et ils donnent, chaque jour, deux belles representations sous un pavillon ample quoique simple, que l'on élève et que l'on ôte tous les jours. De cette manière les hameaux les plus éloignés sont visités tous les étés par plusieurs Cirques qui sont précédés quelques semaines à l'avance par des coureurs qui annoncent au moyen des gazettes et des Affiches le jour de la représentation. Il s'y assemble, au jour fixé, une foule de spectateurs qui viennent de cinquante milles à la ronde, et qui même dans les régions les moins habitées comptent plusieurs milliers.

Parmi les compagnies de Cirque de l'Amérique deux des plus grandes et intreprenantes sont celles de M. M. Smith, Quick & Nathans de New York et des M. M. Spalding et Bidwell de la Nouvelle Orléans. L'un et l'autre de ces compagnies ont déjà envoyé dans les pays lointains, particulièrement en Angleterre, dans l'Amérique du Sud, et aux Indes Occidentales, des expéditions qui ont eu un succès merveilleux; et tous deux maintiennent souvent trois ou quatre divers établissements qui donnent des représentations simultanées dans les diverses parties des États-Unis. Ceux ils possèdent à présent les deux Cirques les plus grands dans ce pays; ils contiennent plus de dix cents personnes et chevaux. L'un d'eux particulièrement (que l'on appelle le "Cirque Européen" parce que la plupart de ses artistes sont Européens) fait les progrès les plus imposants par toute l'étendue du pays. Ceux ci jusqu'à la guerre civile possédaient sur le Mississippi quatre magnifiques bateaux-à-vapeur, que l'on avait fait bâtir pour ces divertissements, et qui y étaient spécialement adaptés. L'un d'eux (le "Floating Palace") une immense amphithéâtre, était fourni d'un auditoire élégant, d'un balcon, d'un par et, de galeries, d'un cirque, d'écuries, de salons. Il était éclairé au gaz, et à même de contenir trois mille personnes. Le second (le "James Raymond") un grand hôtel flottant, servait à l'usage des artistes et des employés du Cirque. Le troisième (le "Banjo") un beau théâtre ayant une scène complète, des décorations etc., était adapté à la production des comédies du Cirque. Enfin, le quatrième (la "Gazelle") un petit bateau-à-vapeur, l'avant coureur lequel devançant par plusieurs milles cette flotte colossale, en annonçait l'approche. Par ces moyens les villes principales sur les bords du fleuve et de ses tributaires (près de vingt mille milles d'eaux navigables) étaient mises à même de jouir chaque année, des représentations du Cirque. Pendant l'été ces représentations avaient lieu dans les parties du Nord, pendant l'hiver dans celles du Sud. Fréquemment la population presque entière d'un comté s'embarquait, et après que l'on avait fait partir le bateau les représentations avaient lieu, et elles ne furent jamais mieux achevées ni mieux appréciés sous quelque pavillon que ce soit sur terre. Il y a d'autres associations administrées avec beaucoup d'entreprise, lesquelles jouissent de grandes ressources et d'une haute consideration. On n'a fait mention que de ces deux parceqú elles sont peut-être celles qui sont les plus dignes de consideration, et se sont fait particulièrement distinguées par leur noble générosité, en s'engageant à payer les depenses pour envoyer à l'Exposition Universelle presque tous les artistes les plus célèbres du Cirque Américain.

Il y a dans les États-Unis près de six cents écuyers et gymnastes de profession, tous plus ou moins célèbres, le rang relatif de chacun étant déterminé et bien connu des directeurs et du public, par le moyen de contestations amicales, l'un avec l'autre pour la suprématie dans leur profession. Un pareil concours détermine de suite le mérite comparatif des principaux artistes. Les appointements des champions sont considerables, celui, par exemple, de M. James Robinson, a été cinq cents piastres par semaine. Toutefois, il n'est pas besoin de dire qu'un pareil salaire n'est pas moins rare qu'un pareil artiste. Les directeurs et les artistes du Cirque Américain de Paris feront leur possible pour aider de leurs avis ou de leur conseil les artistes Européens qui auraient l'intention de faire visite aux États-Unis, ou les artistes étrangers trouvent partout une réception cordiale et une rémunération généreuse.

Comme il arrive à tout le monde, les artistes du Cirque Américain ont tous chéri l'espoir de visiter à quelque époque de leur vie, Paris, cette demeure du bon goût et de l'élégance, ou le peuple sait si bien encourager le courage et l'habilité. De temps en temps quelque artiste Américain qui y a séjourné a rapporté à son retour des récits si glorieux de la splendeur de la capitale du beau monde, de la sympathie des Parisiens pour le génie, et de l'éclat des Cirques Français, que le désir universel d'avoir part à toute cette gloire en est venu au comble lorsque l'on a publié l'annonce de l'Exposition Universelle. Un échange réciproque des idées sur ce sujet eut lieu entre tous les champions et les artistes principaux, et il en resulta la decision que les depenses élevées qu'exigeait une organisation si étendue, et le manque de capacité administrative si nécessaire pour les présenter convenablement au public empêcheraient de faire le voyage souhaité. Les choses en étaient là, lorsque M. M. Spalding et Bidwell et M. M. Smith Quick & Nathans, ces directeurs si riches et si dévoués aux interets du public se présentèrent heureusement. Ils offrirent avec une noble libéralité non seulement d'emener à Paris les champions et leurs rivaux, toutes depenses defrayées, mais de leur payer en outre un salaire liberal, et de pourvoir convenablement à leur introduction au public, à la charge que les artistes se missent sous leur direction et se tinssent prêts à rencontrer leurs frères les artistes de l'Europe dans un concours amical pour la suprématie dans leur profession par tout le monde.

Conformément à ce pacte, les champions des Cirques en Amérique tendent par ceci une invitation cordiale aux artistes de l'Europe, qui excellent dans les départemens variés du Cirque, à un Tournoi International que l'on propose de célébrer à Paris pendant la grande Exposition. Aucun esprit de vanité, de vanterie, ou d'arrogance ne dicte cette proposition; elle provient du désir sincère des artistes Américains de faire connaissance sociale et artistique avec leurs contemporains Trans-Atlantiques, et d'une ambition louable de se mesurer avec les artistes de l'hémisphère oriental, dans une contestation amicale. Même s'ils sont vaincus ils s'estimeront heureux de s'être mesurés avec la chevalerie de la profession en Europe. Des vainqueurs ils tâcheront d'apprendre à vaincre dans les contestations futures. Quelques lauriers qu'ils remportent, ils les porteront modestement. Ils apportent avec eux un Cirque d'Été commode et portatif, unique dans son dessin, élégant dans ses arrangements, et propre à la production des spectacles équestres et à la convenance des spectateurs. On espère qu'un tel concours des artistes du Cirque aura une tendance d'élever la profession et d'inspirer une ambition salutaire, et qu'il sera conforme à l'esprit et aux objets de l'Exposition Universelle, tandis que les vainqueurs remporteront leurs honneurs en présence d'une assemblée des gens les plus distingués de toutes les parties du monde civilisé.

Pour rendre complète cette entreprise, laquelle à cause de son étendue et de sa portée a un caractère national, et pour la rendre tout-à-fait Américaine en personel et en materiel, et aussi afin qu'elle se recommande au public (dont l'interet dans le tournoi est peut être naturellement moindre que celui des artistes) les directeurs apporteront avec eux les spécialités variées qui sont propres à l'Amérique; ils introduiront les caractéristiques des Indiens de l'Ouest, des Nègres du Sud, la chasse au Bison, l'équitation au cheval sauvage, les mystères du War-Trail, les Aborigènes, et les divertissements des affranchis des plantations.

Espérants un bon accueil, les artistes Américains ont l'honneur d'exprimer aux artistes de l'Europe leurs sentiments remplis de respect et de consideration.

A French mid-19th century press clipping on the American circus.

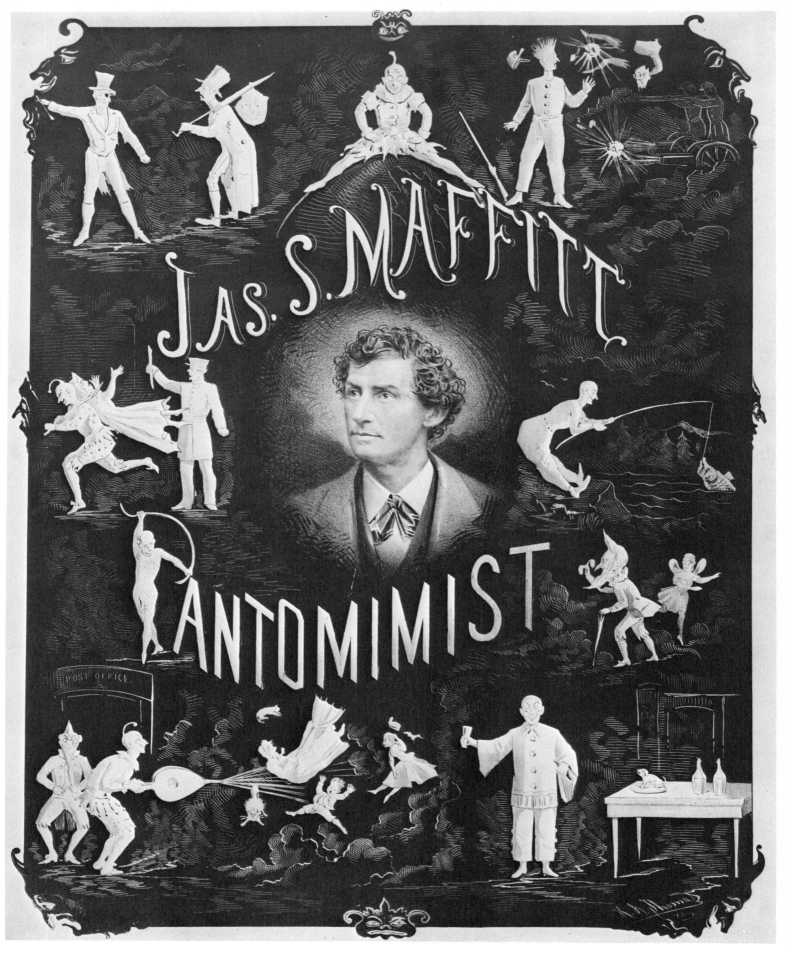

JAMES S. MAFFITT, actor and pantomimist (1832-1897). His style recalls that of Parisian mimes of the same period and the early animated cartoons of Emile Reynaud.

MONSIEUR BIHIN, THE BELGIUM GIANT.

[Now performing at the Adelphi Theatre in the Piece entitled *The Giant of Palestine*, a Spectacle, admirably arranged by MR. EDWARD STIRLING.]

The above Engraving is an exact representation of the manner in which this extraordinary Giant disperses Twelve of his Antagonists, who all beset him at once, but who are all scatteted by the brawny arms of Mons. BIHIN like sand before a hurricane.

Harvard Theatre Collection

MONSIEUR BIHIN, THE BELGIAN GIANT also had melodramas tailored to his dimensions. "The above engraving is an exact representation of the manner in which this extraordinary Giant dispersed Twelve of his Antagonists, who all beset him at once, but who are all scattered by the brawny arms of Mons. Bihin like sand before a hurricane." After having toured al over Europe, he made his New York debut in 1840.

A water color of Harvey (or Hervey) Leach, known as Signor Hervio Nano (1804-1847), as Alnain in "The Gnome Fly," This American dwarf became a brilliant acrobat, with the specialty of seeming to climb up perpendicular walls. He appeared in melodramas built around physique and talents. He played in Paris, London and Brussels, and toured the entire Italian peninsular in the role of Wamba, the Fire Spirit.

Harvard Theatre Collection

CHAPTER II

The Three Styles

THE EXOTIC

FROM the beginning of the 17th century, exotic people and animals were a feature of the travelling charlatan's retinue. The charlatan himself, who might be a quack doctor, dispenser of "cure-alls" or tooth-puller, was usually Italian (genuine or fraudulent—the Italians were greatly reputed as doctors at the time). A "Moroccan" or a "Turk," the one no more authentic than the other, accompanied the master and joined in a short performance called the "parade" before the sales pitch began. A trained monkey usually completed the team. The parade grew in importance, and by mid-18th century it had become so elaborate that Noverre was able to write of the ballets which had been incorporated: ". . . the tricksters and quack medicine peddlers count more on the appeal of their ballets than on that of their nostrums; the entrechats are what attract the public."

The musical accompaniment of trumpets, bugles, violins or guitars, and the exotic aspect of the troupe's female contingent—which the charlatan would recruit from Spain, Italy or England—lured the idlers. The Pont-Neuf, the fairs of Saint-Laurent and Saint-Germain, and certain public squares were the centres of activity in Paris, as the market places were in towns en route. The magician's booth at Saint-Germain in the mid-17th century diverted the public who "walked between a double rank of magic dens, decorated with toads, black cats, skeletons and large stuffed lizards, and where, on payment of a *sou*, the sorcerer in a pointed hat would predict the future through a "Mouth of Truth" in *papier-mâché*."

The public had its first exotic visions spread before it on the fairground; sights such as mummies and "Turks" (who were then a great curiosity in Europe) as well as a tribe of Red Indians—the Osages. The Café Turc with its summer-houses of colored glass, its divans and canopies, in all its brilliant novelty in 1786, contributed to the ensemble. That same year, the Storkenfels, a couple working in the troupe of *Les Grands Danseurs du Roi*, danced a number titled *Marchand d'oignons hongrois (Hungarian Onion Seller)*, wearing boots and spurs, which clicked as accompaniment to their dance. (Fifty years later Fanny Elssler was proclaimed an innovator for performing the same trick.)

Certain of the booths had "historical" displays which usually included a certain number of exotic; i.e., foreign, personages or potentates. There were improbable combinations of waxwork figures grouped in "Circles," such as those of André Benoist, and Clément Lorin's *Cabinet des Grands Voleur's (Collection of Great Thieves, 1774)*, and in Jean-Baptiste Curtius' *Assemblée des Notables (Assembly of Celebrities)* of the same period (the proprietor was father of the Madame Tussaud who founded the London waxworks). The famous showings of automata by Lorget (1786-1789), Henri Droz (1782), Blaise Lagrelet, sculptor and physicist (1750), and the Baron Kempelen (inventor of the famous "Chess Player" and himself sufficiently bizarre to have stepped out of a tale by E. T. A. Hoffmann) touched on the exotic sometimes by their subjects and always by the element of strangeness in a piece of "humanized" machinery.

New décors and properties appeared, ready to be elaborated by the Boulevard theatres: giants created by means of high wigs and ingeniously-constructed boots; a wooden colossus who spoke by means of a small boy concealed in the hollow interior; or fruits, fish and fowl modeled in *papier-mâché*, attached to wires, which could be whisked off the diners' plates and disappear in the wings. In Le Sage's *Théâtre de la Foire* (a famous collection of fairground plays, 1737), the frontispiece for the *Monde Renversé (The Upside Down World)* illustrates this gag which was still amusing audiences in *Les Pillules du Diable (The Devil's Pills)* in 1939.

Literary influences were particularly important to the exotic style, and even the fairground theatres borrowed liberally from contemparary literature. For example, *L'Elève de la Nature (Nature's Pupil)* by Mayeur de Saint-Paul, presented in 1781 by the *Grands Danseurs du Roi*, was taken from the *Sauvage Apprivoisé (The Tamed Savage)* which had just been presented by Audinot's company. And its plot in turn was lifted from a novel by the Abbé Prévost.

Particularly between 1600 and 1660, travel books by missionaries and explorers revealed Africa, Asia and the two Americas to the sedentary Europeans. This vogue was prelude to a popular infatuation with travel books, culminating in the last quarter of the 17th century. Most of these works were fictitious, and are distinguished by two characteristics of the Theatre of Marvels: the voyager always finds a Utopian country whose natives are idealized children of nature "*à la Jean-Jacques Rousseau*," where the "noble savage" reveals qualities that are the pretext for comparisons unflattering to civilized Europeans, and where a "kindly old man," a "respectable," a "venerable" old man is always on hand to greet our explorers, explain the manners and customs of the country, and end up with a moralizing discourse. In 1676, an unfrocked Franciscan, Gabriel de Foigny, invented *La Terre Australe Connue*, supposedly the adventures of a French explorer named Jacques Saxeur, who claimed to have discovered Australia. The details of customs and costumes in certain melodramas, such as *L'Eléphant du Roi de Siam* in 1829, were lifted from Foigny, who himself had made extensive use of the authentic "Voyages" of Théodore de Bry.

A very precise documentation of the voyage is combined with an idealistic description of an earthly paradise: winds, storms, sailors' activities, shipwrecks and encounters with pirates, give an air of probability and interest to the story. Pixérécourt was to make great use of this technique in his *Robinson Crusoe* and *Christopher Columbus*.

The stories of Jean Mocquet, "guardian of the King's Curio Cabinet at the Tuileries," are sufficiently fertile in material to satisfy a taste for the marvelous and the extraordinary: the story of the "beautiful native girl" abandoned by the European whom she had saved from death, makes its first appearance here. The lurid stories of adventurers started to rival the descriptions of Utopian natives in popularity. Jostling the noble savages came other heroes of the exotic novel—the freebooters and buccaneers of Tortoise Island, who strutted through the *Histoire des Antilles* of Père J.-B. du Tertre (1667-1671). The freebooters were so improbable that they lent themselves to no-matter-what extravagant invention. A Dutchman named Oexmelin also sang the praises of the adventurous buccaneers and their exploits in a *Histoire des Flibustiers* (first edition in Holland, 1678, translated and retranslated through an edition of 1772). He found material for his epics in the dashing careers of Montauban, Montbars l'Exterminateur, and Alexandre Bras de Fer.

The *Nouveau Voyage aux Iles de l'Amérique (New Voyage to the Islands of America)*, by Père Labat, a Jacobin preaching brother, was more documentary, but the author described his pirates vividly enough to put them right on the boards at the Ambigu or Porte-Saint-Martin.

Freebooting, officially dead at the end of the 17th century, was still in theatrical favor through the entire 18th and first part of the 19th centuries when the generous brigand began to replace the pirate: *Le Corsaire comme il n y en a point (The Unique Pirate)* in 1790, *Le Corsaire* in 1794, *Saalem ou le Corsaire* in 1808 (revived in 1817) *A-t-il deux femmes ou Les Corsaires barbaresques (Has He Two Wives, or The Barbary Pirates)* in 1813—no other type of stage presentation could contain more spectacular elements, nor abound in more shipwrecks and combats under fringed palm trees, right up to the final ballet of the savages. The "historical" novel of a certain Piqueraud gave the Porte-Saint-Martin in 1807: *Montbars l'Exterminateur ou les Derniers Flibustiers (Montbars The Exterminator, or The Last Freebooters)*, while in 1814, *Lolotte et Fanfan ou les Flibustiers* "pantomime in three acts, with lavish spectacle, taken from the novel of M. Ducrai Duminil by M. Fréderic" enriched the coffers of the Cirque-Olympique. Besides the appeal of child actors—Lolotte was played by *la petite* Godet, the ballet-master's daughter, and Fanfan by *le petit* Blin—there were Caribbean natives, French prisoners of the freebooters, a particularly villainous villain and a large corps de ballet. "The action takes place at the beginning of the XVIIth century on the Ile Saint-Vincent, and on another of the Antilles occupied by the Freebooters . . ."; the decor was by Isidore, the ballets by Jacquinet and the "pidgin" dialogue of the savages by the Franconis.

Savages, above all Caribbeans, grew in popularity until they overshadowed even the freebooters. The scenery of the savage island did not lose its glamour; at the height of the Reign of Terror exotic settings were used to make political propaganda more digestible. In *Les Potentats foudroyés par la Montagne et La Raison ou La Deportation des rois de l'Europe (The Potentates Struck Down by the Mountain and Reason, or The Deportation of the Kings of Europe)*, in 1793, the actor-author Desbarreaux created a heroine who had repulsed the dishonorable proposals of "a monster called a king." *Les Caraibes (The Caribbeans)*, "spectacular production," triumphed at the Gaîté on 24 Floreal An IX (1801), and *Le Sauvage muet ou les Deux Caraibes (The Dumb Savage or The Two Caribbeans)* of Hurtaud and Delorme at the Ambigu in 1806.

The interminable novels of Marin le Roy de Gomberville abound in stageworthy episodes. *Polexandre*, novel in five volumes which appeared over a period of eight years (1620-1637) is the best-known: its knight Polexandre who roams the world and plunges through the unleashed elements to win the beauteous Alcidiane is all set to enter the plot of a *féerie*. Benserade extracted an episode for a ballet scenario: *L'Exil de Polexandre et d'Ericlée (The Exile of Polexandre and Ericlée)*. Gomberville meticulously documented everything from the shell-work ornaments on Carib costumes to the fashioning of Mexican feather capes, or the details of day-to-day shipboard life. This documentation, joined with bewitching memories from the *Images du Monde* and the folklore of the Marvelous was to remain characteristic of the popular theatre. But Gomberville also created an auditory novelty by his evocative use of geographical place names which was to become a theatrical commonplace. The ultimate intoxicating effect of such names was achieved by Charles Charton in his Funambules pantomimes. [4]

Although on a rather higher literary plane, *Les Aventures de Télémaque (The Adventures of Telemachus)* in 1699, still falls within the group of source books, as Fénelon was not content merely to describe his noble savage, product of the study of Nature and Reason, but installed him in his tent and clothed him in an American Indian costume. Excerpts from the adventures of Telemachus rapidly made their way into the fairground theatres.

Brazil, popularized by the Capuchin Fathers Claude d'Abbeville and Yves d'Evreux, in their *Histoire de la Mission des Pères Capucins (History of the Mission of the Capuchin Fathers)*, in 1614, had a renewed vogue beginning in the mid-18th century. The gambols of the little monkeys, which were among the delights of *Jocko* and *Sapajou* in 1825, originated in the chapter on *The She-Monkeys of Brazil* by Père d'Evreux. The Brazilian natives themselves, brought back to France by our Capuchins "as a pious advertisement for their order," were most spectacularly presented to the Parisian public in 1614; the king, the queen regent and a gaping crowd thronged to attend their baptism. In order to accommodate the public, it became necessary to erect a "theatre" or raised altar in the church so that the handsome Brazilians would be visible. (Suffering from the climate, they died shortly thereafter within a few weeks of each other; the stage "Brazilians" were more durable).

Savages and freebooters did not exhaust the resources of the travel books. In 1710, one Simon Tyssot, mathematician and Huguenot surgeon, invented *Les Voyages de Jacques Massé* which introduced that indestructible and endlessly fascinating character—the Wandering Jew. As the enigmatic personage who endures both in popular prints and popular literature (specifically the *"livres de colportage"*—cheap little paper books hawked by peddlers up and down the country), he left his mark on countless solitary travelers of the Boulevard melodrama, wanderers bowed down by remorse for past sins. Tyssot introduces him as a voyager who persuades the fictional Massé to educate himself by traveling the world. [5] The author leans heavily on technical navigational jargon to strengthen the verisimilitude of the *Voyages*. And he uses the typical melodramatic trick of mentioning a fact in passing without any elaboration and using it later as an established reality. He introduces characters speaking dialects as a new source of comic realism in the adventure story. Pixérécourt was to do likewise when he introduced the cheerful simpleton into the horror drama. In a second book, *Voyage de Groënland (Greenland* Trip 1720), Tyssot expanded ancient folklore concerning a great underground kingdom with a cave at the center of the earth, a legend which antedates Greek and Roman mythologies.

The "Savage" as seen by Jean Bérain for "The Triumph of Love" in 1681, then by the choreographer Louis Henry, who documented his ballet "The Savages of Florida" (1807) from the travel account of Père Lafitau (1724). Madame Quériau is the young and rather redoubtable Indian maiden. Almost all research on savage customs and costume was influenced by the "Admiranda narratio fida tamen" . . . of Thomas Hériot, published in Frankfort in 1586 with illustrations by Théodore de Bry. (Below) (Fonds Rondel, Bibl. de l'Arsenal)

Guilbert de Pixérécourt recommended that the costume designer for his melodramatized "Robinson Crusoe" (Gaité, 1805) seek inspiration in the works of Père Lafitau.

Giacomo Pregliasco, in about 1812, designed these exotic costumes for the dancers of La Scala, Milan. They recall the baroque costume designs for the great festivals of 17th-century Turin. Pregliasco knew these albums of costume designs and accessories well, for he occasionally copied or adapted certain sketches during his early years as designer for the theatres of his native city. (Bibloteca Civica, Torino)

Tis tarnation strange-but you cant   beat that no how you can fix it .

Les enfants de M.r Harvey Leach.

OHIO, ARKANSAS, et MISSOURI,

Exécutant les jeux favoris des Aborigènes de l'Amérique.

Imp. d'Aubert & Cie

A normally-scaled homonym of the dwarf, Harvey Leach.

NIAGARA LEAP BY THE WONDERFUL BUISLAY FAMILY.

THE BUISLAY FAMILY rivalled the Hanlons in spectacular trapeze numbers.

This subterranean realm of the Arctic Pole, comprising mysterious mines garnished with stalactites and stalagmites, furnished a startling contrast to the usual sunny isles. [6]

The illustrations and "figures" which adorned so many of the real or fraudulent "voyages" before 1790 were sometimes actually drawn from life or sometimes taken from tenacious old medieval legends as depicted in the *Images du Monde*. The Caribs in Rameau's ballet of that name wore stylized costumes with "savage attributes" (bows, arrows, shells) appliqued on the conventional panniers of the dancers' costumes. The most beautiful of 18th-century ballet-operas, Rameau's *Les Indes Galantes* of 1735, with a libretto by Fuzelier, is an assemblage of stylized Incas, Persians, Red Indians and Turks all dancing and acting *à la française*, with an imagination and fantasy of which Noverre was to write sarcastically and rather unjustly. [7]

Archaeological exactitude was not an 18th century obsession, but it appeared the length and breadth of the Boulevard du Temple in the 19th century.

The technique of documentation, lifted from the travel books, was used in libretti of otherwise improbable ballets such as *Haroun-al-Rashid et Zobeide ou Le Calife généreux (Haroun-al-Rashid and Zobeide, or The Generous Caliph)* by Blache *père* for the Porte-Saint-Martin in 1817. This work scattered details from books of the distinguished archaeologist Caylus throughout its text. Pixérécourt quoted Père Lafitau in his preface to *Robinson Crusoe* and Louis Henry obviously borrowed from him for *Les Sauvages de la Floride (The Florida Savages)*. The illustrations for Père Lafitau's *Moeurs des Sauvages américains comparées aux moeurs des Premiers Temps* (1724) were executed under his direction, but with the avowed intention of showing that the savage Americans were similar to ancient Greeks and Romans, which fitted in well with the Consulate and Empire decorative bias in a transitional theatre. The beautiful and curious prints of Bernard Picard for *Les Cérémonies et Coutumes religieuses de tous les peuples (Ceremonies and Religious Customs of all Peoples)* (1723-1743) were the forerunners of those in the countless "picturesque" works of the 19th century such as Daniell's *L'Inde pittoresque* in 1835, and the *Histoire pittoresque des Religions (Picturesque History of Religions)* illustrated by Jeanron, in 1844.

Among the exotic settings the "savage site" should also be included. This wild landscape or virgin forest, boundless and impressive in its various aspects, is always accompanied by dramatic natural effects—storms, thunder and lightning, sunsets, rosy-fingered dawn (in fact, all of these may still be seen at the Musée Grevin's *Palais des Mirages*). There were also effects of "panoramas," "dioramas," "neoramas" and the whole family of optical illusions which were a show in themselves, and whose techniques passed over into scene design. Water (preferably in falls) and mountains were indispensable; man-made objects were admissible if in ruins—wormeaten bridges, abandoned mills and picturesque "*fabriques*" such as (fake ruined temples, towers and pagodas).

The French techniques for realizing scenic effects were rather primitive until the Florentine Servandoni arrived in 1724. He was decorator and machinist for the Opéra at the Tuileries and for the troupe which was to become the Opéra-Comique at the fairs of Saint-Laurent and Saint-Germain. In *La Pénélope française (The French Penelope)*, performed at the Foire Saint-Germain in 1729, the director Pontau entrusted him with settings in which a castle rises upstage flanked by a torrent which plunges into a waterfall that loses itself in a meadow.

31

Several authors, a goodly number of artists and a few architect-landscape designers paved the way for this type of setting. First came the influence of the 18th-century baroque Italian garden with its "surprises," its grottoes and waterfalls. From 1708 to 1857 treatises and dictionaries on the art of gardens speak of the "pastoral landscape" just as they instruct how to achieve the "heroic landscape" or propose "extraordinary irregularities . . . rocks, torrents, mountains." The impetus came principally from England, whose clearly "Romantic" gardens appeared in the Boulevard theatres, always avid for novelty. [8] Certain rather curious illustrations by Le Rouge, "Engineer-Geographer of His Highness the Count of Clermont" in *"Idées pour la Construction des Rochers dan les Jardins anglais"* astonish by their date, 1734, and their resemblance to the Romantic stage sets of Cicéri.

The English gardens soon got involved with the "Chinese gardens." Already publicized by the travel books, they became celebrated thanks to a long description by Frère Attiret in 1749 and a book by Chambers published in London in 1757 with French and English text.

Although the adjective "romantic" appears in England toward the end of the 17th century, the French preferred the words *"romanesque"* or *"pittoresque."* It was Letourneur, in the foreword to his translation of Shakespeare in 1776, who decided to use the word *"romantique."* " *'Romanesque'* he wrote, 'might make us think of the chimerical and fabulous . . *'pittoresque'* speaks to the eyes, not the soul." Yet the picturesque remains unalterable in the Theatre of Marvels, well before and well after the Romantic period. The "savage site" relates, then, to the "rural gardens," the "untamed landscapes" and the "romantic gardens" whose vogue had been promoted in high society by Watelet and Hirschfeld. Other landscapes were conceived to simulate Swiss mountains and waterfalls, toward which "sensitive" souls, inspired by *La Nouvelle Héloïse*, had been flocking since 1760.

The reaction to these literary flutters reached the noisy Boulevard public chiefly through pictures. Between 1760 and the Revolution more than eighty important books or articles in more than one hundred and thirty editions, mostly illustrated, appeared, and almost all contained the full range of scenic "sublime horrors." There are often analogies between the titles of these illustrations and scenic directions, just as there are between the sub-titles of popular prints and the gibberish of many melodrama scripts.

Originally the privilege of some few ecstatic pre-Romantics, the love of mountain and sea was soon within everyone's consciousness. The machines of Servandoni and his rivals made possible the shipwrecks which were melodramatic accessories: *Jocko, Les Deux Créoles, Christophe Colomb, Polichinelle Vampire* and the *Ile des Pirates* are just a few characteristic examples that we have mentioned. An amalgamation of the "Voyages" and Joseph Vernet's paintings furnished a choice "optical spectacle."

The *"fabriques"* of 18th-century gardens were worthy ancestors of 19th-century scenic marvels. The park of the Count d'Albon at Montmorency, with its Devil's Bridge surmounted by a crumbling cross, reappear in stage sets of Gué and Cicéri, and the *Naumachia* of Monceau inspired another of Cicéri's designs. Belœil, pride of the Prince de Ligne, had enough "ruins" to furnish a dozen or so tableaux for the Cirque-Olympique. Hubert Robert created a garden for the Princess de Monaco at Retz, which contained "a Chinese bridge, a Druid

Ballet costumes engraved by Martin Engelbrecht, which were cut out, pasted on boxes, furniture, screens and decorative objects and varnished over (a process often called "the poor man's lacquer"). The stylistic sources are found in the Bérain costume plates, the Commedia dell'Arte prints and the Larmessin pictorial allegories.

". . . Like "The Elephant of the King of Siam," it concerns a dynastic proboscidian who foils a usurper's intrigues and sets the rightful heir back on his throne. . . . The two elephants of the Circus may not be as talented as the cord-dancing elephants of ancient Rome, but they are perfectly trained; they kneel, get up, give the sceptre to the most worthy, rival Porthos in lifting the bars of a prison in which an innocent victim languishes, carry off one of the supers in their trunks, and at dramatic moments let out terrible snufflings or barks on little brass horns, for which their trunks serve as trombones . . ."

Illustration from the "Recueil des comédies, parodies et opéras-comiques" of Charles-Simon Favart, published by Duschesne, Paris, in 1743. The theme of the "noble savage" dear to Jean-Jacques Rousseau made its appearance at the Opéra-Comique during Favart's directorship, and the Theatre of Marvels in all its various forms continued to exploit "the child of Nature."

The exoticism of 18th century decoration and settings matched the interest in the exotic human being. Designs for gardens scattered with "ruins," gazebos and other ornamental constructions found their way from the landscape architects' treatises to the Boulevard stage.

Anthropomorphic garden, from a design by Le Rouge.

Entrance to the "desert" of Retz, designed by Le Rouge (1785).

The marks in the Center are their Coats of Arms which they use instead of signing their Names.

TEE YEE NEEN HO GA ROW EMPEROUR OF THE SIX NATIONS

SA GA YEAN QUA RAH TOW KING OF THE MAQUAS

E TOW OH KOAM KING OF THE RIVER NATION

O NEE YEATH TOW NO RIOW KING OF GANAJAH HORE

The true Effiges of the Four Indian Kings taken from the Original
Paintings done by Mr. Varelst.

Harvard Theatre Collection

PORTRAITS OF THE FOUR INDIAN KINGS (3 Mohawk Iroquois and one Mohican) who visited London in 1710. "The true Effiges of the Four Indian Kings taken from the Original Paintings done by Mr. Varelst" (John). They visited Queen Anne and delighted the populace when they appeared at the Haymarket to see Mr. Wilks as "Macbeth."

Costume for a Turkish potentate in a ballet at La Scala, Milan, by Giacomo Pregliasco. (Biblioteca Civica, Torino)

temple and a feudal tower, that is cracked and crumbling to perfection . . ." Mausoleums, urns, cenotaphs, tombs inside caverns, mourning statues—in short, the entire range of funerary art works—were soon found on the boards of Audinot, Nicolet and their competitors in *Valther le Cruel, Main de Fer, Hamlet, L'Eléphant du Roi de Siam, Le Petit Poucet*, etc.

In 18th-century pre-Romantic literature and iconography, melodramatic contrasts between a brooding Nature—some dark and sombre forests for example— and the "smiling" country landscape were already present. The village scene with its little hamlet its mill, the cheery goings-and-comings of its rustic populace, followed immediately after settings of a brigand's cave, a hermit's retreat, or a ruined castle crumbling into a lake. From these contrasts came a basic cliché of melodrama and pantomime: there should be complete accord between Nature's moods and those of the protagonists. In the Theatre of Marvels, henceforth, the landscape had to match the actions and emotions of the plot; thus, if the villain walked into a "smiling" landscape, thunder was unleashed and lightning crossed the darkening sky as the wind machines offstage went into action. The effects which followed the evildoer's entrance were as automatic as the musical *leitmotiv* which accompanied him. [9]

THE TROUBADOUR STYLE

The troubadour style, which sometimes overlaps the exotic—especially in subjects drawn from the Crusades—did not furnish many innovations in the techniques of the Marvellous. The novels, ballads, collections of forged epics and rewritten medieval verse chronicles, whose influence on the pre-history of Romantic literature is generally conceded, take their place on our stage primarily for visual qualities. The "Voyages" real or invented, furnished documentary techniques, a gallery of *dramatis personae* and certain fundamental plots, in addition to the sensual aspects of dance, music and scenery.

Troubadour prose, affected and often insipid, with a tendency to long-winded speeches, would have embarrassed the popular stage, but the tournaments, combats, brilliant *cortèges*—in short, all the chivalric panache—were assured of an immediate welcome. Absorbing elements of the anti-clerical plays and the supernatural spectacles, the troubadour style provided these time-tried forms with novelties in costuming, scenery and staging. Finally, it was a means by which Romanticism was to overcome the Opéra's prejudices.

During the 17th century the Italian Comedy had already touched upon troubadour themes; its companies were adept at handling the stage machinery necessary for the functioning of drawbridge, portcullis, and other accessories of the crenelated tower.

Les Plaisirs de l'Ile Enchantée, presented at Versailles in 1664, may be considered as one of the first attempts at reviving equestrian magnificence; and Saint-Aignan, who took a principal part in this *balletto a cavallo*, was himself a survival of yesteryear's valiant knights. The first collection of troubadour poetry, assembled by the Count de Tressan, appeared in 1799. [10] The fairground theatres, dedicated willy-nilly to pantomime, found in these medieval subjects numerous opportunities to use trained animals (false or real), and the ever-popular processions with banners flying and lances glittering. The Ambigu was in the running that same year with *Les Quatre fils Aymon* by Arnould-Mussot; even a half-century did not exhaust the popularity of this epic, which was adapted three times by the Cirque-Franconi during the Empire, twice in a version by Franconi *jeune*. In 1844 Gautier wrote a review of Balfe's opera about the four brothers, with a digression on folk epics and the popular prints devoted to them. He was perhaps the first to understand the analogies between these two forms of the Marvellous buried in the mass subconscious since the Middle Ages.

After the appearance of Tressan's anthology, came two troubadour musical works, whose authors were already well-known as pioneers of the exotic. The first was an *Essai sur la musique ancienne et moderne* by J. B. de la Borde, from which his contemporaries and successors pillaged unashamedly. (Weber extracted a *Danse turque* for the finale of *Oberon*.) It also contained several "medieval" ballads which were very popular at that period. The second work was due to the composer-librettist team of Grétry and Sedaine, the most gifted creators of the troubadour opera. Their first work, *Aucassin et Nicollette*, was greeted with indifference; it was only appreciated some four years later. But *Richard Coeur de Lion* met with universal enthusiasm immediately.

At the Foire Saint-Laurent in August 1781, the Ambigu continued to exploit the troubadour pantomime with *Pierre de Provence ou la Belle Maguelone*, based on a story which had appeared in the Tressan collection; this time it was a lion, favourite menace of the fairground theatre, which was involved in the ups and downs of the plot. That same year the Théâtre de la Gaîté launched *Geneviève de Brabant* on a long theatrical career; the popular printmakers took her into their repertoire as well. In 1782 the *"pantomime à spectacle"* *Dorothée*, preceded by the *Preux-Chevaliers*, *"prologue-pantomime de M. Audinot"* presented their heroine enclosed—obviously—in a Gothic tower, to crowds that overflowed the Ambigu at its Foire Saint-Laurent booth. This "beautiful pantomime *Dorothée"* as Grimm called it, was to enjoy a decade or so of popularity; in 1790 a procession of monks and archbishops was added for further color. [11]

Although the troubadour style was in evidence long before the more extreme forms of Romantic "Gothick," the Countess Dash (as did many of her contemporaries) associated it with the Restoration (Louis-Philippe) in her memoirs. This can be justified primarily in the realm of decorative arts, by the thousands or ormolu clocks surmounted by statuettes of Isabeau of Bavaria, inkwells in the shape of miniature cathedrals, the popular Provencal figurines of painted clay and the prints of the rue Saint-Jacques (center of the *imagerie parisienne*). In the provinces, between 1840-1850 the vestiges of Empire and troubadour styles—both long out of fashion in Paris—were still current in the craftsman's atelier.

But the troubadour style, born in the 18th century and eclipsed during the Revolution, reappeared in force about 1795 and reached its apogee toward 1813.

In 1796 the great architect Alexandre Lenoir established his Museum of French Monuments; that is, he assembled in a former monastery of the Petits-Augustins all the fragments of ancient French architecture that had managed to survive the Revolutionary looting and destruction. This was of considerable importance because of its influence on painters and consequently on scene design. Pupils of David deserted the Louvre for the Petits-Augustins, where they could see the "Sepulchre of Héloise and Abélard," 12th century in style, constructed from what had been saved from the Basilica of Saint-Denis. The columns were

This statuette from Marseilles was doubtless produced in a Proyençal atelier which made "santons" (religious figurines), for he is made in the same style and of the same "barbotine" (painted clay). His troubadour-style costume may have been copied from a Martinet print of costumes for Aumer's ballet "Astolphe et Joconde" (Paris Opera, 1827). Taking into account the usual time lag between Paris and the provinces, he probably dates from about 1835. Yet the costume, and his manner of carrying it, reappear in this Second Empire lithograph of the prestidigitator Lassaigne, that "pleasant enchanter."

Dans un salon doré, poétique demeure
LASSAIGNE, sous son charme, a su faire plier
Sa pendule docile à nous rappeler l'heure
Que l'aimable enchanteur nous ferait oublier

Troubadour

Set with a luxury characteristic of the great Italian theatres—La Scala of Milan, the Teatro Regio of Turin, the San Carlo of Naples and the Fenice in Venice—the ballets of the expatriate French choreographers would eventually influence the Parisian scene designers. The "Gothick" setting for Louis Henry's "Hamlet" (La Scala, 1817) was typical. The production of "le Drapier" at the Paris Opera in 1840 had one of the innumerable period sets designed by Philastre and Cambon, both strongly influenced by the Italians.

Robertson inspired a whole series of fantas-magoric scenes and personages: the phantoms in the Gaité's "Blue-Beard" (1823) were on stage some eight years earlier than the phantom nuns of "Robert le Diable" at the Opéra. As for the "Bleeding Nun," she reap-peared toward 1810, impersonated by Madame Jacquinet in "La Soeur de la Miséricorde," described by the Martinet engraver as "a fair-ground scene, théâtre Montansier."

Print of a performance of the "Fantasmagoria" (1797) from Robertson's "Mémoires" (1831).

Two very different techniques for presenting a magic turn: the first (Viennese print) in a colorful and downright pretty setting, with luxurious accessories, was launched toward 1820 by the French prestidigitator Philippe, and further developed by Robert-Houdin; the other background is bleak and banal, yet its two realistic doorways are menacing and disquieting. (Italian lithograph, 19th century, Collection Bertarelli, Milano)

"The Procuress," illustration by Binet from Restif de la Bretonne's "The Contemporaries," combines the modishly terrifying with the author's amiable eroticism.

MADAME LECOMPTE (LECOMTE) "Princi-pal Danseuse at the Theatres Royal, Paris, London, St. Petersburgh." As the Abbess in "The Nun's Ballet" of "Robert le Diable." A Lithograph drawn by E. W. Clay and issued by Robinson in 1837, brought both artist and publisher to the attention of the Public Prose-cutor. Madame Lecomte and her brother, Jules Martin, headed a ballet company which, in 1839, brought not only Jean and Marius Petipa to America but also the acrobatic dancer Klischnigg. The ballerina and her brother became permanent U.S. residents and ran a dancing school in Philadelphia.

surmounted by ogives pierced with trefoil openings through which the light filtered dimly upon statues of the couple, lying side by side. It was Lenoir who had previously obtained an authentic "Gothic ruin" for Josephine, patroness of the troubadour-style painters, as well as similar items for Prince Eugene and Queen Hortense. But his influence on the theatre was far more direct, for the records state that on 20 Floreal of the Year VI (May 10th, 1797), "Citizen Lenoir, architect-owner and director of the Cité-Variétés theatre" profitably ceded his enterprise to a new administration in which Cuvelier, "man of letters" who had already furnished Lenoir with many pantomimes, made an appearance. The theatre's settings continued to evidence his preoccupation with archaeological research. [12] The Lenoir productions of historical, exotic, melodramatic and always spectacular pantomimes had met with such success that the new administration made a point of announcing that it would carry on with the same type of programs. To emphasize this point the theatre was re-baptized "Théâtre de la Pantomime Nationale." Lenoir was on hand to supervise the opening program and the public to applaud *La Naissance de la Pantomime* by the "Citizens Cuvelier and Hapdé with music by the Citizens Navoigille and Banneux." Its reputation once established, the theatre soon reverted to its former name of Cité-Variétés. It continued thus with pantomimes such as *Frédegilde* and *Montoni*, which retained their popularity through the Empire, when the pre-Romanticism of the troubadour style began to give way to the heroes of Walter Scott.

Out of fashion in literature and art, the troubadour style persisted in the theatre. Always behindhand, the Opéra staged Meyerbeer's *Robert le Diable* in 1831. Dance historians consider the *Ballet of the Nuns* in *Robert* as the point of departure for the Romantic Ballet. Actually, the "innovations" in *Robert* had been fixtures in the secondary theatres for the past twenty years, and the Opéra only endowed them with its prestige and elegance. In conformity with Boulevard stagecraft was the faithful reproduction of the cloisters of Montfort l'Amaury with chiaroscuro effects made possible by gas lights which Cicéri had ordered installed for this setting. The "English traps" for sudden apparitions had been standard equipment in Boulevard theatres since 1824; and finally the "white phantoms of the nuns" recalled the restless ghosts in the Revolutionary anti-religious dramas, compounding the troubadour and the supernatural.

The troubadour style fulfilled its historic mission. Its contributions to the Theatre of Marvels continued in evidence until the 1850s, and its iconography, including book illustrations, calendars, almanachs, "cathedral" bookbindings, popular prints, scene designs and Salon paintings, have an aesthetic merit which even today is vastly more interesting than its literary output. In spite of the little it offered in new techniques, the mystery of its decors and the flourish of its parades remained a part of popular spectacular entertainment.

THE SUPERNATURAL

From the 16th century up to the Foire du Trône of today, magic has been inseparable from the great European fairs, just as the wizard was inevitable in the magic plays of the Italian Comedy and the French fairground theatres. According to instructions for the scene designer, the magician's laboratory was modest in *Les Forces de l'Amour et de la Magie* of 1678, expanded in *Le Petit Poucet* of 1798, and became positively cumbersome in *Le Diable boiteux* of 1836. But it never varied in its characteristics.

Marie-Joseph Chénier was one of the first to insist on the French preference for the defined, logical, "explained" supernatural, as it occurs in Ann Radcliffe's novels: Gautier, Janin, Ginisty and many others ventured the same opinion. However, at certain periods the "pure," unexplained supernatural seems to have imposed itself on the logical French with unusual force; the century of Voltaire was after all that of Cagliostro, Mesmer and the Count of Saint-Germain; the Goddess Reason never managed to banish superstition. In 1791, conjurors and fortune-tellers held forth in the public gardens while the prestidigitator Perrin performed his magic feats at the Delassements-Comiques—while the Revolution pursued its course.

The illustrated books of the period are linked as closely to the Boulevard theatre as they are to the works on romantic gardens. In *Les Nuits de Paris ou le Spectateur nocturne* of Restif de la Bretonne, for instance, the illustrations of Binet unite the supernatural, the *noir* and "Gothick." [13] The influence of the English "Gothick" novel, especially Walpole's *Castle of Otranto*, *The Monk* of Lewis (Matthew called "Monk") and the *Mysteries of Udolpho* colored the troubadour productions of the French popular theatre, where some traces of Germanic macabre supernaturalism crop up as well. Walpole went back, as had the Count de Tressan, to the old technique of Foigny and Tyssot—the "journal" written by a supposed traveller which his family turned over to an "editor." [14]

It is nevertheless remarkable that in the abundant output of such Boulevard masters as Cuvelier and Hapdé, the pure and unexplained supernatural plays an important part, particularly in dream sequences. The persistence of the supernatural as an important component in pantomime and melodrama was due particularly to the influence of one man, Robertson, whose *Fantasmagoria* was known to all the Boulevard purveyors.

Born in Liège, E.-G. Robert, called Robertson, was one of the most exceptional physicists of his period; his genuine passion for scientific knowledge, his balloon ascensions and his serious research work had no taint of charlatanism. Having come to France as a student in experimental physics with Charles, he earned his living by painting cameos for a dealer in the Palais-Royal arcade and became interested in Freemasonry and the Rosicrucians. His studies in physics and the phenomena of light inspired his creation of the *Fantasmagoria*.

In 1797 he established himself in a vast derelict chapel at the center of a cloister in a Capuchin church. He writes in his *Mémoires* that its arrangement and bygone function "inspired a favorable inclination to meditation": one entered a chamber draped in black, dimly lit by a sepulchral lamp with a few lugubrious paintings to set the mood; "deep calm, absolute silence, sudden isolation on coming out of a noisy street, were like preludes to an ideal world."

Robertson made a short speech stating that his program was not frivolous, and then after having sketched a learned and contemptuous history of false apparitions, said that he proposed to offer something very different to the public. As he finished, an ancient lamp suspended above the spectators flickered out, plunging the room into utter darkness. The elements (sounds of thunder and rain, effects of dawn and sunset) became "actors" just as they were in pre-Romantic landscape painting and the Romantic theatre. By means of adroit lighting effects and the use of projections, Robertson presented a *Petit Répertoire fantasmagorique*. Dream episodes were used throughout as they were to be in the Boulevard theatre—pretexts for apparitions. An episode which shows Cupid curing a maiden who has been stabbed by her jealous lover, and which closes with a shower of rose petals, remains unique.

The 18th century pre-Romantics never wearied of Young's *Night Thoughts* (repeatedly translated), nor of the episode *Young enterrant sa fille*. Robertson's version had a setting worthy of Lenoir's Cité-Variétés, or of the Funambules at a later date, when Deburau adopted the English mimes' comic macabre and brought on stage undertakers, ghosts and skeletons. "Bells sound from a belfry" begins Robertson's program, "view of a cemetery by moonlight—Young bearing the inanimate body of his daughter. He enters a cavern and discovers a series of elaborate tombs. Young raps on the first one; a skeleton appears: Young flees, returns and starts digging with a pick; a second apparition materializes to terrify him anew. He knocks on the third tombstone; a ghost rises up and asks him: 'What do you wish of me?'—'A grave for my daughter,' replies Young. The ghost recognizes him and cedes his place. Young deposes his daughter in the vacated grave. Scarcely is the lid closed when one sees her spirit rising toward Heaven. Young prostrates himself and remains in ecstasy. . . ."

The episode of *La Nonne Sanglante* was taken from contemporary pantomime. "Victim of her sensibility," she returns to "fly about the cloister where her lover (who betrayed her and repented) is devoting his remaining days to acts of piety." The *Ballet of the Nuns* in *Robert* and the phantoms in *Giselle* are not unrelated to this erring and errant nun.

Unfortunately the process for producing the *Fantasmagoria*, although jealously guarded by their inventor, were stolen by one of his assistants, who put on a similar program. Robertson won a lawsuit for plagiarism but the public learned his secrets; the Boulevard theatres took over his effects and his subjects. With an eager public awaiting him all over Europe, he left Paris, lived for some time in Spain and Portugal, and travelled extensively. His *Mémoires* were published shortly before his death, with diagrams and explanations of all the wonders performed by the *Fantasmagoria* and his other magic tricks.

In contrast to the magicians Philippe and Robert Houdin, who pioneered a new style of magic performances in 1836 and 1844 respectively, but had no influence in the theatre proper, Robertson made contributions of techniques and themes which dovetailed with all the types of the Theatre of Marvels. His use of a lighted screen and manipulation of projected shadows earned him the title cinema pioneer.

Jean-Georges Noverre was the great theoretician of the ballet d'action; his "Letters" are still celebrated—and even read. (Autograph letter, Fonds Rondel, Bibl de l'Arsénal)

CHAPTER III

The Forerunners

❧ JEAN-GEORGES NOVERRE ☙

INETEENTH-CENTURY choreographers were to find in the *Letters on the Dance* of Jean-Georges Noverre a key work for their guidance and the point of departure for their innovations.

A native Parisian, born in 1727, pupil of the great Dupré at the Opéra, Noverre made a modest début in Fontainebleau. After a brief stay at Potsdam he signed as a dancer with the Opéra-Comique at the Foire Saint-Laurent in 1743. This company, offshoot of the Italian Comedians and several other fairground troupes, was to receive its letters of nobility (that is, become a state theatre such as the Opéra and Théâtre Français) in 1762. Noverre joined the company at the very time when that gifted man of the theatre Favart began to raise the level of both repertory and production; and the choreographer profited by learning the mime techniques of the actors.

The Opéra-Comique was already renowned for its ballets and ballet-pantomimes. Its roster of ballet-masters since the beginning of the century included the names of Nivelon *fils*, Boudet, Raymond-Balthazar Dourdé, Haughton l'Anglais and Pierre-Louis Lachaussée.

The fairground spurred Noverre's inventiveness. The introduction of craftsmen and apprentices in ballet, urged in his *Letters*, came directly from the fairground theatres. The *métiers* had already appeared as fantastic figures in 16th and 17th century court ballets, wearing costumes composed of "attributes" ("tools, utensils and equipment") of their professions, and were recorded in elegant prints by Nicolas Larmessin. But the fair presented them realistically, at work and at play. In 1752 Cosimo Marinesi danced in a series of ballet-pantomimes staged by the Italian Soldi at the Foire Saint Laurent, titled *Les Batteurs en Grange*, *Les Tailleurs* and *Les Savetiers* (threshers, tailors and shoemakers). In 1780, Hamoire, ballet-master at the Variétés-Amusantes, staged *Les Forgerons*, *Les Jardiniers protegés par l'Amour* and *La Place Publique* (blacksmiths, gardeners and the populace at ease). Nivelon *fils*, who inherited the choreographic gifts of his father Louis, appeared in a peasant ballet wearing wooden clogs. When Noverre enlarged the scope of ballet by incorporating these unaristocratic dances, the contribution was greater than that of his complicated pantomime—which theoretically enabled a ballerina to recount the destruction of Rome.

Engaged yet again as ballet-master of the Opéra-Comique by Jean Monnet, in 1747, he proceeded next to Berlin for an important two-year contract. On his return, ignored by the Opéra, he rejoined the Opéra-Comique, where his two ballets—*Les Fêtes chinoises* and *La Fontaine de Jouvence*—with sets by Boucher and costumes by Bocquet, were the artistic sensations of 1754. The *chinoiserie* was so successful that David Garrick took Noverre to London with him. Noverre's first ballet there coincided with one of those recurrent difficult political situations: a riot cut short the performance and Noverre's engagement. Garrick continued to admire Noverre who, for his part, learned much from the great English performer.

Any history of the arts is studded with persistent ironies. Thus Noverre, the great innovator honored by Lessing and Garrick, praised by Diderot and considered a genius by Voltaire, was kept out of the Paris Opéra for thirty years by a coalition of his adversaries. Incapable of paying court to powerful officials, or sacrificing the plan and execution of a ballet to satisfy the caprices of a highly-protected ballerina, or intriguing for the support of politically-useful partisans,—he was eternally thwarted by the Gardel clan, artistically his inferiors but most certainly more adroit diplomats. Maximilien Gardel, followed by his brother Pierre, made the Opéra first un-enterable and then untenable; Alexandre Gardel tried—without success—to damage Noverre's reputation in Germany and Italy.

Excluded by the Opéra on his return from London, and obliged to go to Lyon for an engagement in 1758, he was fortunately summoned to Stuttgart in 1760 by the Duke Charles-Eugène of Wurtemberg. A hundred dancers, twenty feature dancers, the scene designer Servandoni, the costume designer Bocquet and the conductor Jomelli were placed at his disposal. Stuttgart became the capital of ballet and Noverre was even able to hold his own against the ducal mistress—Agathe Gardel. That same year he launched the first edition of his *Letters*, "which are a tract, a plan of action, a movement and the rough outline of an aesthetic, all rolled into one." He himself was never able to bring all his theories to realization on the stage, although he precisely indicated elements that the choreographer might use in constructing his ballet.

"A ballet-master should see everything" he wrote, and went on to mention crowded streets, public walks, country excursions, a village wedding, hunting, fishing, craftsmen and apprentices, and "youthful fops who are the apes and caricature copies of those whose age, rank and fortune seem to give them the rights of frivolity, irresponsibility and self-satisfaction!" . . . "Everything" he exulted "offers him picturesque and varied tableaux of different style and color."

He stressed the lessons to be learned from painting, and exhorted ballet-masters to study great works of art so that they might master the techniques of asymmetry. His plea for asymmetry was far in advance of contemporary choreography: "I would ask those who are prejudiced as a matter of course if they find symmetry in a troop of sheep fleeing the murderous jaws of a wolf, or in a band of peasants in flight from field and village before an army's onslaught. Certainly not: but Art lies in knowing how to conceal Art." [15]

Early in his career Noverre was interested by the possibilities of a conventional sign language drawn from the deaf-and-dumb alphabet of the Abbé de l'Epée. This was a mimed language "without choreographic or emotional content" which permitted actual dialogues between the dancers, with words set down in the scenario and translated on stage by matching gestures. The result is equivalent

50

to the gesture language of Hindu dancing, and thus requires either a religious discipline or a physical handicap to insure that the language is mastered.

Noverre thought as a complete man of the theatre. *Letter VI* is devoted to stage sets, costumes and direction, which he considered integral parts of the production (a point of view so commonplace today that it seems odd anyone should ever have been obliged to state it). Directing masses of extras who appeared in ballets of the period was another of his particular interests, shared by his compatriots Dauberval, Aumer, Henry and Perrot, and by his great Italian disciple Salvatore Viganó.

He insisted that stage machinery should be employed only if it functioned so perfectly that the marvels it was meant to achieve seemed to have been accomplished magically. He advised his colleagues to give up mythological ballets based on Ovid, with their flights and metamorphoses, unless they were actually competent machinists themselves.

Noverre attempted to put his theories into practice on the grand opera stages of all Europe: he succeeded partially in Germany, Austria, Italy and England; yet in Paris it was not the Opéra but the theatres of the "Boulevard du Crime" which realized his theories. He knew those theatres so well from his fairground days, and so utterly despised them! The term *"ballet d'action"* was not yet in current usage, so his contemporaries found no apter way to refer to his work than "ballet-pantomimes" or "pantomimes of the celebrated Noverre." And the word "pantomime" infuriated him; speaking of the English he said: "It is especially in their pantomimes, a trivial form, without taste, without interest, and with vulgar plots, that their masterpieces of stage machinery are deployed." [16]

The Opéra stalwarts spoke of him as "the little Noverre, good for the fairground and the provinces." The reforms he preached in the *Letters* offended many of his colleagues, and the "outmoded methods" he attacked did not give way before his eloquence.

Honored beyond the frontiers of Paris—or rather of the Paris Opéra—he reigned at Stuttgart from 1760 to 1767, then for seven years in Vienna and Naples, followed by two years in Milan. In 1776, through the intercession of Marie-Antoinette, he at long last received the appointment to which he so ardently aspired: *maître de ballet* at the Académie Royale de la Musique, the Paris Opéra.

The Gardel partisans did not consider this first victory as their final defeat. Their conversational gambits were deprecating references to his debut at the Opéra-Comique, or dismissing his seasons at the great European courts as "provincial engagements." Even Dauberval, his favorite pupil and disciple, joined the implacable cabale. The originality and exotic charm of a Chinese divertissement, which he composed for Piccini's *Roland* in 1778, were termed "worthy of the fair." His ballet *Medea*, created in Stuttgart, had been plagiarized by Gaetan Vestris, who presented it under his own name at the Opéra. When Noverre tried to put on his complete original version the cabale went into action. La Guimard, the powerful ballerina who refused to take orders from any choreographer, got her lover J.-E. Despréaux to write a parody which was launched when the ballet itself was produced in 1780. "*Medea and Jason*, terrifying ballet, garnished with dances, suspicion, gloom, pleasure, stupidity, horror, gaiety, treason, jokes, poison, dagger, mix-up, love, death, murder and fireworks." This reads like one of the more or less witty parodies of 19th-century melodrama.

Extravagantly praised by the writers, painters and the most brilliant intellectuals of his day, Noverre was to struggle five years against the Gardel coalition, supported by officials who were—on principle—against change, and dancers too lazy to meet his exigent demands. In 1781, completely frustrated, he retired from the Opéra with a modest pension, and spent ten years as a European celebrity exiled from Paris. The many editions of his *Letters* may not have increased his income by much or reinstated him at the Opéra, but they continued to build his reputation. His last creation in London opened on the very day of Louis XVI's death. [17]

Noverre often committed the same excesses as the melodramatists of a later date, searching to ennoble the dance by complicating the pantomime when visual language alone could not possibly suffice to translate the tortuous plots. Nevertheless, he made possible the *ballet d'action*, first evolved by the Englishman John Weaver with *The Loves of Mars and Venus* in 1717, and later attempted by the ballerina Marie Sallé. [18] By his own experiments as well as his theoretical writing he succeeded in perfecting the *ballet d'action*, pushing his mimed actions to extremes which called for some sort of equilibrium. At the end of his life (1810) he was just beginning to reconcile mimed and danced actions.

If this rather difficult, disagreeable and eminent personage did not succeed in making an impression at the Paris Opéra, his *Letters* and his disciples were to influence the entire contemporary theatre; thanks to him, all the European theatre world and many interested scholars began to consider the problems posed by mime.

JACQUES-LOUIS DAVID

It would seem that everything that needed to be said about David as artist must have been said. And there are pamphlets and theses concerning David as "Director of Revolutionary Festivals" which emphasize the political uses of "mass media" that he employed before the term even existed. Masterful organizer of the Revolution's national festivals, author, director and scene designer, he is the link between Noverre and Pixérécourt, second of the triumvirs who were to determine the future of theatrical staging. And in this role he is too little known.

On June 8th, 1790, the National Assembly voted to celebrate the National Confederation. David and Marie-Joseph Chénier, both members of the Convention, advocated a grandoise program. David was named official director of all the government-sponsored festivals and retained this post until the 9th of Thermidor.

The *Fête de la Fédération*, voted for on July 14th, 1790, dazzled the public with a procession of dragoons, riflemen, hussars, naval gunners (uniforms of that period were as colorful as costumes), disabled soldiers preceding a drum corps, musicians and official deputations following the heroes of the celebration: 18,000 federal deputies with their eighty-three banners (the oldest deputy of each district carried a white banner on which was painted the name of his region encircled by an oak wreath.) At the center of the Champs de Mars an "Altar of the Nation" had been erected, ornamented with perfume burners (a favorite accessory taken over from the Romans) and with inscriptions on all four facades; this was a rudimentary version of what these "altars" were to become. As for the spectators, shaken to their depths by these ceremonials—they were the very public of the Boulevard du Temple. This is apparent on comparing a print by Helman, after an eyewitness drawing by C. Monnet, with later lithographs by Pruche (*Physiognomies théâtrales, Boulevard du Temple*), Damorette, Boilly and Daumier. There is a whole group of these Revolutionary prints, oblong panoramas, signed Prieur, Simon, Bourjot, Swebach-Desfontaines and Girardet, which show the crowd and the performance of these pioneer "organized spontaneous demonstrations."

On September 18th, 1791, *The Fête of the Completion of the Constitution* opened with a band followed by heralds-at-arms in striking costumes, with national guardsmen afoot and ahorse, and closed with a balloon ascension, the car of the balloon trailing a variety of allegorical emblems. The ascension is, of course, the archtypical apotheosis which was already current practice in Servandoni's "theatre of machines."

David established the plan—one is tempted to write "scenario"—for the *Fête of the Unity and Indivisibility of the Republic* which took place on August 10th, 1793, early in the Reign of Terror. "The French people will rise at dawn" he wrote, "and the touching scene of their meeting will be illumined by the sun's first rays." (Daybreak was particularly popular for bringing up the curtain on pantomimes, melodramas and ballets for half a century.) The meeting place was set at the site of the destroyed Bastille where, amidst the ruins, David had erected "the fountain of Regeneration represented by Nature," in the form of a gigantic sphinx whose hands pressed her breasts from which streams of water jetted. The President of the Convention (Robespierre) and the delegates, one after another, drank a goblet of the regenerative waters. The cortege, composed of Conventionnels carrying ears of wheat, delegates each holding an olive branch, the *Enfants Trouvés* (abandoned or lost children being cared for by the State) in their cradles, and students of the Institute for the Blind singing hymns, proceeded to the Champ de Mars. On a triumphal chariot symbolizing Filial Piety, pulled along by a group of children, sat two aged people (this was one of the basic themes of melodrama, as were lost and abandoned children and the blind). These very themes were among those proposed by Robespierre in a speech on 18 Floreal An II (May 3rd, 1794) for celebrating the festivals of the *décadis* (according to the Revolutionary calendar). They included: to Love of Country—to Hatred of Tyrants and Traitors—to Modesty—to Glory and Immortality—to Friendship—to Conjugal Love—to Paternal Love—to Maternal Tenderness—to Filial Piety—to Misfortune—as well to the ages of man, agriculture and industry and finally—as in melodrama—to Happiness. And disavowing atheism, Robespierre introduced a celebration dedicated to the Supreme Being.

Getting back to the *Fête de l'Unité*, its success was such that the Conventionnel Bouquieur, member of the Committee for Public Education, in collaboration with the Citizen Moline, "secretary-clerk assigned to the Convention," worked it into a *"sans-culottide dramatique"* in five acts, titled *The Reunion of August 10th or the Inauguration of the French Republic*, based on the scenario and scenic effects of David. The President of the Convention and all the notables of the day, including the director of the ceremony, were depicted on stage; in the second act there was a ballet of the "Heroines of the 5th and 6th of October"; in the third, as two doves took shelter in the draperies of a statue of Liberty, the stage directions note: "Emotion of the director (the painter David)." The Com-

The paper cut-out theatres beloved in the 19th century faithfully reproduced all the characteristic scenery of the Theatre of Marvels.

Noverre introduced craftsmen and apprentices on stage in a realistic fashion which made the stylized costume covered with "attributes"—such as this 17th century design by Bérain for "a Sculptor"—seem outmoded.

Noverre was disdained for his début on the fairground stage. Yet his ballet "Medea" was plagiarized the very year of its creation by Gaetan Vestris, who presented it under his own name.

VUE DE LA MONTAGNE ELEVÉE AU CHAMP DE LA REUNION

pour la fête qui y a été célébrée en l'honneur de l'Être Suprême le Decadi 20 Prairial de l'an 2e de la République Française.

A Paris chez Chéreau Rue Jacques, aux deux Colonnes, près la Fontaine Severin. N.° 257.

The "practicable" set pieces of Moench, Gué, Ciceri and their competitors were the descendants of J.-L. David's "Mountain," awaiting only the garnishments of bushes, trees or the necessary bits of architecture for the apotheosis. This was a French element which was introduced into the Italian-influenced scene designs. A late 19th century arrangement in the Arena of Beziers, using a natural hillside, achieved the same sort of perspective. And in the 20th century, Cinemascope would move its crowds, put up and take down its mountains and light its skies according to the same system.

GUILBERT DE PIXÉRÉCOURT

"Le Mont Sauvage ou le duc de Bourgogne" ("The Wild Mountain or the Duke of Burgundy"). Stage set by Gué (Gaité, 1821).

THÉÂTRE DE LA GAITÉ.
3.e Acte du Mont Sauvage, songe du solitaire.

mittee of Public Safety underwrote the expenses of the production for three series of performances at the Opéra, the Opéra-Comique and the Théâtre Molière. It held the stage from March 13th, 1794 to January 21st, 1795 (after the 9th of Thermidor!).

The *Fête of the Supreme Being* on June 8th, 1794, was the last brilliant appearance of a powerful and self-assured Robespierre and the last triumph of David during the Revolutionary period. All Paris was either actor or spectator. The city was adorned with flowers; musicians were directed to start playing at daybreak as the various groups taking part in the ceremony assembled, section by section. The cortège stopped first at the Jardin National where Robespierre, leading the group—a long plume streaming from his Conventionnel's hat—set fire to a monument representing the "Enemies of Public Welfare," surmounted by Atheism. From the debris arose a statue of Wisdom. Columns of marchers, representing the different ages of man, joined the procession as it headed toward the Champ de Mars, accompanied by an ox-drawn chariot bearing tools of the arts and crafts. In the middle of the Champ de Mars a tremendous "practicable mountain" had been constructed, which the Cirque-Olympique might well have coveted for its pantomimes. In fact, the circus and all the theatres began to construct this type of usable scenery, but it was literally a landmark when it first appeared. It rose in six levels, masked by caves and crags modeled in the "rock." A "Tree of Liberty" perched on the summit. Members of the Convention, decked out in their curious official costume (a cross between ancient Rome and the troubadour style) were thus able to make their ascension up its "paths." The actor-athletes of the Boulevard were later to achieve all sorts of stunning effects—leaping chasms, fencing up and down its sides, scaling precipices—with versions of David's "mountain."

The Opéra ballet, led by Pierre Gardel, took part in this festival. Of all the innovations which David lavished on his productions only one appealed to Gardel—the use of classic Greek and Roman costumes—which he was to adopt for his mythological ballets such as *Hero and Leander* and *Telemachus*.

The upheaval of the 9th of Thermidor which reversed Robespierre and ended the Reign of Terror also put so staunch a Jacobin as David in prison—luckily only for four months. He was then set free and stayed quietly under cover until Bonaparte decreed him the leading artist and artistic arbiter of the Empire. In the interim he was replaced by Marie-Joseph Chénier, who had become his mortal enemy, and who never touched the grandeur of David's productions. *La Fête de la Victoire* on October 21st, 1794, made use of the mountain and column left over from the apotheosis of the Supreme Being; there were some impressive moments when the military schools, in mock combat, took a fortress by assault. A dramatic effect, in which a thousand voices repeated the vows after the President of the Convention, became a standard device in melodrama (the brigands vowing loyalty to their chief, loyal soldiers vowing to follow their unjustly-deposed prince and so forth).

Still a third director of public festivals was named, who followed the Davidian formula closely. Antoine-Marie Peyre, member of a well-known family of architects, had just been named to a post in the Beaux-Arts administration and is supposed to have assisted Alexandre Lenoir with the installations in the Museum of French Monuments. His *Fête de l'Agriculture* on June 28th, 1796, far surpassed the skimpy programs of J.-M. Chénier as well as the later festivals of the

Directorate. As in the pageants of David, village festivals were a feature. Statues, chariots, children and young girls representing either some farm attribute or occupation, were decorated with garlands and baskets of fruit. At the end of the celebration the President of the Convention plowed a furrow around the chariot of Liberty and Agriculture and then proceeded to sow—presumably seeds of peace and prosperity—while a ballet accompanied by songs of Jean-Jacques Rousseau was performed. The only novelty added thereafter was a chariot race in 1796 coinciding with the general popularity of the Cirque Franconi's equestrian performances, and foot races whose contestants were weighted down by toques garnished with towering ostrich plumes. The imposing phalanxes, resplendent in uniforms of a generation which regretted war and loved military glory, the manoeuvres of columns afoot and ahorse, all the "production numbers" set in motion by David, gave many pointers to the Franconis and their mimodramatists of the Cirque Olympique. The grandiose spectacles in which musicians from the Conservatoire, corps de ballet from the Opéra and innumerable troop units all circulated around the Champ de Mars in step, were to bring the Cirque-Olympique orchestra out of the limbo to which such musicians are usually relegated into rivalry with the tremendous groups dedicated to performing the works of Berlioz and Félicien David. [19]

We owe to Jacques-Louis David, in sum, usable scenery made to be climbed up, into and over to a degree not previously imagined. We also owe him the marshaling and management of those hordes of extras who appeared in battle, ballroom, parade and harvest scenes, filing through the streets, squares and public gardens, and finally onto the stage itself. Many of the pre-Romantic authors who survived him had attended his civic pageants and profited thereby. David prepared the stage for Pixérécourt.

GUILBERT DE PIXÉRÉCOURT

Today, when the director of a play or film rivals the author in importance, the name of Guilbert de Pixérécourt has emerged from oblivion. Without claiming any great literary value for his prose, once so popular and certainly so characteristic of its period, we must still recognize that no French theatre historian—in fact no historian of the occidental theatre—can ignore the melodrama and its most celebrated author. Pixérécourt furnished the Theatre of Marvels with its most stunning effects, and brought the classic situations of fairground comedy up-to-date. He determined the structure of a popular theatre which was to last through the 19th century. [20]

His first play, *Selico or the Generous Negroes* (1793) is typical of the Revolutionary negrophilia, and in conformity with the spectacular pantomimes that followed the opening of the Reign of Terror. "During the Directorate" recalled Charles Nodier, "there played in Paris for several years, under the bizarre name of *dialogued pantomimes,* a collection of formless scenes, abortive and monstrous; stormy as a riot, mysterious as a conspiracy, noisy and murderous as a battle; in them; one always found ghosts, caverns, cells and the marvelous; briefly, everything characteristic of an art form in its early infancy."

58

The public of the secondary Paris theatres—Pixérécourt's public—was drawn more and more from all classes, and if there was a public which wanted to be "attracted particularly by its eyes" according to Gautier, there were more demanding ones Saint Petersburg and the patent theatres of London, where Pixérécourt was also honored in the repertories.

America, which heretofore had not developed large-scale spectacular stagecraft, was to find in Pixérécourt the inspiration for enlarging the scope of Alexandre Placide's early experiments in lavishness.

It was thus for this multiple public with a variety of tastes that Pixérécourt, by the ingenuity of his treatment, his marvellous grasp of theatrical effects, and by the well-arranged progression of scenes, began to remodel the riches of the popular theatre. As Noverre had called for unity in elements of ballet, so Pixérécourt determined that scenery, music, dance, lighting and the very movements of his actors should no longer be left to chance but made integral parts of his plays.

In 1800 *Coelina or the Child of Mystery* seemed to anticipate the Romantic background by its décors and the alternation of calm countryside scenes with catastrophes. The following year *The White Pilgrim*, adapted, as *Coelina* had been, from a novel by the indefatigable Ducray-Duminil (who had found *his* inspiration in *The Little Savoyards* of Marsollier and Dalayrac) gave yet another opportunity for staging a village festival. Only ten years after the Revolution, it is curious to find in the cast a heroic and good-hearted nobleman attended by a faithful old retainer. In 1830, *The Polish Mines*, which was to be translated into Italian, Polish, German and English, supplied Cherubini with the libretto of his opera *Faniska*. In the stage directions Pixérécourt outlines an early version of what was to become a spectacular feature in later productions—the stage divided horizontally in two levels, both usable. *The Wife of Two Husbands*, set in Antwerp, featured a Flemish *kermesse* "in the style of Teniers."

Pixérécourt, still fulfilling his self-appointed destiny as "the complete man of the theatre," directed all his own plays. Not only did he supervise the usual production staff found in secondary theatres of the period—scene designer, costumer, machinist, composer and ballet master—but he annotated his scripts with directions for mime, lighting effects and background music. In 1804, he himself laid out the choreographic schema for *The Moors of Spain or the Power of Childhood*, alternating dances by a retinue of maidens with those by a group of warriors. At the close of the ballet a dove flies across to the heroine who removes the message tucked in its wing—which, of course, announces a catastrophe.

In 1805, Pixérécourt's *Robinson Crusoe*, brimming over with local color and sumptuous effects, was the hit of the season. Finding it difficult to reconcile Defoe's theme of solitude and the exigencies of melodrama, the author set out to populate the desert isle. A shipload of mutineers, led by one Atkins, stops to abandon the captain (who turns out to be Robinson's brother-in-law Don Diego), Isadore (Robinson's son!), a loyal sailor from Provence (dialect comedian), the old nurse of Robinson's wife and a few supers. Things look dark, but Pixérécourt brings on Igloue, father of Friday, who has had friendly relations with French traders in the past. Igloue brings his tribe to foil the perfidious Atkins. A letter of homage by the composer Alexandre Piccini, which precedes the published text, tells us that the entrance of Robinson in his goatskin costume—carrying his parasol and with a superb parrot that made apt comments on the action (a ventriloquist?—parrots are not that infallibly obliging)—was greeted with an ovation.

In his preface Pixérécourt refers those who are interested to the source of his ethnographic information: *Les Moeurs des Sauvages américains comparés aux Moeurs des Premiers Temps* of the Reverend Père Lafitau. In all, ". . . Three acts of gaiety, sentiment, . . . strictly authentic costumes, magnificent décors, varied dances, well-managed extras . . ." enthused Piccini.

The machinery, and particularly the lighting techniques, of Gué's settings for *The Savage Mountain or the Duke of Burgundy* in 1821 were much the same as Robertson's magic lantern techniques for the dream of repentance in the *Fantasmagoria*. In *The Guardian Angel or the Female Demon* (1808), Pixérécourt follows the old fairground players' formula (an old Plautus formula, for that matter) of highborn persons who hide their rank either to watch over and protect a loved one, or to be loved for their qualities alone. *The Guardian Angel* was tailored to measure for Mademoiselle Bourgeois, champion lady fencer of the Boulevard, famous in *travesti* roles (what the English used to call "breeches parts"), and for her changes from audacity and energy in masculine characters to gentleness and submission in her woman's costumes. She appeared as a gipsy, a page, an old man, a court lady, a magician. The other novelty of *The Guardian Angel* was its children's ballets, which were to continue in high favor through the 1850's. *The Union of Mars and Venus, The Marvelous Lamp, The Underground Cistern* (this title really should stay in French—*La Citerne* sounds so much pleasanter), *Polichinelle Swallowed by the Whale* and the *Polka of the Salons* featured the youthful dancers disguised—turn by turn—as little cupids, little blackamoors, dwarfs and little worldlings. Child performers are regarded rather squeamishly by any sophisticated audience today, although the general public still loves them. Yet the European travelling companies' system of putting the child—acrobat, juggler, dancer—to work in public at the earliest possible age has valid advantages. For that matter, the great Russian ballet schools even today put the child pupils on stage whenever possible, with no detriment to their health or education.

It would be too long a matter to list all the surprises that Pixérécourt conjured up: in *La Citerne*, composed of elements from the Italian Comedy and Revolutionary pantomime, one stage set collapsed completely into artistic ruins [21]; the grotesque ballet in *The Ruins of Babylon* in 1810; the death of the villain by fire in *Marguerite d'Anjou* the same year; the trained dog in *The Forest of Bondy* in 1814 [22]; life on shipboard in *Christopher Columbus* in 1815; volcanos erupting—Mount Etna in *The Belvedere* of 1818, Vesuvius in *The Death's Head or the Ruins of Pompei* of 1827; the flood followed by a tempest in *The Daughter of the Exile or Eight Months in Two Hours* in 1819 [23]. For each title there was a new effect, and by his ingenuity as a director and his skillful use of supers (the equivalent of extras), Pixérécourt was not unworthy of the designation given recently by Marcel Astruc: "forerunner of the cinema."

In addition to his melodramas, Pixérécourt collaborated on several fairy spectacles, which in technique and subject are inseparable from the Theatre of Marvels: *Ondine or the Water Nymph* in 1830 (where the underwater creature who appeared in French ballets since the period of Louis XIV, reappeared); *The Four Elements* in 1833, with a weak plot but fantastically rich tableaux, and finally *Bijou or the Child of Paris* in 1835, indirect cause of Pixérécourt's retirement, as the Gaîté burned down on the day it opened. [24]

Toward the end of his life an embittered Pixérécourt heard his melodramas judged out of fashion and too far in spirit from the Romantic concept. Yet he left his personal mark on the entire popular theatre, by the introduction of realistic details, the importance assigned to background music, and the cohesiveness imposed on all the other elements of melodrama.

"Series of Exercises by the Famous Monkey trained by Sr Spinacuta, premier rope dancer, who has had the honour of dancing before the King of France and the Royal Family at the Menus Plaisirs of Choisy. Sr Spinacuta has had them engraved in this manner for ornamenting the Collector's study and placing under glass." At the bottom of the 16th and last plate it states: "Sr Spinacuta, when requested, will show this Divertissement in Schools and Convents for the convenience of persons who cannot go to public performances." (1766)

WAITING FOR THE BELL.—A SCENE UNDER THE STAGE AT NIBLO'S GARDEN.—MISS MARIE MAJILTON WAITING FOR THE SIGNAL TO MAKE HER APPEARANCE THROUGH THE STAR TRAP IN "THE BLACK CROOK."—SEE PAGE 3.

CHAPTER IV

Techniques of the Theatre of Marvels

MONG the "techniques of the Marvelous," that is to say the means for its realization, mime and direction (the nearest equivalent to the French *"mise en scène"* or the ordering of everything which is on stage or takes place there), seem inseparable. If, during the first half of the 18th century, the term *"mise en scène"* applied primarily to scenery and costumes, it finished by including the "supers," the principals, and mimed as well as spoken language. In France this mimed language, which goes back to the medieval "mysteries" and the *"Soties de la Confrérie de la Passion,"* has the same traditions as the comic dance. Dance, mime and direction are thus united in the same historical perspective. The 14th century was already rich in royal pageants with splendid allegorical décors, triumph wagons laden with trophies. The crowds of brilliantly-costumed dancing and acrobatic demons, delight of populace and nobles alike, were still having the same success four hundred years later in the acrobatic dance interludes of itinerant troupes.

Mime and *mise en scène* had two sources. The first was Italian court ballets which were introduced by Catherine de Medici in the 16th century. Under Henri IV these mythological ballets took a more fanciful turn—with *Les Echecs (The Chessboard)* for example, all the dancers represented chessmen and moved in their appointed ploys. Under Louis XIV, however, the mythological-allegorical subjects were again fashionable. The second source was the pantomimes or comedies of the itinerant companies. These were particularly important because the laws prohibited these companies from allowing their actors to speak or sing; the Italian Comedians, protected by powerful nobles, were permitted to speak, but acrobatics still played a major part in their comedies. In fact, the humor of regional Italian dialects (Harelquin from Bergamo, Pantaloon from Venice, and so on) did not transplant too well, so that the license to speak meant less than it would have to a French company.

The perfect example of a fairground theatre production was *Les Forces de l'Amour et de la Magie (The Powers of Love and Magic)* presented at the Saint-Germain and Saint-Laurent fairs in 1678. This buffoonery was a bizarre parade of twenty-four acrobats of various nationalities from the troupe of Allard and Maurice, in which eccentric dances, sleight-of-hand tricks, leaps and sarabands succeeded one another. The first-act decor was an early example of the characteristic "untamed landscape." Here and there, costumed as Polichinelles or demons, were tall thin acrobats standing on pedestals, immobile as statues. Merlin, servant to the Magician Zoroaster who is in love with the shepherdess Gresinda, is the butt of countless tricks. The first act ends with an explosion of forward somersaults.

In the second act, Zoroaster orders a series of divertissements to amuse Gresinda, including an eccentric dance by acrobatic shepherds, a sleight-of-hand number with three goblets from which three monkeys emerge, and a pile which contains winged serpents. Gresinda, more frightened than seduced by this performance, implores the aid of Juno (!) who intervenes. When the magician tries to clasp the recalcitrant shepherdess in his arms, he finds himself face to face with a demon who drops from the flies. Merlin then recites the moral of this story: "Everything by love, nothing by force!" and the curtain falls on a saraband in nine parts.

Scholarly research also contributed to the development of the pantomime language so indispensable to a "visual" theatre. This was due to the Swiss, Jean-Gaspard Lavater, and the German, J. J. Engel, whose works reached a wide public in France at the very time when the popular theatre was evolving new forms.

Lavater, whose treatise on physiognomy with explanatory illustrations created a sensation in France, became something of a seer during his own lifetime. Under the Directorate a series of almanachs were dedicated to him, the first of which, edited by Madame Mérard de Saint-Just, was issued in the Year VIII (1799-1800). The second appeared in the Year IX with a frontispiece that looked like a pantomime setting: (*Le Petit Lavater ou Tablettes mystérieuses*) (*The Pocket Lavater, or Mystic Tablets*) a vaulted cavern complete with a flickering suspended lamp, and a gypsy fortune teller reading the cards for a young maiden. The abuse of Lavater's dictum: "The face is the principal reflection of the soul's impulses," caused certain exaggerated facial grimaces which verged on the ridiculous, but his influence was unquestionable.

Engel, member of the Berlin Royal Academy of Sciences in his *Idées* on gesture and theatrical action, took into consideration not only the face but the actor's entire body. To elucidate his theories, he calls for legends and fables familiar to everyone since the days of Greek and Roman pantomime, and proposes to the actors that they work on these cliché-plots, insisting that "one must avoid choosing an unknown subject for a pantomime" but adopt instead "imitations of daily, very ordinary events, which can be understood without explanation." In this he approached the theories of Diderot, who was one of the earliest to search for acting effects that could render "the realities of daily life." To that end Diderot had introduced his "composite scenes," analogous to Noverre's compositions of craftsmen and apprentices, at the same time recommending the use of "tableux"—those frozen groups which brought down a curtain, introduced a transformation scene or formed an apotheosis. During the Directorate the tableau was incorporated in all theatrical forms. Overworked for the rest of the century, it was finally eliminated by the realistic theatre.

In all honesty, taking seven of the most successful comic ballet-pantomimes— *La Fille mal gardée, Les Six Ingénus, Rosine et Almaviva, La Neige, Une Visite à Bedlam, Les Artistes* and *Le Diable boiteux*—which were well above the ordinary level, it must be admitted that five of them came from sources already well-

"Der Kobold," the first ballet for which Jules Perrot was named as choreographer, presented in Vienna with Carlotta Grisi, in 1838.

Print from the Parisian series, "Le Bon Genre:" "The Incomparable Ravel." "Watching them, we thought of what prodigious suppleness and serpentine flexibility the human body could attain by these exercises, that same body which a routine school education renders so awkward, so stiff, so heavy and so ungraceful . . ."

known: two from the Opéra-Comique, two from popular farce, a third from Le Sage's celebrated tale, another from a popular print, etc. It is really quite apparent that all the plots of all the entertainments comprising the Theatre of Marvels more or less resemble each other, and when by chance such is not the case, the protagonists remain clearly identifiable: hero, villain, simpleton, heroine, noble father and their confidants.

Engel demanded that theatrical background music have the same associative and evocative qualities as the pantomime plots: joy should be expressed by piercing notes (!) and "only the drums and trumpet" could evoke "the idea of a noble and majestic fête." Finally, he urges transferring scenes from famous paintings onto the stage, incorporating them as appropriate or even making the occasion to use them.

If mime at this period was as limited in its means of expression as Engel claims, by what miracle was it able to enrich the work of so imposing a group of actors and dancer-choreographers as Fréderick Lemaître, Edmund Marie Dorval, Mélingue, Aumer, Mazilier, Mazurier, Henry, Perrot . . . without forgetting the genius of pantomime, Deburau?

What Engel seems to forget is the influence of the itinerant troupes: it was acrobatic stylization which would enable the great mimed scenes to bridge the gap from pantomime to melodrama and thence to the Romantic *ballet d'action*. Moreover, if the fairground mimes were obliged to perform feats of strength and skill, the dancers, rope dancers, and acrobats in turn were usually obliged to take lessons in mime.

Actually, actors and dancers of the Boulevard were often obliged to fill three jobs: mime and dancer in pantomimes and mimodramas, actor in melodramas. In the pantomimes, gestures which represented certain "key" emotions tended to become stylized, while the dancers, by dint of working with acrobat-actors, achieved the expressive mime demanded by Noverre. The fact that Emilie Bigottini of the Ambigu-Comique, who preceded Mme Quériau as queen of mime during the pre-Romantic period, was also *première danseuse* at the same time, is but one telling point to indicate the close relationship of the two arts. Thus, when the Decree of 1807 compelled most of the theatres that had not been closed to resume their original programs of "acrobatic scenes," trained animal acts, gymnastic feats and rope dancing, the fairground school was enabled to continue its instruction. Whence the renewal of the acrobatic theatre's influence which lasted through the height of the Romantic period.

The administration of Louis XVIII, favorable to returning lost privileges to the old-established secondary theatres, was less charitable to newcomers. In 1816, Bertrand and Fabien, when they established their Théâtre des Funambules, in order to present pantomimes were obliged to make every actor enter by means of a tight rope, permanently stretched across the stage. Fréderick Lemaître, in his début at the Variétés-Amusantes, was concealed in a bear skin; at the Funambules he entered walking on his hands and made a forward somersault, even if he was supposed to be a "Count Adolph" of illustrious lineage. In 1821, the Theatre of the Panorama-Dramatique, despite the support of Baron Taylor, Alaux and Charles Nodier, could not obtain authorization to present more than two speaking actors on stage at a time, and had to be content with ballet-pantomimes or hybrid, partially-mimed plays.

Nevertheless, acrobatics, dance and stylized mime were the arts by which a Deburau, a Mazurier, a Fréderick Lemaître an Edmund Kean and a Perrot were to create their masterful performances; these five great artists had all been acrobat-dancers. The celebrated Fréderick, whether in his frenetic race through *Robert Macaire,* or in the walzt of *Mephistopheles* never lost the wonderful suppleness from his days at the Funambules or the Cirque-Olympique. "In *Cartouche,*" wrote the Countess Dash, "one often noted the way in which he used his hands and the way in which he danced a sort of *chaconne.*"

The iconography of this period is rich enough to constitute a veritable "gallery of gestures": the frontispiece for Le Sage's *Théâtre de la Foire* illustrated the emergence of mime and dance in little comedies and interludes; the thirty-four plates scattered throughout the two volumes of Engel were primarily a theoretician's observations. But the alphabet of extravagant gestures that characterized 19th-century mime were set down for posterity in the *Petite Galerie Dramatique* of Martinet (later Martinet-Hautecoeur) in the first series (1796-1843) and in Mme Masson's untitled plagiarism published from 1810—1813. (In England the "penny plain, tuppence coloured" popular prints recorded the same gestures.) In spite of the stiffness of the attitudes and the exaggerations or poor drawing of these portraits, the Masson series caught the inner conviction of the actors expressing noble or base sentiments.

Series of porcelain or faience dishes appeared representing "the twelve emotions," one per plate (including "gluttony"); each represented by a Pierrot who bore a tolerable resemblance to Deburau. Their manufacture began toward 1840 and continued to the end of the 19th century. The quality of the drawing and of the china itself was extremely variable: porcelain, opaque porcelain and iron ware, from the factories of Creil, Gien, Choisy-le-Roi and Sarreguemines. These plates, in black and white or touched with color, document many aspects of the Theatre of Marvels. They are rather pretty things, and becoming hard to find.

The *metteur en scène,* who would be called "director" in English today, was already the subject of a chapter in the *Code théâtral* of Pierre-Joseph Rousseau in 1829; in 1835, *le Monde dramatique* published a series of studies entitled: *Inside our Theatres: Mise en Scène,* especially devoted to examining the functions of the director, stage manager, scene and costume designers and machinist; it emphasized the complexities inherent in the preparation of any type of stage spectacle.

The *metteur en scène,* or "master of ceremonies" according to Jules Janin, was already as indispensable to the 19th-century theatre as he is to that of the 20th. His creation owes much to the Revolutionary period and to that man of genius who had a city, a people and an epoch at his disposal—Jacques-Louis David.

The term *mise en scène* itself seems to have been synonymous at first with "decoration," and Grimm in 1786, as had Favert in 1760, uses it in connection with sets and costumes. Discussing a troubadour play by Monvel, Grimm remarked that the Théâtre Français had rivalled the fairground pantomimes' opulence: *"Le Chevalier sans peur et sans reproche (The Fearless and Irreproachable Knight)* offers the pomp of a true spectacle. Nothing was spared for the *mise en scène* of this play; the period costumes were perfectly reproduced, and with a magnificence that rivalled their exactitude."

The term, in its complete sense, appears on the title page of an 1800 libretto with the authors' names: *"Les Chevaliers du Soleil (The Knights of the Sun)*

66

This print, dated 1741, of Grimaldi's Acrobatic Theatre, shows some thirty-five different traditional numbers, many of which were essential to the development of 19th century acrobatic mime. This print would seem to have influenced later ones by the Bassets, Langlume, Ledowyen and other ateliers of the rue Saint-Jacques.

Ioh. Iacob Schübler delin.   Ioh. Balth. Probst Sculpsit   Cum Pr. Sac. Cæs. Maj.   Hæred. Ier. Wolffii exc. A.V.

I. Iacob Schübler del.   Ioh. Balth. Probst Sculpsit   Cum Pr. Sac. Cæs. Maj.   Hæred. Ier. Wolffii exc. A.V.

The gamut of moods which pantomime commands:—the mad anarchy of the Italian Comedians, the poised coquetry of Barrault, the insouciance of Deburau and the basic comic catastrophe photographed by Louis Lumière.

A commemorative lithograph of Baptiste Deburau in his most famous roles by his colleague at the Funambules—Désiré Vautier. The pantomimes represented are: "Love and Despair," "The 1000-Franc Note," "Black and White," "The Pretty Soldiers," "The Dupes or the Two Georgettes," "The Trials," "The Devil's Hair," "The Female Elf," "The Golden Dream," "The Salad Vendor," "Pierrot in Africa," and "Perrette or the Two Poachers." (Bibl. de l'Op.)

Le Capitaine fracasse   Turlupin   Gros Guillaume   Gaultier Garguille

The gross gaities of the 16th-century "parade," with its monologues, monkeys, sketches, hard-selling sales talks and adroit shills, might overnight be consigned by constituted authority to dumbshow, and the comic interludes entrusted to mime. In either case stock characters of the Italian Comedy appear and reappear. The 17th century Pulcinella, the Italo-French mime Delpini and Marcel Marceau convey even in the immobility of print and photo both subtlety and forthrightness.

Carlo Delpini, celebrated pantomime dancer and clown, performed in England from 1785 to about 1828. In this London print as Pierrot pretending to weep for the death of his master, his style seems close to that of Deburau. He was author of "Don Juan or the Libertine Destroyed," a pantomime ballet based on Gluck's ballet, first presented in London in 1787, and in Philadelphia, with refurbishments of scenery, costumes, music and dances, from 1792 through the remainder of the century.

The "Galerie Martinet" prints of Boulevard stars expressing "states of the soul" have the same emphatic gestures as their English colleagues in the "penny plain tuppence coloured" or their Italian confrères in the popular woodcuts: scorn and anger by Franconi "jeune" in "The Renegade"; grandeur of spirit and contempt of death by Marty in "The Forest of Edinburg"; vengefulness and murderous intent by Fresnoy in "The Count of Glethorn"; and concentrated hatred by Philippe as "Montbars the Exterminator."

The Ambigu-Comique Theatre.

Mlle Elisa Gougibus, aged six, as "la petite Nichon."

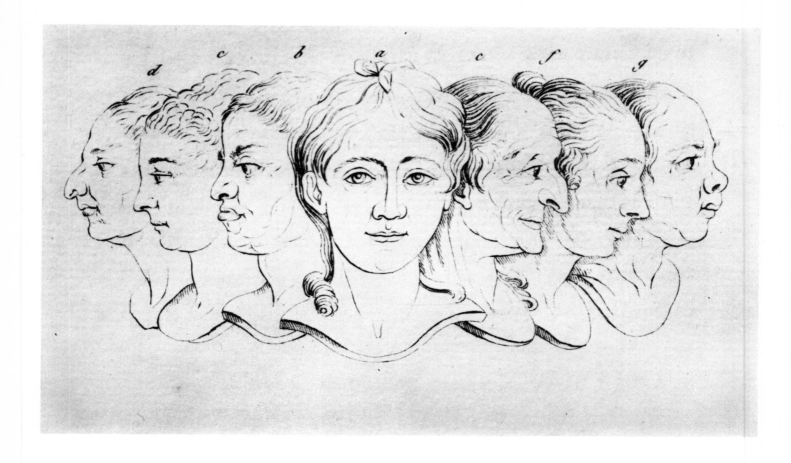

Facial characteristics and movements which constitute facial play, an essential element of mime, became modish subjects for research by the end of the 18th century with the publication of Lavater's "Treatise on Physiognomy." This carried on the work of Rubens' "Theory of the Human Face," of Charles Le Brun's "Physiognomical Geometry" and the handsome studies by Morel d'Arleux on "Animal Physiognomy" after Le Brun.

The evolution from frog to Apollo in the 1803 edition of Lavater followed the same line as had Camper in 1791. These studies of human and animal physiognomies had a vogue which greatly benefited the art of pantomime—and later furnished inspiration for the drawings of Grandville.

of Bignon and Eugène Hus, *mise en scène* and combats by Citizen Gougibus the elder." The Gougibus brothers (or Gougy or Gougi) came from an old family of itinerant performers. In 1788 they were members of Audinot's company on the Boulevard du Temple, at the period when his success was crowned by the construction of his theatre "in the Gothic style." The Gougibus brothers were dancers: Pierre-Toussaint, the younger, was to remain just that; but Jean-Toussaint, the elder, quickly acquired an enviable reputation in the new theatre world. Mime, dramatic author, specialist in staged combats, and director, he tried for striking effects from his very first one-act pantomime, *Zelly ou le Naufrage* (*Zelly, or The Shipwreck*). Then he left to join Nicolet's company, as mime and *metteur en scène*; he turns up almost everywhere on the Boulevard until about 1830. His daughter, aged 6, who played *La Petite Nichon* at the Jeux-Gymniques became a star of fairy spectacles under the name of Madame Lémenil. In 1820, Gougibus the elder signed a contract with the Funambules, from which its proprietors, Fabien and Bertrand, derived more satisfaction than when they signed Deburau, who actually was making their fortune.

Other names became celebrated as *metteurs en scène* of the Romantic period: Ferdinand Laloue of the Cirque-Olympique shared critical laurels with his collaborator Adolphe Franconi. With him, and Théodore Nézel, Léopold Chandezon, Henri Villemot, Prosper Lepoitevin de Saint-Almé, Anicet Bourgeois and *tutti quanti*, that is "in collaboration," Laloue wrote his famous works starring dogs and horses.

According to the *Repertoire* of the Cirque-Olympique, Laloue began his career as *metteur en scène* in 1835, although he had been an author-in-title of the circus since 1820. Henri Franconi (nicknamed Minette) and his son Adolphe began to establish the formulas for moving masses of men and horses in the circus arena. Minette, having established his reputation as *metteur en scène* between 1802 and 1827, turned the direction over to his son, who brought in Laloue and Villain de Saint-Hilaire as associates.

The transposition of celebrated paintings into "living" tableaux was a specialty of the Cirque-Olympique. When Cuvelier was inspired to use a painting of General Lejeune—the attack on the convoy near Salinas—the critic Chaalons d'Argé wrote that "the idea had all Paris flocking—it would be impossible to stage the movements and manoeuvres of troops more expertly. The Franconis have no rivals in this field."

Although Laloue was less an innovator than the collaborator of an already-renowned master, he nevertheless developed the idea of reproducing contemporary paintings by Gros, Charlet, Horace Vernet and their rivals. He was also fascinated by stage machinery, and induced the elder Laurent, acrobat-dancer-author, to leave the Funambules. Famous for his fantastic pantomimes with extensive use of machinery, Laurent became Laloue's collaborator in the celebrated *féerie Les Pillules du Diable* (*The Devil's Pills*) in 1839.

The number of scene designers and painters who worked for the Franconi-Laloue administration far exceeded that of the Opéra or the Porte-Saint-Martin. The prosperous days of Minette Franconi produced a list of names including those of Moench (or Moenk, or Munch or Munich), and Isidore, and the younger group: Gué, Blanchard, Justin Leys, Demay (or Dumay), and Gosse; then the deans of the profession: Cicéri, Philastre and Cambon, Wagner, Leroux, Martin and Thierry. The machinist, who regularly received his own ovation, was named Sacré.

He made possible the grandiose visions of the Franconi, of Laloue and of Dejean, who took over direction of the circus in 1835 when it was in financial difficulties due to its lavish productions, and managed to increase not only the splendor but also the profits.

Another *metteur en scène* was the dashing François-Antoine Harel, who produced *Dick-Radjah,* a melodrama by Saint-Hilaire with an elephant as star, on the stage of the Odéon or second Théâtre Français, in 1832. Harel, friend of the great Romantic authors, verged continually on bankruptcy because of the luxury with which he produced their plays. He was a legendary figure of the Boulevard. After having emptied his purse at the Odéon, he started anew at the Porte-Saint-Martin, where his mimo-dramas rivalled those of the circus. In one of his frequent moments of financial embarrassment he even thought of pulling in the crowds by presenting an animal trainer with his whole menagerie on stage.

At the Opéra, an improvement was visible under its new director, Dr. Véron, and his associate (later his successor) Edmond Duponchel, architect, artistic director and costume designer. These two were instrumental in raising the Opéra's scenery and *mise en scène* to Boulevard standards. They brought in the Boulevard designers and choreographers who created *Giselle, La Peri, Le Diable boiteux (The Devil on Two Sticks)* and *La Filleule des Fées (The Fairies' Goddaughter).* But after 1850 the Opéra again began to settle into its ancient set of prejudices. [26]

The so-called "classic" mime of the 19th century, which reached its apogee with artists such as Deburau, Mazurier and Fréderick Lemaître no longer exists except in the ballet and certain circus and magicians' acts. In the early cinema, vestiges of classic mime reappeared; the talking film eliminated them. Farina, Séverin and the master Georges Wague carried on the tradition against odds; Jean-Louis Barrault, Pierre Etaix and Jacques Tati in their recent films, certain choreographers, and above all Marceau, remain the great exponents of mime.

The *metteur en scène* so well served by mime, gradually turned toward the new school of realism. His techniques may have changed but not his professional procedures.

CHAPTER V

Boulevard Du Temple
Versus Opera

WHETHER melodrama, pantomime, ballet or circus mimodrama, the plots and techniques of the "marvellous" repertory were quite familiar to its public at the beginning of the 19th century. Between 1789 and 1800 the various forms of popular entertainment emerged at the very time that a new struggle was impending between the secondary theatres which had absorbed the fairground companies and the State-subsidized houses with their official prerogatives. The Opéra, led by Pierre Gardel, spearheaded the persecution of the Boulevard theatres.

Although the famous fairs of Saint-Germain and Saint-Laurent had disappeared since 1786, their principal theatrical leasees such as Audinot and Nicolet, were already established on the Boulevard du Temple, as well as others of the fairground performers.

The great families of travelling performers, all of whose specialties were based on acrobatics and who handed on the traditions of popular art from generation to generation, are a most singular phenomenon. Ballet, and later the circus, which recruited from them, would keep the same dynastic pride. They were sometimes veritable royal families, with international alliances in which a caravan or a lease at a particular fair were as carefully considered in matrimonial arrangements as a duchy in an alliance of the House of Valois. Guardians of techniques and traditions, they also became artistic innovators, often by trying to outwit the laws that plagued them.

Nicolet's hall, built in 1764 next to the former site of a mechanical spectacle put on by Fourré, was the future Gaîté theatre; for a time, after a performance at Versailles in 1779, it was known as *"Les Grands Danseurs du Roi."*

In 1769, Nicolet's Theatre was taken over by his great competitor Audinot, who teamed up with Arnould-Mussot. Unlike Nicolet, Audinot was not a member of a theatrical family: he abandoned the trade of wigmaker in order to join the Italian Comedians. The Parisians were as amused by his marionettes as by his vaudevilles and ballets performed by child actors. These ill-defined entertainments—a mixture of parody, drama, comedy, singing and dancing—were then known as *"ambigus."* Audinot's theatre accordingly became the Ambigu-Comique.

The third of the great Boulevard theatres, the Porte-Saint-Martin, opened its doors in 1802. Let us only mention here that it was heir to all the theatres of the preceding period.

Some posters preserved in the Musée Carnavalet reveal the continuity of the subjects treated and the artistes' work. In their program for January 20th, 1779, the "Grands Danseurs du Roi" announced a ballet, *La Rose et le Bouton (The Rose and the Bud)*, interposed between a rope dance by "*Le Petit Diable*" (Pol Rédigé) and the first performance of a pantomime "interspersed with fighting and dancing": *Les Contrebandiers (The Smugglers)*.

Indeed, a taste for ballet and pantomime was infecting the public which had originally come to see the acrobats and enjoy the horseplay of the charlatan's parade. Originating in the success of mythological ballets and their brilliant interpreters at the Opéra, this type of spectacle, previously reserved for aristocratic patrons, spread to the Boulevard theatres.

The success of the allegorical fantasy *La Rose et le Bouton* was durable: it appears in the program of the "*Grands Danseurs*" after the taking of the Bastille, when Parisians were invited to see this ballet, sandwiched between *Le Raisin d'Amour* and the misfortunes of *Cupidon Puni par Vénus*.

On January 24th, 1785, the eve of the Revolution, *Le Ravissement d'Europe (The Rape of Europa)*, a subject which would have delighted Gardel, shared the evening with a harlequinade and rope dancing. On October 26th, 1787, the "*Grands Danseurs*" again announced "*The Rape of Europa—by Jupiter in the Form of a Bull*, an Heroic Pantomime in Five Acts, with a wealth of Spectacle."

However, amid the rope dancing, springboard jumping and juggling, signs of the new interest in folklore began to appear in 1787. They can be noted in *A Flemish Festival, The Port of London*, a "Great Pantomime-Ballet," the Béarn ballet, introduced by the "*Petits Comédiens*" of the Duke of Beaujolais in *The Béarn Wedding*, and *The American Hero*, that noble savage who continued his exploits with the "*Grands Danseurs.*"

The constant rivalry between Nicolet and Audinot gave the spectators their money's worth.

Nicolet kept the spoken word in the background; Audinot, however, began to introduce a bastard form, "dialogue pantomime." Thereupon Nicolet resorted to *Leitmotiv*, the expression of mood by an appropriate musical phrase. This tradition persisted with Deburau at the Funambules, but was also a feature of most forms in the popular theatre.

During the last years of Louis XVI, the theatres enjoyed much greater freedom than during the First Republic and the Empire. How did the Revolution affect the secondary theatres? After promising the most complete freedom, the Convention insisted upon a little propaganda; during the Terror, this minimum became a maximum.

Beffroy de Reigny, known to the tenderhearted by the nickname of "Cousin Jacques," was the popular dramatic writer at the beginning of the Revolution. Before the flight to Varennes, the constitutional monarchy seemed fairly stable on the whole. *Nicodemus in the Moon or the Peaceful Revolution* (1790), was inspired by this short-lived equilibrium. The 19th-century fairy play owes much to "Cousin Jacques," who added the goodhearted simpleton of *Nicodemus* to the characters such as Harlequin, Pierrot, Columbine and Pantaloon inherited from Italian Comedy. Devoted as he was to the idea of constitutional monarchy, "Cousin Jacques" makes use of a lunar kingdom to which his hero ascends in a

Par permission de Monseigneur le Lieutenant-Général de Police.

AMPHITHEATRE ANGLOIS,
DES SIEURS ASTLEY.
Rue & Faubourg du Temple.

Les quatre dernieres Représentations, c'est-à-dire, aujourd'hui Vendredi 1er Avril, Samedi 2, Dimanche 3, & Lundi 4, pour la Clôture.

PLUSIEURS EXERCICES EXTRAORDINAIRES D'EQUITATION.

Dans les intervalles,

LE COMBAT NAVAL, &c.

TOUS LES TOURS PAR LES SAUTEURS.

PLUSIEURS EQUILIBRES SUR LE FIL-D'ARCHAL PAR LE SIEUR SAUNDERS.

LA SCENE COMIQUE DES DEUX PAILLASSES,

ET LE RÔLE DU TAILLEUR ET SON CHEVAL,

Avec tous les Exercices du Sieur ASTLEY, fils, & la Troupe Angloise.

Une jeune Demoiselle Américaine [Eleve du Sieur ASTLEY, fils] aura l'honneur de faire différens tours sur un & deux chevaux.

On ouvrira à cinq heures, & on commencera à six heures précises par les OMBRES.

Premieres Loges 3 livres: Secondes 36 sols: Troisiemes 24 sols: uatriemes 12 s.

Perm. d'imp. & distr. ce 7 Mars 1785. LE NOIR.   De l'imp. de P. DE LORMEL, rue du Foin.

38

A program from the first circus established in France by Philip Astley, featuring an equestrian interlude, "The Tailor and His Horse," forerunner of the full-length shows with animal stars. (1785) (Bibl Natl, Cabinet des Estampes)

Des cendres d'Ilion renait une autre Troye : VUE DE LA NOUVELLE DECORATION Un Prince bienfaisant pour récréer Paris,
Venés de toutes parts livrés vous à la Joye ; DE LA FOIRE S.t GERMAIN A rétabli ce lieu, digne séjour des Ris.

A Paris chez Basset rue S. Jacques a S.t Geneviève

More than a century lies between these two prints—the first of Nicolet's theatre at the Foire Saint-Germain and the second of a "Grand Cirque Paillasson" in a popular print of a fairground in the early 1900's—but the atmosphere is unchanged.

"Jocko the Brazilian Ape," ballet by Philippe Taglioni, taken from Mazurier's vehicle, the "Jocko" of MM. Gabriel and Rochefort.
". . . the charming aspect of this sort of performance is taking a tremendous voyage with one's eyes alone, never quitting one's box."

BELLEROPHON TRAGEDIE

Partisan's of the mythological and allegorical ballets of the Paris Opéra, which had remained almost unchanged in style since the period of this handsome setting (1686) inspired by Bérain, were faced with a new stagecraft derived from the popular theatre.

This Parisian poster shows a number which is often described—badly—in contemporary reviews: The Equilibrist and the Windmill. The costumes and accessories, troubadour or exotic in style, and the windmill itself, would fit nicely into any number of melodrama settings.

"... The great charm of the Opéra, one scarcely perceived and which keeps it standing amid the ruins of the other theatres, is that nowhere else is convention so forced and so far removed from all that is natural. In fact, what more unnatural than to see a conspirator demanding silence by singing at the top of his voice or a persecuted woman expressing her despair in a cabriole."

Pierre Gardel in the title role of "Telemachus," ballet presented at the Paris Opéra in 1790.

The Paris Opéra of the rue Le Peletier, designed by the architect Debret, constructed in 1821 and destroyed by fire in 1873.

"Montgolfier balloon," foreshadowing the scientific fairy plays influenced by Jules Verne. A mixture of spoken and sung couplets explained that the King of the Moon is kindhearted and devoted to his subjects, but that his ministers are the cause of misfortunes of which he knows nothing. The novel feature of *Nicodemus* is a comic ballet in the second act, in which two fishwives, *Mère Bahu* and *Mère Cassecroute*, dance a grotesque *pas de deux*.

Until the reaction of the 9th of Thermidor, the "jacobinized" theatre was under the yoke of the Committee of Public Safety and required to serve as a weapon of revolutionary propaganda. Managers were "requested" to consult it on the plays they presented. As the word "censorship" had a rather unpleasant sound, even to the followers of Robespierre, the word "supervision" was substituted.

The Law of August 2nd, 1793, ordained that the tragedies of *Brutus, William Tell, Caius Gracchus* and other plays "relating the glorious events of liberty" were to be given in the Paris theatres three times a week at the Republic's expense. Political reliability was supervised by the Committee of Public Instruction and a regular team of official and voluntary censors. Old and new plays were revised and corrected in accordance with the views of the Jacobin Club.

"Cousin Jacques," who was suspected of the crime of "moderation," obviated this dangerous situation by means of an opera whose libretto, published before the actual performance, flattered the established authorities: "*All Greece, or the Achievements of Liberty*, a civic episode in two acts (written expressly for the Opéra), was accepted for production with acclaim on September 14th last at the Academy of Music and will be given there at the first opportunity. The work is dedicated to the National Convention, the Paris Commune and Sections William Tell and Bonne Nouvelle where the two authors are registered. Words by Cousin Jacques, music by Lemoyne." The play was performed on January 5th, 1794, with various scenic effects—"Freedom Embracing the Children" and a ballet at the end of the second act.

It is astonishing that these productions, instigated by contemporary politics, were able to reach the realm of the "Marvellous" and its accompanying escapism. The properties, scenery, dancing, fighting and processions were employed to make Jacobin propaganda palatable. Allegory was also used to provide a little pleasure for the senses and a little revolutionary propaganda for the soul.

Despite the scorn Hébert poured on the "*Grands Danseurs*" and similar companies, the circus and former fairground shows maintained a certain balance. With the twofold disability of its English origin under Philip Astley and its former aristocratic patronage, the circus was taken over by the redoubtable Antonio Franconi. On March 21st, 1793, he opened the Amphithéâtre Franconi, offering the beautiful rider Angélique Chiarini to the city of Paris, then a raging holocaust. Such originality overshadowed the productions of writers, composers and actors who had to work for a theatre tolerated by the Jacobins only as a pillar of their authority; the fanatics of the Committee of Public Safety had to fall back upon the Opéra, whose personnel was more docile; although in the grip of demagogic officials, it was distinguished by a degree of complaisance which bordered on obsequiousness and merited the accolade of Père Duchesne.

As the repertory of revolutionary propaganda encountered an increasingly indifferent public, the Committee of Public Safety called for supplementary performances. Accordingly, on December 26th, 1793, at the Opéra, there was a revival of *The Feast of Reason,* first performed in the church of St. Roch during the previous month. Grétry was now older, and terrified of a regime opposed to all his beliefs; his score is based on a text by S. Maréchal. The plot is no more nor less unworthy than a hundred others of the period. A village mayor is preparing an anti-Catholic demonstration. The "old mothers of families" refuse to take part in it, and wait outside the church porch for the parish priest, singing the *Pater, Ave* and *Credo, sotto voce.* The priest appears, announces that he too has abjured "the cult of fanaticism in favor of that of Reason," and reveals the costume of a *sans-culotte* under his half-open cassock. The church porch collapses and its place is taken by an altar dedicated to the Goddess of Reason. The success of the finale was assured by a troupe of *"sans-culottes"*— dancers, including Nivelon, Vestris and Beaupré.

If these former dandies of the ballet stooped to appear as *sans-culottes,* their leader went much further: Gardel decked himself out as Master of Ceremonies for another *Feast of Reason,* with a score by Méhul, performed at St. Roch with the assistance of the Théâtre de la République (Théâtre Français), which was far from enjoying the official support that the Opera had succeeded in acquiring.

The *sans-culotte* authors, even as they celebrated the destruction of Gothic masterpieces, unwittingly fostered a taste for the medieval. Some anxiety over the influence of anti-clerical plays affected the people who had urged their production. Perhaps the similarity of the processions, choirs and blasphemous ceremonies intended as parody, produced a certain nostalgia. In its November 23rd, 1793 issue, *La Feuille du Salut Public (The Public Safety Journal)* pontificates thus: "We adjure the female citizens, especially those connected with the stage, to stop wearing crucifixes when playing the parts of country girls. This sign of fanaticism, which the fair sex has turned into an adornment, must be proscribed forever." These same crucifixes were to become compulsory in "village maiden" parts for the nineteenth century exotic folklore.

The scenic directions were fairly precise, and almost official in their requirements; for example, those for *The Festival of Equality* in 1794: "The theatre represents the Place de la Commune. Upstage, the statue of Liberty, on one side, and the statue of Equality on the other. In front of each of these statues the busts of the Martyrs to Liberty. In the center, the platform arched over with greenery; and downstage, a small mound for the bust of Jean-Jacques Rousseau."

Pierre-Gabriel Gardel, the Opéra ballet-master, a perfect political weathercock, at once put himself at the disposal of the Committee of Public Safety. During nine regimes, beginning with Louis XVI and ending with Charles X in 1829, h seerved the statesmen of the moment with adroitness and even servility, never relaxing his authoritarian control at the Opéra.

He disliked Noverre's innovations as much as those of the pantomimes and the secondary theatres' melodramas and ballets. His great objective, which he almost realized, was to suppress ballet on the Boulevard and to stubbornly maintain the tradition that the Opéra alone had the right to crown any aspiring dancer; that a reputation established elsewhere was worthless without the seal of approval from Paris. Reinforced by a veritable galaxy of star dancers, he achieved the latter result, for even in Italy, until about 1850, *primi ballerini* had to be *di rango francese.*

The French male dancers, especially before the time of the ballerina *sur la pointe* were the leading dancers throughout Europe owing to the dazzling virtuosity achieved by new techniques. Gaétan and Auguste Vestris (although they were of Italian origin), Dupré, Dauberval and Nivelon reached perfection with their *tours de force* and were in demand at all the European courts.

Pierre Gardel, like Gardel the Elder before him, fiercely resisted the slightest encroachment on his prerogatives, and always found political support. During the Empire, moreover, Napoleon approved of his conservatism and his views for the abolishment of the secondary theatres' privileges, especially that of putting on ballets. By his craftiness and with the help of complaisant officials, Gardel crushed his colleagues, stopped their productions at the Opéra and was at the root of the many destructive clauses in the Decree of 1807 which closed the majority of secondary theatres.

Despite his apparent admiration for the great choreographer, Gardel helped his brother to keep Noverre out of Paris for good. In 1798 he munificently lent the Opéra for a benefit performance for the former ballet-master; but after Noverre's *Galatea's Caprices*, the finale was reserved, by Gardel himself, for a divertissement of his own composition.

In 1783, the Gardels also encouraged the departure of the great choreographer Dauberval, who took refuge at Bordeaux as ballet-master of its Grand Théâtres, where he created several masterpieces, such as *La Fille Mal gardée* (1786), which is still performed. He transmitted the teachings of Noverre to his pupils Viganò, Eugene Hus and Jean Aumer, who contributed to the downfall of the Gardelian empire.

The comic dancer Beaupré, who had begun to explore the new vein of folklore with *The Mountaineers* and *A Provençal Tambourine* at the Théâtre de la Cité around 1792, was also kept out of the Opéra, and so, for nineteen years, was *Flora and Zephyr*, Didelot's masterpiece which was greatly superior to similar works of Gardel. In 1815, Gardel finally gave way, but he made Didelot pay the expenses of wires for the flying scenes, which amounted to 400 Francs—more than what he earned as choreographer. Didelot therefore had to return to Saint Petersburg, where he continued imposing the French school of ballet at the Imperial Academy of the Dance.

Louis Duport, the great *demi-caractère* dancer, had the good fortune to succeed in getting three of his ballets on the Opéra stage; but he too eventually succumbed to the standard intrigues and had to take temporary refuge in Italy and Austria. When the Opéra refused him leave, in 1806, he crossed the border disguised as a woman and sought refuge with Philippe Taglioni in Vienna.

Milon, a docile younger colleague of Gardel's, began his Opéra career in the troubled times of 1790. Like Aumer and Henry at a later date, he kept his post of dancer at the Opéra and in 1796 entered a Boulevard theatre, the Ambigu-Comique, as choreographer, with immediate success. Gardel found his gentle character reassuring and wished to keep him as dancer at the Opéra. He therefore permitted Milon to become second choreographer in 1799. Milon's first ballets, *Héro et Léandre* (1799) and *Pygmalion* (1800), did not obtain the success anticipated. Why did the latter ballet in particular with a brilliant cast mentioned in newspapers of the day, have only twelve performances?

Indeed, neither Milon nor any other choreographer in the annals of the

Opéra had as many ballets performed as many times as did Gardel. This cultivated despot and excellent musician, whose talent in composing divertissements was admitted even by hostile critics, was nevertheless not on the same plane as Milon, Aumer or Perrot. And yet his three best ballets had almost miraculously long runs. Was it rather due to the all-powerful Gardel's prerogatives in choice of repertory? During the thirty-six years of his "reign," *Psyché* was performed 905 times after its first performance in 1790; *Dansomanie* was more or less continuously performed for twenty years after its first performance in 1800; and *Paul et Virginie*, which dates from 1806, was danced for more than ten years. The recurrence of Gardel's name on the program, bringing as it did enormous royalties and lasting prestige, explains his interest in maintaining his own works in repertory.

Yet his struggle against the young exponents of Romantic ballet recalls that of the king who ordered the waves to recede: his obstinate refusal to give way before the new order resulted only in helping it to take hold.

Three theatres of the Boulevard du Temple opposed Gardel: two survivors of the fairgrounds, the Gaîté and Ambigu-Comique, and the new Porte-Saint-Martin, the most interesting of the three. [27] To the number of houses devoted to pure spectacle may be added the Cirque-Olympique, where the Franconis specialized in gigantic spectacles while keeping their clowns, jugglers and equilibrists for interludes. [28] All employed the "melodramatists." They had the standard permanent teams of composer-conductor, painter-scene designer, machinist, ballet-master, first dancers of both sexes and corps de ballet. The Cirque-Olympique added a specialist in cavalry evolutions. The director—*metteur en scène*—makes his appearance everywhere; sometimes he was an author, such as Pixérécourt, sometimes the theatre manager, such as Harel; often the ballet-master—Aumer and Coralli for example. At the Cirque-Olympique it was usually an equestrian cum-librettist—Minette Franconi or his son Adolphe.

Comparison of the four repertories suggests that the Gaîté and Ambigu presented the same type of performance, whereas the Porte-Saint-Martin and Cirque-Olympique created specialties peculiar to themselves. The Gaîté may have engaged Perrot to compete with the illustrious Mazurier at the Porte-Saint-Martin, but the latter theatre retained supremacy in ballet for some thirty years. The Franconis could hire out a few horses here and there on the Boulevard without damage to their takings, for no one else had the arena-theatre in which to stage gigantic mimodramas and plays with performing animals which were long their monopoly.

The Porte-Saint-Martin—"this literary theatre" as Gautier dubbed it, presented a number of the new Romantic authors' most important plays—*Marino Faliero, Marion Delorme, Lucrezia Borgia* among them. As it looked ahead of the State theatres in its choice of plays, so it did with its ballets. As soon as the Romantic ballet had triumphed at the Opéra, the Porte-Saint-Martin seems almost to have lost interest in it and began to compete with the Gaîté for supremacy in "*la féerie.*" When the Cogniard brothers began the confection of fairy spectacles toward mid-century they did indeed surpass the Gaîté, establishing the pattern of the Châtelet super-productions.

At the very beginning of the 19th century, then, the Opéra was the last stronghold of mythological and allegorical ballets. Foreign tourists, accustomed

86

to innovations of the peripatetic French choreographers and their disciples at home, would arrive in Paris hoping to see some fine examples of the new choreography at its presumed fountainhead—the Opéra, only to be bitterly disappointed. The German novelist August Kotzebue permitted himself some tart remarks on the subject: "*Le Jugement de Paris (The Judgement of Paris)*, a pantomime ballet by Gardel, is ill-conceived and ill-written. . . . The first act has no connection with the action: it consists entirely of games and exercises in which Paris annoys a flock of shepherdesses." He also comments on Milon's *Les Noces de Camache (Wedding of Camacho)*, created in 1801: "Another colorless and insipid ballet. The artist who plays the part of Don Quixote comes off very well. Rosinante and Sancho Panza's ass are live animals, to the great joy of the Parisian public." These live animals, probably hired from Franconi, were actually an unusual concession to the Boulevard!

However, the performers' virtuosity remained astonishing: "The ballet titled *Retour de Zéphyre (Zephyr's Return)* is bad; it would certainly have been hissed in Vienna. It is only tolerated in Paris on account of the pleasure given by Duport's dancing, which is really astounding; although very young he already outclasses Vestris. Among other things, he has the marvelous and extraordinary talent of pirouetting forty or fifty times on end with remarkable skill and agility. As he is certain of thunderous applause, he regrettably uses his *tour de force* too often, but the Parisians do not weary of seeing him." But the Parisians *did* weary of the Opéra, if an examination of its account books and the measures taken to suppress competition by the secondary theatres are used in judgment. Again, Kotzebue made a serious mistake in writing: "The ballets *Télémaque* and *Psyché* (1790) are still put on from time to time; but they are no longer performed as when I saw them thirteen years ago." It was not the ballets, but the world and the literary current which had undergone a change since 1791; during the intervening period the works of Dauberval and his pupil Salvatore Viganò had been well received in Vienna, where Kotzebue had seen them. *Psyché* must have appeared old-fashioned indeed to the admirer of a ballet-pantomime such as *Richard Coeur de Lion*, with a dream episode for the anguished heroine, "soldiers of the guard running in from all directions, their lanterns lighting the night sky as they formed picturesque groups" and "a procession so well rehearsed that the horses' hoofs struck the ground in cadence."

Further on Kotzebue expounds one of the tenets of Romanticism, later stated as a principle by Gautier and other critics, concerning the role of the poet in composing libretti for opera and ballet, briefly, that he was indispensable: ". . . for the plan of a good ballet is almost as difficult to plot as that of a drama." While it is true that movement alone in itself is the basic element in ballet, it is nevertheless impossible not to agree with the German critic and his partisans, given the sad decadence of the allegorical-mythological ballets, whose libretti had become mere combinations of clichés. [29]

Kotzebue, as a foreigner long-familiar with the work of Dauberval, Viganò and the followers of Noverre, was more severe than contemporary French critics. It was not until some fifteen years later that the Paris press set upon Gardel. Thenceforth, the ballet-master's rehearsal baton—known as "the Marshal's baton"—could no longer strike down hostile journalists, for they reflected the views of a large section of the public.

The reviews of A. Delaforest, who not only passed judgment on Gardel's defects but also revealed some of the problems of this transitional period, unleashed a veritable cabale against Gardel in 1822: "If the chorus of favorable claims which greet every work of Gardel could be stilled—claims which have been strengthened by the exile to which he has for so long a time condemned all those who wanted to follow the same career as he at the Opéra—it will soon be perceived that while he is superior to his rivals in divertissements, his ballet-pantomimes are unimaginative and dull. All of his compositions lack unity." This is not a reference to Aristotelian unities, but to the Romantics' unity of spirit—dance, mime, music, costume and scenery composing a harmonious whole. Already, without realizing it, Delaforest was looking forward to the arrival of the Romantic ballet as it was to materialize in 1830-1850.

Meanwhile, the hostility of officialdom and the disdain of the press did not prevent the birth of many lively works in the secondary theatres. At a deeper level than these surface clashes, the Boulevard, like the Opéra, believed in its specific historic role. While the one remained the guardian of previous traditions the other was to be, for some time, an innovator whose contributions were visible in a variety of forms.

CHAPTER VI
Pantomime

JEAN-FRANCOIS ARNOULD-MUSSOT

ARNOULD-MUSSOT, co-manager with Audinot of the Ambigu-Comique and a regular contributor to its repertory from 1769 until his death, was the very prototype of the prolific Boulevard author. His pantomimes are particularly important in the development and clarification of mime, for speech played no part in them. He was an innovator by virtue of his interpretations of the troubadour style (*Pierre de Provence, Les Quatre fils Aymon,* etc), the exotic style (*L'Héroïne Américaine*), and also the lurid adventure story replete with brigands in a wild forest pockmarked with caves and underground passages. His pantomime *La Fôret Noire* is of particular interest as one of the first French pantomimes performed in America (Philadelphia, 1794, with its title in French) and one often revived during the next fifteen years. Its first *recorded* performance in Paris would seem to date from 1801: a text published for an 1807 revival describes it as "A Most Spectacular Pantomime in Three Acts by Arnould, revived at the Ambigu-Comique Theatre with New Scenes, on 20 Frimaire, Year X (1801) and on Thursday, February 5th, 1807." It was probably created in 1787-1789. The text states that the music was arranged by M. Quaisain and the ballet by M. Richard, "Pensioner of the Imperial Academy of Music."

This 18th-century pantomime contains almost all the elements [30]—which were to be developed during the 19th century; its career spanned the two centuries and its scenario merited translation in England and America, while the many revivals were considered financially attractive.

CUVELIER DE TRYE

Cuvelier was the typical author of pantomimes in which the supernatural plays a principal part and even constitutes an ingredient in the psychological portrait of the villain.

Among the mediocre throng of dramatist-officials who gravitated around the Committee of Public Safety in 1793, he was a man of the theatre who stood out by virtue of his innate sense of dramatic contrasts. Jean-Guillaume-Antoine Cuvelier de Trye, known as Cuvelier, was born on January 15th, 1766, at Boulogne-sur-Mer. Like Pixérécourt, "the Corneille of the Boulevards," and

Caigniez, "the Racine of the Boulevards," he whom the minor press and the almanachs were to dub "the Crébillon of the Boulevards" began his career as a lawyer. During and immediately following the Revolution there was a great increase in speechmaking generally and "pleas for the defense" in particular. It was no accident that many of the melodramatists had had legal training.

Cuvelier was sent to the Convention, and soon found himself "Adjudant-Major, 2nd Paris Battalion in the Vendée." However, his health was never very good and he was released on his return to Paris. He started his literary career with two plays which had the singular good fortune of finding favor both with the Committee and the public: *L'Enlèvement ou La Caverne dans les Pyrénées* (*Kidnapped, or The Cavern in the Pyrenees*), performed in 1792—author at first unnamed; then, in September 1793, for the architect-impresario Lenoir, *Les Royalistes de la Vendée ou Les Époux républicains* (*The Vendée Royalists, or The Republican Couple*). The latter was a distinctly anti-monastic "dialogue pantomime" terminated by resounding thunderclaps: a Republican colonel and his wife are captured by Royalists and a Capuchin; dungeon scenes are followed by battle scenes; the Royalists are exterminated and the "Cowled Monk" is "struck by deadly lead" and disappears in the torrent, to prolonged cries of "Perish the tyrants! Long live Freedom!" The *Tribunal d'Apollon* apostrophized Cuvelier in these terms: "Machinists, designers, costume makers, whale-oil vendors, painters and paint sellers, bow down before the father who suckles you!"

Thus encouraged, Cuvelier sped along the road which led his effervescent creativeness to produce some hundred plays, novels, and two texts for the Opéra. With Loiasel de Tréogate, he shared the honor of familiarizing the public with "historical events," a term which was to include the most miscellaneous subjects whose historical authenticity is not always beyond discussion.

He was one of the first to take an interest in the rebirth of the troubadour theme, and his "little fifteenth-century piece," *Damoiselle et Bergerette* (published in 1795) furnished him the outline of an equestrian pantomime in 1809. In 1797 he was represented in the catalogues by nine titles. The most famous of these was *C'est le Diable, ou La Bohémienne* (*'Tis the Devil's Doing, or The Gypsy Woman*), in which, amid Gothic scenery by Moench, an almost fairytale version of a terror story is performed, with scenic effects derived from Robertson (it was the very year of *Fantasmagoria*). The prodigious success of this "drama," as the libretto calls it, owes much to the local color of the troubadour style. *L'Indicateur Dramatique* for Year VI (1797) comments: "'Twas the Devil who had the patience to study antiquity for the period furnishings seen therein, and to give each actor historically-correct costumes. . . ." We shall see that in 1836 the Opéra, under Duponchel, managed to send its tailors "to study Léopold Robert's paintings in order to copy the fishermen's and harvesters' costumes, which it used for the divertissements in. . . . *Stradella ou Venise et Rome.* The painters were also consulted for their settings of Italian sites and monuments."

In 1797, Cuvelier began his collaboration with the Franconis; it was to last throughout his life. His great success *La fille Hussard* (*The Girl Hussar*), was already being revived on 9 Frimaire, Year VII (1798), "with equestrian combats and evolutions executed by Citizen Franconi's troupe."

Although he began as an out-and-out Republican, Cuvelier soon became an enthusiastic Bonapartist. During the Consulate, he was a captain in the Guides

Harlequin and Sprite in the English 19th century pantomimes reconciled the merry and the supernatural in the same manner as they had in the royal ballets of the 16th and 17th centuries.

"William Tell" (1810), a ballet by Louis Henry, which had a long career in the European repertory. Battle scenes ("combats réglés") such as this were specialties of the great choreographers and of many directors; the cinema has a monopoly of such large-scale battle scenes today (with the exception of the Peking Opera).

MAZURIER ARTISTE
de la Porte St. Martin D.

Mazurier, the great dancer—and the greatest 19th century comic dancer—of the Porte-Saint-Martin company. Below: The Porte-Saint-Martin Theatre in 1829.

". . . The habitués of the popular theatres desire above all to be lured by the visual. We are convinced that not a single melodrama with splendid settings, costumes and Bengal fire has failed to return at least its production costs. The masses love the beautiful, the brilliant and the majestic precisely because their own lives are shabby, obscure and wretched!"

The Gaité.

Soissons in "Main de Fer," presented at the Gaité.

THÉÂTRE DES FUNAMBULES,
Boulevart du temple, 54.
VACANCES DE 1858
tous les soirs :

LA FÉE CARABOSSE
PANTOMIME ARLEQUINADE EN 12 TABLEAUX,
M. KALPESTRI jouera le rôle de Pierrot.

LITH. VAN CELEYE ET SONS, 19, PARIS

and Interpreters Corps, which led him to study English. This in turn impelled him to translate Shakespeare into a series of situations—there was no longer any element of poetry—which he arranged into melodramas.

He had the good fortune, denied to Pixérécourt, of not surviving his own vogue. The Cuvelier of the Cirque-Olympique, who died in Paris on May 27th, 1824, artisan of the spectacle of marvels, veritable lion of the Boulevard theatre, was still the leading writer of pantomimes. One of his early successes was written in collaboration with Augustin Hapdé, another author of pantomimes, fairy plays and melodramas: *Le Petit Poucet ou L'Orphelin de la Fôret (Tom Thumb, or The Orphan of the Forest)*, a curious attempt at a fairy play called a "drama" on the title page. Hapdé's sole contribution was probably the dialogue and songs. Performed for the first time at the Théâtre des Jeunes Artistes on 24 Ventôse, Year VI (1798), *Tom Thumb* reached its 230th performance, as mentioned in a third edition of the libretto, on 13 Germinal, Year VIII (1800). At this time, the title "Citizen" was still in use, as witness hundreds of title pages. The first performance took place barely five years after the law of August 2nd, 1793, and barely five years after *Les Royalistes de la Vendée* had been welcomed by the powerful Comitée. Cuvelier and Hapdé were neither dishonest nor exceptional in the reversal—or perhaps the development—of their ideology. As popular writers, they expressed views which were common currency at the time, and their *Tom Thumb*, "of no ordinary stock,"—another way of saying "noble"—represented the new social class reinstated by Bonaparte.

Tom Thumb recalls countless predecessors by its scenery of dark forests, Gothic castles and village festivals. The ghosts and shades—like the "Good Fairy"—go back to the fairground rather than to the English supernatural tradition; scenes of "wild beasts," wearing *papier-mâché* masks recall the fairground plays of Anthony de Sceaux, as well as the performing (real) animals of the Franconis. The description of the pepperpot tower, lair of the miscreant who practises black magic, is of fairground origin, and the walls covered with hieroglyphics and cabbalistic signs, as well as the enormous silver bell with a raven soaring above it evidence a revived interest in occult sciences.

Although the starting point in Perrault's fairy tale is overlaid with complications that have completely transformed the plot, Cuvelier's beloved horrors are played down in *Tom Thumb*. Was this owing to Hapdé's influence or to a real desire to retain, for once, something of the magic world of childhood? In any case, the agony of uncertainty plays no part here. What is the explanation of the 230 performances of *Tom Thumb*, the success of its sequel *Rosaure de Valencourt, ou Les Nouveaux Malheurs du Petit Poucet (Rosaure de Valencourt, or The Further Misadventures of Tom Thumb)* (1801), and of its plagiarized version *La Botte de sept lieues ou L'Enfant précoce (The Seven League Boots, or The Precocious Child)* (1812)? The singing and dancing of the child players, the impressive new scenic resources, the torture scene with "fierce beasts" in cardboard masks—these are probably some of the reasons. Examination of contemporary libretti indicates that this was the first attempt at reproducing an arena to accommodate animals on stage; henceforth, an imitation lion or bear simply bounding out of the wings would lack verisimilitude. It was not until *Les Lions de Mysore* (1831) that the arena was filled with real wild beasts.

La Botte de sept lieues, a pantomime by Monsieur Hullin, ballet-master at the Gaîté, revealed the talent of his daughter Felicity, aged four and a half. Although this libretto is closer to Perrault, the simplicity of his text could not be respected in a spectacular production with "Gothick" chamber, combats, a reception at the Aragonese court, and thunderclaps at suitable moments. Despite its date— 1818—the classic of "modern" fairy plays, *Le Pied de Mouton* (*The Sheep's Foot*), influenced it not at all. The Hullin pantomime remained a primitive fairy tale with an outmoded text and stylish scenery.

On the title page of his libretti, Cuvelier liked to have his name followed by the title "Corresponding Member of the Philotechnic Society" of which he seems to have been inordinately proud, or by quotations from Horace, Racine or simply the "Master" himself. In the last case he usually expounds his theories and justifies the plays which follow. Thus, the title page of *Valther le Cruel ou La Géolière de Mergentheim* (*Valther the Cruel or The Lady Jailer of Mergentheim*) is adorned with the following text: "Pantomime is a picture wherein virtue is represented and becomes tangible, as it were, and vice is punished and inspires the crowd with righteous revulsion; its arguments go straight to the soul, and it is difficult to refute them; it must delight the eye while satisfying the heart, whereas its noble rivals, in greater finery, often speak but to the mind, which, alas, they sometimes dupe. (Extract from an unpublished work by the Author)."

Valther le Cruel, a spectacular pantomime with ballets by Hullin, was yet another of the Gaîté productions designed to show off the fencing talent of Mlle Bourgeois who played a wide range of leading parts, from the perfidious Régilde in *Main de Fer* to the noble Alexina in *Tékéli*, and *L'Ange Tutélaire* (The *Guardian Angel*) of many disguises. "One of our most celebrated termagents" wrote Harel in the *Dictionnaire Théâtral* of 1825, "Mlle Bourgeois' talent is outstanding. Few women have wielded the rapier with such mastery."

The two remarkable features of *Valther le Cruel* are the arrangement of its combat scenes, in which Mlle Bourgeois starred, and its manner of borrowing Banquo's ghost from *Macbeth*. For this provided another opportunity (or rather Cuvelier manufactured one where it would hardly have been expected) to rework a Shakespearean effect: the use of spectres. A note attempts to explain what Cuvelier believed to be a novelty in France: "There is nothing magic in this scene: the author's only intention was to make palpable, as it were, the workings of conscience in a great criminal overwhelmed with remorse and horrified at the sight of his own crimes." The note also explains at length that the spectre is visible only to the guilty man; his pantomime had to express strong emotions before the other persons present, and was thus admirably adapted to the new school of dynamic directing.

The return of a person supposedly dead; a victim left dying by hired assassins in an ambush scene; a man saved from poisoning by a kindly hermit's antidote; an unfortunate, abandoned in a desolate forest, who miraculously escapes from wild beasts; a poor wretch immolated in a tower which is set on fire, escaping unperceived by his enemies; an innocent captive, buried alive in a sealed-up cell, who escapes on touching a flagstone that swings aside to reveal a providential tunnel leading right into her persecutor's castle; a ghost who returns to haunt and exact vengeance—all these are so many aspects of a pillar of melodramatic structure: symbols of the triumph of virtue and right and the punishment of the powers of evil. This is an aspect which lends itself, incidentally, to those effects of the "explained supernatural" so dear to French hearts.

In the little time left him by his output for the Franconis, Cuvelier concocted a classic of this kind for the Gaîté: *La Main de Fer ou l'Epouse Criminelle (The Iron Hand or The Criminal Wife)*. It has highly flavored Boulevard prose, an overloaded plot and an unerring sense of theatre: masses moving across stage, silhouettes of fugitives, tableaux that follow one another like exclamation points—the entire production foreshadows Romantic drama. It is true that Cuvelier, translator and devotee of Shakespeare, drew upon the master's work for his horrific details because, like most Frenchmen of the period, he considered Shakespeare primarily as a melodramatist, although the morality of the tragic has nothing in common with melodrama's "Good will triumph, Evil will be punished." The Shakespearean tragedy for Cuvelier was related to the Boulevard by virtue of its horrors; hence he ignored poetry, philosophy and sublimity in favor of bloodstained tableaux, murders and the supernatural. Thus in *Main de Fer*, Lady Macbeth gives birth to a strange sleepwalking descendant whose function is still the same as in the majority of late 18th-century works: to reveal the guilty soul harrowed by remorse. Parenthetically, wish-fulfillment dreams occur rarely, and then usually in the *"féeries,"* as a sort of first-act apotheosis. Cuvelier makes the following acknowledgment for the bloodcurdling vision in *Main de Fer*: "This scene is borrowed from the English play *Macbeth*, and I have endeavored to renovate it by means of additional effects: in any case, I believe such a situation better suited to the Boulevard than to the first theatre of the Empire." (The young intellectuals were beginning to clamor for performances of Shakespeare at the Théâtre Français).

Any surprise at the revision of Shakespeare by a Cuvelier should be lessened by the recollection of the English Dr. Thomas Bowdler who revised Shakespeare for the "polite society" of 1818. In England and America as in France, the most bloodthirsty melodramas held the stage while the English poet was represented in mutilated versions.

The inevitable reward of virtue which concludes *Main de Fer* and the whole body of this theatrical "literature" is an example of the curious reaction by the melodrama, speaking for its public, against the religious scepticism of the late 18th century. It is not a question of a logic such as that of the Englishman John Bunyan in the 17th century, who accepted that wrongdoers might well not be punished during their lifetime and even die in the odor of sanctity but believed that a terrible and just punishment awaited them in Hell, because the classic Dantesque conception of Hell had faded away during the 18th century. Melodrama's public wanted to see vice punished and virtue rewarded all at the end of the last act.

THE TYPICAL PANTOMIMES OF HUS, HAPDE AND HULLIN

While Cuvelier is certainly the most typical author of works—whether "dialogued" or entirely mimed—certain of his contemporaries' pantomimes are interesting from the production standpoint and because, in order to be fully understood, they require mime by the whole body; that is, the acrobatic mime of the old fairground theatre.

P.-J. Stapleton, known as Eugène Hus, belonged to the tribe of Hus with its complicated genealogical branches, and was one of the most original choreographer-producers. He boasted with justifiable pride that he was a pupil of Dauberval's and a dancer at the Opéra.

In his struggle against the Gardels, Noverre could count two generations of the Hus family among his supporters. The first, Auguste Hus (1733-1805), son of a provincial actress, made his debut on the Paris stage as the author of *Plutus rival de l'Amour (Plutus Rival of Love)*, staged by the Comédie Italienne in 1756; as a pupil of Dupré, he was then engaged by the Opéra which he quit to become ballet-master in the provinces and abroad; eventually he settled at the court of Turin as first dancer and ballet-master. In 1760, Noverre's *Letters* spare "Sire Hus" the somewhat caustic comments which he often lavished on his colleagues. Indeed, Noverre congratulated the Comédie Française on its perspicacity in having just engaged him as ballet-master. Between two trips to Italy, Hus returned briefly as ballet-master at the Comédie Italienne.

At the end of the 18th century there were already three Huses—two of them, Pierre and Auguste II, probably sons of Auguste I, and the other, Eugène, an adopted son. Pierre and Eugène had been trained in the Italian techniques so strongly influenced by Noverre. [31]

The name of the energetic Eugène Hus is associated with developments in production and miming on the Boulevard. However, he began with an Anacreontic ballet at the Opéra in 1793, *Les Muses ou Le Triomphe d'Apollon (The Muses, or The Triumph of Apollo)*. He then joined the Gaîté, where he was writer, choreographer and director, sometimes all three simultaneously. He appears on the title pages of libretti, and in the *Répertoire de la Gaîté*, as "Stapleton, known as 'Eugène Hus' or 'Hus the Younger'." He revived *Le Déserteur*, by his master Dauberval in 1799, occasionally assisted Aumer in 1803, and then settled down for a time at the Théâtre des Jeunes Artistes. He reappeared at the Gaîté, where we find him in 1819, and died, according to Quérard, on February 24th, 1823.

Eugène Hus appears as choreographer in *Les Chevaliers du Soleil ou Amour et Dangers (The Knights of the Sun or Love and Dangers)*, a pantomime by the author Bignon who formerly wrote for Nicolet. The director, celebrated for his "regulated" (or staged) combats, was Gougibus the Elder. The action takes place on "an island beside the sea" (sic), a rather indefinite place in an unspecified century. (This vagueness as to time and place was supplanted later in the century by a vogue for the most specific details.) The costumes, minutely described werein troubadour style. Moreover, numerous directions were given concerning the music which was composed to underscore the action. It foreshadows program music with realistic details which could not be more precise. For example, the action is opened by "mood music": "Act 1—Introduction and Overture. It begins with an adagio, depicting the awakening of Nature in a wild countryside. The roaring of wild beasts, the calls of the hoot owl and screech owl, and the sound of the storm-tossed sea are heard. Gradually the mood changes, together with the tempo of the music, which, as it modulates becomes more rapid. It is a battle between two large armies: Alert, Stand to Arms, Fall In, and then a most violent clash; this is followed by the screams of the wounded and dying, the victorious army's songs of triumph, and finally the complete rout of the army of the Knights of the Sun."

Thus the Boulevard prepared the way for recorded nightingales and auto

horns in modern symphony and concerto and for the scoring of locomotives. The most curious thing is the transformation of an essentially popular form of realism into an *avant-garde* musical technique, a rather precious and highly esteemed technique, fashionable a century later in film music.

Similarly, there are signs of the new school of directing—intensification of emotion by sudden changes of groupings and a dynamism which contrasts with the pre-Revolutionary use of static "supers."

At times, too, the pantomime seems to have been composed from Noverre's *Letters*; for example, this passage of the *Letters* is followed almost literally by the scenario: "A camp; military movements; drilling; attack and defense of fortifications; a seaport; an anchorage; embarkation and landing—these are pictures which must compel our attention and carry our art to perfection, if the execution is to be believable." "As the curtain rises," Bignon's scenario continues, "some wounded men from the defeated army pass by. They are without weapons, and fleeing in the utmost disorder. They are followed by a platoon of the same army, which, like them, rapidly crosses the stage. One of the soldiers drops the threadbare cloak which he was wearing, and retreats precipitately."

L'Ingénu ou Le Sauvage du Canada is a work entirely created and produced by Eugène Hus. On 27 Nivôse Year XIII (1804), the Théâtre des Jeunes Artistes launched this spectacular pantomime with the usual accompaniment of dancing, marching, military evolutions and tableaux. The Hus scenario is based on the love story of a "noble savage" known as "*l'Ingénu*" ("the Innocent"), and various military exploits of courageous Frenchmen. The libretto title page describes Hus as "Ballet-Master, Dramatic Author and Teacher, Pupil and Successor of the Famous d'Auberval (sic) at the former Theatre of the Royal Academy of Music," but neglects to mention Voltaire's well-known tale by which Hus was manifestly inspired.

In this work attention to details of mime were carried to such lengths that the directions have an unconscious humor of which neither the artists nor the good-natured public were aware. The same is true of the curious use of the word *sensible* ("sensitive") which, having begun its triumphant career in the 18th century continued its popularity in such effusions as the following *Dramatis Personae*: "Ingénu, a young Canadian, very amorous, brave and grateful . . . Mlle de Saint-Yves, modest, tender and sensitive . . . M. de Saint-Yves, her father, a retired military man, noble and stern, but sensitive . . . Mlle de Kerkabon, lively, animated, philanthropic and good-hearted . . . M. de Kerkabon, her brother, a rich tradesman, plain dealing, jovial and kindly . . . Gilotin, the bailiff's son, a ridiculous and pretentious fool . . . A French officer, brave and sensitive."

The plot concerns the romance of the young savage and the young French girl Mlle de Saint-Yves. The child of nature is a better match than might be supposed. After a gavotte danced by all the Europeans "*l'Ingénu*" is asked to perform one of his native dances. "His dance is vigorous and strongly rhythmical. He strikes the ground with force, assumes a number of picturesque attitudes and spins around with agility; the dexterity of his movements is equalled by the vivacity of his steps; he delights the spectators and ends his dance with a pirouette, stopping in a picturesque attitude."

All this is a bit insipid and the author, imitating Voltaire, soon gives it some savor: as l'Ingénu dances a medallion he is wearing falls to the ground. It depicts M. de Kerkebon's missing brother and his wife, whose features the young savage undoubtedly possesses. On the strength of this hoary stratagem, the pantomime can now march to its apotheosis with the French flag unfurled.

Augustin Hapdé seems to have tried all theatrical forms for all the theatres: with more than fifty of his works in print and others written for odd occasions as well, he equalled the productivity of Cuvelier and Pixérécourt. Hybrid plays, a combination of melodrama, pantomime and ballet, were his specialty, to which may be added some *"féeries"* which were frequently revived during the first decade of the 19th century. Traces of Pixérécourt abound and no cliché is ever omitted. Neither Cuvelier's pithy prose nor Pixérécourt's genuine dramatic power and novelty are to be found in Hapdé's work. He went on as he had begun at the end of the 18th century, making a potpourri of everything fashionable on the Paris stage.

Thus the basic elements of the "Gothick" novel are to be found in one of his most typical confections in three acts: "A highly spectacular medley of pantomime, song and dance, with combats, military evolutions, explosion, fire and demolition; new scenery and costumes." *Elizabeth du Tyrol ou Les Hermites muets (Elizabeth of the Tyrol, or The Dumb Hermits)* (1804), enjoyed considerable success; its "book" ran into several editions. The clichés in which this pantomime abounds were evidently enough at the time to establish a Boulevard literary reputation. The story, complicated to the point of incomprehensibility, takes place in a setting of Tyrolian mine galleries in about 1700. *Elizabeth* verges on a parody despite an "N.B." in which the author states that the subject is not adapted from any novel and that he himself had brought back the waltz music from the Tyrol.

In 1788, *Estelle*, the novel by Florian, who was born too late for the great wave of sensibility in the 18th century and too early for the sentimentality of the 19th, met with a tepid reception. The love story of the shepherdess Estelle and the shepherd Némorin had to wait until the Restoration to obtain a celebrity incomprehensible today in the theatre and in popular prints.

On the stage, *Estelle et Némorin, ou Les Bergers de Massane (Estelle and Némorin, or The Shepherds of Massane)*, a pantomime "manufactured" by the ballet-master Hullin, is tricked out with fighting, drilling and brigands. The tableau in the second act, which was warmly received, must rank as the most involved specimen of all the improbable moments in 19th-century pantomime. Némorin, compelled by Estelle's father to relinquish his love, decides to go soldiering with Gaston de Foix, and they capture a band of brigands. His companions in arms have just awarded Némorin a laurel wreath as prize for his skill with sword and rapier. At this point, enter the marriage procession of Estelle and Méril, the suitor approved by Estelle's father. The soldiers ask the young beauty to present the wreath to the new recruit. Almost fainting at the sight of her lover, she agrees, and the soldiers observe their reunion with interest. "The brigands, taking advantage of the relaxed surveillance, fall upon the sentries and seize their weapons, and a general melee ensues." On one side, the French soldiers led by Némorin charge the brigands, and on the other, Estelle desperately encourages him. "This final tableau presents the twofold picture of a military engagement and a truly heartrending domestic scene," the author modestly remarks. If *Estelle* had often been characterized as "a pastoral without a wolf," Hullin certainly repaired the omission.

This Viennese· print of the Averino family (c. 1838) unites balletic grace and acrobatic skill, and gives yet another indication of the fairground theatre's contribution in technique—this time mechanical—to the Romantic Ballet. The flights of willis, sylphides, sprites and other supernatural creatures of the Romantic ballets and "féeries" were made possible by mechanical devices which owed as much to their development by the popular theatres as to their originator Servandoni. These machines required great adroitness from the performers. Defying gravity is an essential element of acrobacy and the materiel for more complicated numbers was continually being developed (and still is, particularly by the Soviet State Circuses). The Averinos were originally from Ancona, and constituted a circus dynasty proficient in many specialties. Eugenio Averino and his "mimic-choreo-graphic-excentric-acrobatic and plastic" troupe introduced Pantomime-Harlequinades to Central Europe and Turkey in the 1870s. Orlando Averino was a popular clown early in the century.

Piere Magarieu
Sancenr ve Corles
el Gri anen Torce

Non plus ultra.

3.008

UNICA SOLI NON IMPAR.

At the left: Pierre Magarieni, "master rope-dancer" and acrobat (Nuremburg print, c. 1775). Above: "the famous Prussian" ballerina on the tight and slack rope (French print, c. 1789).

The tiny Madame Pierson, wife of the comedian-dancing star of the Porte-Saint-Martin and mother of the ballerina Louise Pierson, in the travesty role of Felix in "Pupils on Vacation," ballet by Jacquinet with music by Piccini. (Galerie Martinet) The Piersons in "the Girl Soldier" of Blache "père" and "fils" (1818). Choreographers always accentuated the comic contrast between Madame and her tall thin husband.

"Der erste May im Prater": Viennese print (1826-1827) of a "magic pantomime"
by Rainoldi, showing the corps de ballet in that perennial favorite—a shawl dance
(the Soviet choreographers are still turning them out).

The parade of Cupid-soldiers was the big hit of 1811 at the Cirque-Olympique in
a pantomime-ballet "L'Enfant de Mars et de Flore" celebrating the birth of the King
of Rome (son of Napoleon and Marie-Louise). "Mars, wishing to test the inclinations
of his son, invites Love to lead his army of Cupids in formation," wrote Hapdé. The
ballet-master Renauzy revived this successful number in "The Marvelous Lamp," a
"féerie" by Merle, Carmouche and Saintine (Panorama Dramatique, 1822), recorded
in the souvenir lithograph opposite.

Virginia Chiarini. Flora Chiarini S
la Sera del '21. Nᵇʳᵉ 1831. nel Teatro degli Intrepidi in Firenze

Since ancient Rome, rope dancers had executed movements and attitudes which form part of ballet's basic vocabulary (and long before the development of "classic" ballet): pirouettes, jetés, ronds de jambe, entrechats, etc. All the oldest of the great circus dynasties featured rope dancers (as they would later feature equestrians). The oldest recorded dynasty, the Chiarini, were not only circus celebrities but numbered many performers who cleared with ease the barrier between fairground booth and great opera houses such as La Scala. For over 300 years the Chiarinis were top performers in every specialty of the Theatre of Marvels. Among the family's notables were Angélique the equestrienne, Giovanni the choreographer, Antonio, premier danseur at La Scala, and Flora and Virginia—dancers on stage and on the tight-rope. There was even a branch of the Chiarinis which ran a school of mime in Vienna, particularly for circus children.

Virginia and Flora Chiarini on stage.

"Aglaë or Love's Pupil," a ballet mounted by Philippe Taglioni at Stuttgart in 1825. This lithograph, edited at Stuttgart in a souvenir album, is of interest because it actually gives some idea of the choreography. The young Mlle Mées who is shown lower right would seem to be the same who figures as a child in the earliest known lithograph (Paris, 1821) showing a ballerina "sur la pointe." (Below) Her father Mées (more often written Maze) became "maître de ballet" at Saint Petersburg. A comparison with the Roman souvenir print of Teresa and Luigi Maglietta (1838) shows the difficulty that a reasonably mature ballerina could have in acquiring the new technique.

MR DUCROW AS ZEPHYR.

London, Pub July 13th 1830, by R. LLOYD, Dramatic Repository, 40, Gibson Street, Lambeth.

The Ducrow family was particularly notable for the feats of Peter Ducrow, the "Flemish Hercules," until his son Andrew Ducrow (1793-1842) became one of the greatest equestrian artists in circus history. He was known for his abilities as mime and dancer, which he used to develop a unique type of pantomime on horseback ("The Dying Brigand," "Vicissitudes of a Tar," "The Patriotic Greek" etc.) This portrait of Andrew Ducrow as Zephyr might be that of any well-known dancer of the period. (London, 1830) He also danced a "Persian Menuet" with his horse in the pantomime "Charlemagne" (!) (London, 1839).

The illustration from the "Bon Genre Parisien," Empire period, shows one of the numerous delicate acrobatic exercises, "The Equilibrium Of The Chandelier."

The 1837 Viennese engraving depicting Madame Romanini is another example of the transition from one medium to another.

Assassini Valacchi al Seguito di Store

The Valacchis had a reputation as assassins—a reputation exploited by the melodramas and ballets of the nineteenth century. They figure in "La Forêt d'Hermanstadt" (Amigu-Comique, 1796), and in the ballet "Il Bosco d'Ermanstadt O La Falsa Sposa" staged in 1814 at La Scala, Milan. Here the assassin is seen in a costume created by Pregliasco.

Three ballet masters of the Boulevard—Millot, Rhénon and Jacquinet—who are not among the renowned choreographers of their period. Their use of excess and popularization (as mimes-dancers-choreographers and, when necessary, actors) prepared the way for Aumer, Henry, and other future "greats" of the Boulevard and Opéra. (prints from the Galerie Martinet.)

RHENON, rôle du CHASSOMANE dans la Chassomanie. Pantomime.
Th. de la Porte St Martin.

N° 26.
Théâtre de l'Ambigu Com.
Melodrame.

Mr MILLOT et Mr GERARD
Dans le Ballot de la Forêt d'Hermanstadt.

Sangodemi!......
A Paris chez Martinet, Libraire, rue du Coq N° 3 et 15.

MISS: DEBLIN.   MR: CONWAY.   MRS: CONWAY.

OF THE PARK THEATRE NEW YORK.

Drawn by H Reinagle Etch.d by Wright. Published May 1.st 1827 New York.

MR. AND MRS. E. H. CONWAY, dancers from the Surrey Theatre in London, made their first American appearance at the Chatham Garden Theatre of New York in 1825. Conway became Ballet Master of the Park Theatre that same year and presented his pupil, Miss Deblin. Drawing by H. Reinagle, etched by Wright, New York, 1827. There is a close kinship between this print, the drawings in the Blasis "Manual," and those of Thomas in his album "Un An à Rome et dans les environs."

"Ottavio Pinelli or Insults and Vengeance" was created by Paul Samengo for the Vienna Opera in 1827. In it Fanny Elssler scored one of her earliest triumphs. The "pas de cinq" included Amalia Brugnoli, Samengo's wife, who was one of the first and most gifted ballerinas to dance "sur la pointe." In 1823 Marie Taglioni wrote of her that "she introduced a new style; she did very extraordinary things on the point of her foot."

Carlo Blasis was the first to actually set down definitions, with appropriate illustrations and instructions, of the figures and techniques of the classic ballet, in his "Manual" published in 1830 (amplified from his "Traité de l'Art de la Danse," Milan, 1820). Although ballerinas were already dancing on the point, the new technique was not yet widespread, and the illustrations showed the ballerina dancing on the 1/2 point. The closeness of the new technique to that already perfected by the dancing acrobats is very clear if one compares almost any figure in the Blasis "Manual" with this illustration from A.-J.-B. Thomas's album, "Un an à Rome et dans les environs." (1822)

THE BOUQUET OF LOVE—EQUESTRIAN EXERCISES BY DUCROW AND HIS YOUNG SISTER Like his "Flore et Zéphire," this baroque number, performed shortly after his French tour, would seem to have emptied the theatrical property shops of Paris. Drawn by Bergmann and lithographed at Geneva in 1820.

CHAPTER VII

The Romantic Ballet
of the Boulevard du Crime

F the Porte-Saint-Martin had been nothing more than "the people's Opéra," as it was often called, Gardel and the Opéra officials would have been less vindictive. However, the regular Opéra-goers—the prosperous middle class and aristocracy of the Empire—sometimes transferred their distinguished presence to the Boulevard. Another significant indication of the popularity of the Porte-Saint-Martin ballets is that Martinet's *Galerie Théâtrale*, in which thirty-six pictures a year were devoted to productions of the Paris stage, had the following number of dance prints between 1802 and 1807: one for the Ambigu-Comique, one for the Gaîté, three for the Opéra and four for the Porte-Saint-Martin.

At first Gardel seems to have been convinced that the secondary theatres' success came from their choice of subjects; hence the Decree of June 8th, 1806:

"*The Opéra*. It alone may perform plays with music throughout, and ballets of a noble and gracious style, such as those whose subjects derive from mythology or history and whose chief characters are gods, kings and heroes. It may also (but not to the exclusion of other theatres) stage ballets representing rural scenes or scenes from everyday life."

"*The Porte-Saint-Martin*. It is especially assigned the category of Melodrama, and highly spectacular plays. However, in this theatre's repertory of plays, as in all the secondary theatres' repertories, only songs in the common domain may be used. Ballets of historic or noble style may not be given at this theatre, that category, as stated above, being reserved solely for the Grand Opéra."

"*The Gaîté*. It is primarily intended for pantomimes of all kinds, but without ballet, and for "harlequinades" and other farces of the kind formerly given by Nicolet at this theatre."

The Ambigu-Comique is not even mentioned in the Decree, according to the *Annuaire dramatique ou Etrennes Théâtrales* for 1807. However, the Gaîté still kept its ballet company and sometimes circumvented the Decree.

Between 1802 and 1807, the first period of the Porte-Saint-Martin, its personnel, although they were often trained at the school of the former Royal Academy of Music (while other children trained on the Boulevard were engaged by the Opéra), never rivalled the dazzling virtuosos of the national theatre. The latter possessed exceptional artists at that time even among the "*remplacements*" and "*doubles*," with *premiers danseurs* such as Vestris, Duport, Beaupré and

Mlle Clotilde. Apart from its *première danseuse*, Mme Queriau, who was equal to Mlle Bigottini of the Opéra according to contemporary accounts, the dancers of the Porte-Saint-Martin were not better than those of the Gaîté or the Ambigu-Comique. The Gaîté could boast of the infant prodigy Albert, shortly to be engaged by the Opéra and the Ambigu-Comique had Jacquinet, already a dancer and mime of repute. The "supers" at all three theatres were of the same calibre. The Gaîté also prided itself on its permanent ballet-master Eugène Hus, who had been an Opéra choreographer. In 1800, Charles Taglioni came to Paris to engage a few dancers for Italy, see his son Philippe who was a junior member of the Opéra company, and enter his children Salvatore and Louise in the classes of Coulon *père*. While in Paris, he arranged two pantomime-ballets for the Gaîté: *Le Jour de Noce ou L'Enlèvement* (*The Wedding Day, or the Elopement*) and *L'Amant statue ou L'Ecole Hollandaise* (*The Statue Lover, or The Dutch School*).

M. Richard, ballet-master at the Ambigu-Comique, and formerly of the Opéra, where his choreographic talents had been ignored, caused no anxiety to Gardel. Jean Aumer and Louis Henry of the Porte-Saint-Martin, and Eugène Hus who appeared frequently on its programs, did.

Gardel's early tactics were to prevent his rivals from using subjects and types of ballet that he favored. Thus he hoped that the Opéra would win back its public. The Porte-Saint-Martin, which obeyed the Decree scrupulously, continued to compete with the Opéra and even outclass it. So in 1807 a new Decree closed this theatre, that of the Jeunes Elèves and some others less important. The Ambigu-Comique and the Gaîté (the latter after Eugène Hus had left) kept their ballet-masters and dancers, who were no danger to the Opéra.

On January 1st, 1810, Augustin Hapdé and Dugas *fils* obtained authorization to present pantomimes at the former Porte-Saint-Martin, rechristened Salle des Jeux-Gymniques. The names of its personnel appeared in the almanachs under the heading "mimes," but Gardel should have been alerted for they included already well-known dancers who reintroduced ballet into the repertory under cover of this equivocal title.

On March 24th, 1810, *L'Union de Mars et Flore et les bosquets de Lauriers* (*The Union of Mars and Flora and the Laurel Groves*) "allegorical tableaux" by Hapdé with divertissements by Camus and music by Piccini and Darondeau, was a brilliant success. All Paris enthused over its ballet of soldier-Cupids danced by children, which was to be revived several times on other stages. This topical piece (it concerned the Emperor's marriage) did not go unnoticed, and it aroused jealousy and complaints from the Opéra officials. Yet, the ballet-master Camus, a competent Boulevard practitioner, was not in the class of the famous pre-1807 Porte-Saint-Martin choreographers and might have seemed incapable of competing with Gardel and Milon of the Opéra. No doubt the old name of the theatre, which still appeared below the new one, was enough to attract an immense public.

On June 13th, 1810, the Jeux-Gymniques presented *Lapeyrouse ou Le Voyageur autour du mond* (*Lapeyrouse, or The Globe Trotter*), in which a troupe of performing monkeys, forerunner of the monkey ballet in *Jocko*, was joyously received. But the "historical," "allegorical" and "comic" tableaux were beginning to cause their powerful competitor serious alarm. In 1811, the triumph of *Les Chevaliers de la Table Ronde ou Roger et Naïda* (*The Knights of the Round*

Table, or Roger and Naïda) a troubadour pantomime with ballets by Camus for which the Jeux-Gymniques had secured the services of the Franconis and their horses, was followed by an admonition after a complaint from the Opéra.

Still more imprudently, the Jeux-Gymniques put on *La Fille mal gardée (The Ill-Guarded Maiden)*, advertised as "A Village Tableau in Two Parts by the Late Dauberval, revived by Eugène Hus." The euphemism did not conceal the fact that this was the famous ballet. Then the dancer Soissons put on a curious choreographical account of his stay in a nursing home: *Momus dans la maison des fous ou Le Retour à la raison (Momus in the Madhouse, or The Return to Reason)*.

Finally, on May 19th, 1812, appeared *Lise et Colin dans leur ménage ou La Suite de La Fille mal gardée (Lise and Colin's Married Life: A Sequel to "The Ill Guarded Maiden")*, "village tableaux followed by a divertissement." This was so patently a ballet in the style of the Porte-Saint-Martin that everyone expected the Opéra to take its revenge. The stars were the young Hoguet (an excellent dancer who went as ballet-master to Vienna in 1835 and later settled in Russia) and Mme Darcourt. Jacquinet was the ballet-master, and he must have been a remarkable mime, with a highly individual style, judging from an engraving of his Harlequin in Martinet's *Galerie Théâtrale*. The anticipated third complaint by the Opéra closed the theatre on June 4th, 1812.

The re-opening of the Porte-Saint-Martin under its own name followed not many months after the restoration of Louis XVIII. The *Annuaire Dramatique* gives the composition of its ballet company for 1815: Rhénon *aîné*, a former member of the Opéra, and Rhénon *jeune* were respectively First and Second ballet-masters; they were competent Boulevard practitioners. The *premiers danseurs* Rhénon and Jacquinet were reinforced by Toussaint aîné, who had recently resigned from the Opéra and Clairançon, a talented young dancer who subsequently became ballet-master at the Grand Théâtre of Bordeau. The *premières danseuses* were Mme Darcourt, the Dresden china Mme Pierson, and Aline Dorlé who soon moved over to the Opéra. Among other names in the company, certain sometimes appeared at the Opéra and sometimes on the Boulevard. Their careers can be followed through a century from father to son and mother to daughter, by means of the theatrical almanachs; such were the Tournois, Poidevaints (Potdevins, Poidevins, etc), Laurents, the Petits and their tribe, the Bartholomins, Richards, Saulniers, etc.

The Porte-Saint-Martin School of Dance produced other names which were to reappear: among the men—Monnet, Bégrand, Hutin, Ahn; among the women—Courtois, Leroy, Lingot. At the end of the Almanach the titles of first performances and names of debutant dancers followed by those of their teachers were listed in the same manner as those of the Opéra. In 1816, a distinguished visitor—Louis Henry—is mentioned, as well as a prominent staff choreographer, Frédéric Blanche. The latter was a son of Jean-Baptiste Blache (known as Blache *père*), an excellent choreographer who preferred to remain in the provinces, whence he sent his ballets to Paris and even across Europe. His sons, Frédéric—Auguste and Alexis Scipion, profitably devoted part of their careers to reviving their father's ballets.

Les Meuniers (The Millers), by Blache *père*, described by Saint-Léon in 1852 as "a fundamental type of farce which, without the aid of scenery and costumes, without the luxury supposedly essential to ballet, has been and is still being played at theatres everywhere, large and small," is the pattern of a success which, still according to Saint-Léon, earned more than 60,000 francs "for the fortunate composer and his family." Blache was the first to introduce a skating dance (in *La Laitière Polonaise (The Polish Milkmaid)*: Porte-Saint-Martin, 1817). In *Rosine et Almaviva*, first composed with Duport at the Opéra in 1806 and then revised by Blache alone, the famous *pas de huit scénique*, reproduced by "reflections" in a mirror, was his invention. All the works of this "elite among choreographers," who was satisfied with having replaced Dauberval in the dance-mad city of Bordeaux, were revived by his son Frédéric in Paris.

On only one occasion did Blache *père* himself put on a ballet at the Opéra, after a career devoted mainly to the new type of popular ballet. Then he achieved a "mythological" *tour de force* in the purest eighteenth-century style. This was *Mars et Vénus ou les Filets de Vulcain (Mars and Venus, or Vulcan's Nets)*, which was staged at a time—1826—when Gardel himself would have hesitated to do it. Most improbably, this Anacreontic ballet held the stage until 1837, with 105 performances, and was immortalized in Paris by the popular prints.

Making use of the Blaches' prestige, the Porte-Saint-Martin played a decisive part in the development of Romantic ballet between 1816 and 1830. "Possessing a corps de ballet as well constituted as the present one," said the *Journal des Théâtres*, "the Porte-Saint-Martin will be able to achieve its former splendor. . . . Everything in the past season demonstrated that for choreography the Porte-Saint-Martin was really a branch of the Opéra." In addition, the *Galerie Martinet* continued to devote a number of plates to its ballets; between 1816 and 1830, sixteen plates were devoted to ballet at the Opéra, thirteen to that of the Porte-Saint-Martin; the Gaîté and the Ambigu-Comique did not even appear in this category.

Among Blache *père's* ballets mounted by Blache *fils* from 1816 until 1825 (when Jean Coralli succeeded him as chief ballet-master at the Porte-Saint-Martin), were the following: *Suzanne et les Vieillards (Susanna and the Elders)*, *Les Meuniers (The Millers)*, *Le Sculpteur (The Sculptor)*, *Rosine et Almaviva*, *L'Amour et la Folie (Love and Madness)*, *Haroun al-Rashid*, and *L'Amour au village (Love in the Village)*. Frédéric Blache himself composed all ballets for the melodramas, as well as the series of vehicles for Mazurier.

At that period, the Porte-Saint-Martin presented an imposing repertory, in addition to the works of its "resident" ballet-masters and their guest, Louis Henry: *Les six Ingénus (The Six Innocents)* (Duport, revived by Jean Petipa in 1815), *Le Berger de la Sierra Morena (The Shepherd of the Sierra Morena)* (Petipa, 1815), *Les Ecoliers en vacances (School Holidays)* (Jacquinet, 1815), *Le Moulin d'Andre ou Les Meuniers et les Meunières (Andre's Mill, or Love Among the Millers)* (Rhénon and Blache *fils*, 1817), two melodrama ballets by Labottière of Bordeaux (1818), a revival of *Les Vendangeurs (The Grape Harvesters)* by Eugène Hus of the Gaîté (1819, first performance 1804), *Annette et Lubin* (Dauberval, revived by J.-B. Blache in 1821), *Une nuit de carnaval (Carnival Night)* (Télémaque, "after Taglioni"—père?—1822), *La Laitière suisse (The Swiss Milkmaid)* (Titus, of the Berlin Opera, later ballet-master at St. Petersburg, 1823), *Le Déserteur (The Deserter)* (Dauberval, "revived with alterations by Blache *fils*" in 1824), *Les Deux Petites Soeurs (The Two Little Sisters)* (Hullin, 1825), several melodrama ballets and *Scaramouche ou La Statue du Commandeur (Scaramouche, or The Commander's Statue)* by Aniel (1825, 1826).

In 1829, when Coralli was certain of his contract at the Opéra under the new director, Dr. Véron, he was replaced at the Porte-Saint-Martin by Petit (called Anatole) of the Opéra, where he had already choreographed *Le Sicilien* (*The Sicilian*).

Toward 1841, the Porte-Saint-Martin launched a series of fairy plays and "*revues fantastiques*" by the Cogniard brothers. In 1845, Ragaine's name appeared on the programs. A pupil of Coulon *père*, he appeared in the corps de ballet at the Opéra in 1816, was promoted in 1819, took posts as ballet-master in the provinces and on the Boulevard, and finally joined the Porte-Saint-Martin.

In these spectacular fairy plays, *pas seuls* and *pas de deux* were only divertissements, in which the corps de ballet was given a star role, in which male dancers were almost entirely replaced by ballerinas in "*travesti*" and remained only in "grotesque" or comic ensembles such as the Kingdoms of Vegetables, Fishes, Demons, Undertakers, etc. The Châtelet style, in short, became established at the Porte-Saint-Martin, outclassing the rival spectacles at the Gaîté and Cirque-Olympique. Some Porte-Saint-Martin fairy plays, such as *La Biche au Bois* (*The Hind in the Forest*) (1845) and *La Belle aux cheveux d'or* (*The Golden Haired Beauty*) (1847), were revived some twenty years after their *premières*.

Sometimes the Porte-Saint-Martin paid tribute to the *ballet d'action* with *L'Ombre* (*The Shadow*) in 1843, *Trilby ou Le Lutin de la chaumière* (*Trilby, or The Cottage Sprite*) in 1846 and *L'Etoile du marin* (*The Sailor's Star*) in 1849, with Eugène Lerouge, Ragaine's successor, as ballet-master—and it could still afford the luxury of engaging the star Flora Fabbri in 1855 and of putting on Perrot's *La Esmeralda*, in 1856. [33]

In the *Moniteur Universel* of December 29th, 1856, Théophile Gautier stated the chief reason for the decay of the Romantic ballet, particularly the *ballet d'action*, until its rebirth under Diaghilev: "The Porte-Saint-Martin's license includes, of course, permission to perform ballet, but it rarely makes use of it because the addition of a choreographic troupe to a drama company is a costly affair. *Esmeralda*, which is showing this week, was originally performed in London at Her Majesty's Theatre; it is the masterpiece of Perrot, the last man who really danced; Perrot, who designs dances as brilliantly as he once performed them!" And he ends with this significant sentence: "The dancer, M. Paul, has great elevation; he soars up to the flys and stays there; but today the public pays little attention to the male dancer."

Gautier's point about the addition of a troop of dancers to a company of actors was not really serious until 1850. Previously, secondary theatres, which had to stage a great variety of spectacles, did not need to maintain two or three complete companies. Because every performer at that time was, by virtue of his training, able to appear as a dancer or at any rate a "super." Thus, actor-dancers, singer-dancers and mime-dancers rubbed shoulders with dancer-dancers. This mixture of dancing personnel, which reduced running expenses, did no harm to ballet as a whole; under Aumer's direction, for example, such a corps de ballet could outclass the listless nonentities of the Opéra.

The decline of the *ballet d'action* was inevitable after the apotheosis of the ballerina in the Romantic period: male dancing was almost eliminated, and *ballet d'action*, thus unbalanced, could not survive. Only in Italy did the male dancers resist being completely submerged by the ballerinas; there they carried acrobatic feats to such heights that Italian critics, around 1856, called a *premier danseur* such as Carlo Foriani, "vulgar." It was precisely these acrobatic feats, which were cultivated in Italy and Russia but neglected in France under Louis Mérante's reign at the Opéra, that were to restore male dancing and consequently the *ballet d'action.*

During the period of the Romantic ballet, which extended until about 1860, a number of choreographers worked for the Boulevard stages. Milon was ballet-master at the Ambigu-Comique from 1796 until 1799 before he submitted to Gardel and returned to the Opéra. Two ballets spread his fame to Italy, England, Germany, Russia, Denmark and America: *Nina ou La Folle par amour (Nina, or Love Mad),* first presented in 1813 and performed 191 times until 1837, and *Clari,* presented in 1820 and given 92 times up to 1830. From Aumer came *Les Pages du Duc de Vendôme (The Duke of Vendôme's Pages),* performed at Vienna in 1815 and at Paris in 1820 (115 performances until 1830), *La Somnambule (The Sleepwalker),* performed in 1827 (119 performances until 1857) and his ballets for *La Muette de Portici (The Dumb Girl of Portici),* which were performed about 500 times between 1828 and 1882. All these ballets were danced in Europe and the chief cities of America.

Ferdinand Albert Decombe, called "Albert," a famous dancer of the pre-Romantic period and later a great choreographer, performed on the Boulevard during his adolescence; his ballet *Cendrillon (Cinderella)* (1823), remained in repertory until 1830, with 104 performances. Born in Bordeaux, he came to Paris and was at once billed as *premier danseur* by the Gaîté ballet-master Eugène Hus. He remained there until 1806, working with Vestris at the Opéra and attended the classes of Coulon *père.* He was invited back to Bordeaux but returned to Paris almost at once, where he was appointed *"double"* on joining the Opéra on July 1st 1808. In 1810 he was a *"remplacement"* and two years later *premier danseur* with Vestris and Beaupré.

Unfortunately, as a choreographer, Albert could not win acceptance from the Opéra; apart from an attempt in 1818 with *Le Séducteur du village ou Claire et Mectal (The Village Seducer, or Claire and Mectal),* and afterward with *Cendrillon* in 1823. He had to wait nineteen years before producing another ballet there—his masterpiece, *La Jolie Fille de Ghent (The Fair Maid of Ghent),* in 1842. However, he spent his holidays in London where he had an opportunity to stage his creations: *Finette* in 1821, *Amynthe et L'Amour (Amynthe and Cupid),* *L'Anneau magique (The Magic Ring),* *Une heure à Naples (An Hour in Naples)* and *Daphnis et Cephis,* all in 1832, *La Coquette soumise (The Coquette Subdued)* in 1834, *Le Corsaire (The Buccaneer)* in 1837 (rearranged and signed by Mazilier in 1856), *La Fille de Marbre (The Marble Maiden)* in 1845, and *L'Odalisque* and *La Reine des Fées (The Fairy Queen)* in 1847.

Passionately interested in the history of his art, according to Léopold Adice, he delved for all possible information by questioning his oldest colleagues concerning the development of dancing and choreography. (Incidentally, he invented the system of "stenochorégraphie," for which Saint-Léon claimed paternity.) He died in 1865, having witnessed the decline of the *ballet d'action,* which he loved so greatly, and the triumph of Saint-Léon who had done much to hasten its decadence.

The origins of toe-dancing are still open to discussion, and the actual date at which it made its appearance will probably never be definitely known.

While it is clear that the training of dancers in France assimilated certain acrobatic exercises, is the ballerina's dancing *on pointe* a department of pure acrobatics? This aspect in the development of classic ballet should be greatly clarified when Léopold Adice's four manuscripts are published.

A *demi-caractère* dancer of Italian origin, after an honorable career as performer he was appointed teacher of the advanced class at the Opéra by Nestor Roqueplan. His good relations with Coralli, Albert and Mazilier kept him out of difficulties until the arrival of Saint-Léon and the administrator Perrin. The latter retired him prematurely. His manuscript volumes, finished in 1873, amplify his *Théorie de la Gymnastique de la Danse Théâtrale* (Paris, 1859), the only real technical exposition of dance technique for this period.

However, *pointe* work in France goes back to at least 1817 or 1818, when the elder Mlle Gosselin was dancing at the Opéra. An English engraving of 1821 shows Fanny Bias on *pointes,* and a French lithograph of the same year shows Mlle Mees in a similar posture. Moreover, Marie Taglioni seems to have seen Mlle Amalia Brugnoli, an Italian-trained ballerina already famous in Naples and Milan and a protégée of Armand Vestris, dancing on *pointes* in 1823. [34]

The testimony of A. J. B. Thomas concerning the development of dancing on *pointe* in Italy is interesting: in Rome during 1822 he made a collection of his own drawings of costumes, customs, ceremonies and "in general, everything of note that is to be seen." The collection, lithographed by Villain under the title: *Un An à Rome et dans les Environs (A Year in Rome and its Surroundings),* was published by Firmin-Didot in 1823. One plate, titled *Polichinelle et Grotesques,* shows a couple of dancers on quarter *pointes* beside Pulcinella; the three characters are surrounded by *acrobats.* May not the origin of classic pointe dancing therefore go back to the fairground companies, the *atleti danzatori Zanfretta* and the *Compagnia mimica-acrobatica-dansante dei fratelli Chiarini,* to mention only two of the travelling companies as well known in France as in Italy? That men should also at one time or another have gone in for toe dancing seems an overemphasis of its acrobatic side; but the influence of fairground on the development of dancing on pointe seems certain.

Leaving speculations on technique for a factual note about some of the choreographers who bridged the transitional period, it would seem that certain ballet masters did not appear at the Paris Opéra, but made their careers on the Boulevard, in the provinces or abroad. These included Millot, Jacquinet, Camus, Thierry (the future ballet-master at Warsaw), Adam, Morand, Hullin (ballet-master in London), Télémaque, Renauzy, Paul Maximilien (future ballet-master at the Opéra-Comique), Lefèvre (ballet-master in London), Ragaine, Laurent ainé, Chap, Bertotto, Laurençon, Blondin, and E. Lerouge. Mazilier danced on the Boulevard and, although no innovator, played an important part in the history of Romantic ballet as dancer and choreographer. Philippe Taglioni, whose choreography has been considered the cornerstone of Romanticism, was no innovator either. His part in the creation of Marie Taglioni's style consisted in using the discoveries of the period with a slight delay for *La Sylphide,* as subject and choreography, had already evolved on the Boulevard. Her personal genius as a performer made the true stylistic innovations.

Actually, five men were to determine the direction taken by ballet for over a century through artistic formulas which fall entirely within the domain of the Theatre of Marvels: Jean Aumer, Louis Henry, Mazurier, Jean Coralli and Jules Perrot.

THEATRE OLYMPIQUE

Erigé dans les Arènes de Nîmes par M. Belfort, directeur des Théâtres.

St. Dédie par lui à la Ville. An 1828.

M. Belfort, "Director of Theatres," tried to reproduce the splendors of the Cirque-Olympique mimodramas and the Porte-Saint-Martin ballets in the arena amphitheatre at Nîmes, which had for some time been given over to bullfights. He engaged the dancer Girel, who had been performing all of Mazurier's roles at the Royal Theatre of Brussels (La Monnaie) to do the same at Nîmes. The decorative motifs on the proscenium pediment are vestiges of the Empire ornamental vocabulary which remained popular in the provinces until about 1850. At Nîmes they were appropriate to the setting and the pro-Napoleonic sentiments of Belfort.

Jean Aumer as the Dulce of Vendôme in his ballet "The Pages of the Duke of Vendôme" (1815).

Although somnambulism was as much a part of the Boulevard theatre as madness (Deburau even played in an anonymous pantomime "Pierrot Somnambule" at the Funambules in 1823), Jean Aumer's ballet "La Somnambule" was considered a novelty on the grand opera stages in 1827.

This lithograph of Aumer's ballet "Alfred le Grand" (Paris Opera 1822, created Vienna 1820) sets forth explicitly the handling of the masses of supernumeraries in an important ballet d'action (comparably to the Vienna print of Henry's "William Tell.") This print shows the scenery designed to facilitate the action in four degrees of depth and on several levels formed by solidly constructed set pieces. The perspective backdrop with its "trompe l'oeil" details, was lighted by crossed beams "by reflection and refraction" according to the scenic instructions.

Mazilier (Marseille, 1797—Paris, 1868), made his début at the Grand Theatre of Bordeaux in 1820, and his Parisian début at the Porte-Saint-Martin as premier danseur in 1823. Dr. Véron engaged him for the Paris Opéra in 1831 in the same capacity and he became an Opéra choreographer in 1839. He created vehicles for the greatest ballerinas of his day: "La Gypsy" (1839), "Le Diable Amoureux" (1840), "Paquita" (1846), "Vert-Vert" (1851) "Les Elfes" and "Le Corsaire" (1856) and "Marco Spada" in 1857. His subject matter and techniques were clearly influenced by his eight years on the Boulevard. This lithograph, the first known print of Mazilier, shows him in a revival of Dauberval's celebrated ballet "The Deserter" "as put on with changes by Blache "fils" at the Porte-Saint-Martin in 1824.

Louis Henry and Marie Quériau were starred almost immediately on their arrival in Italy. Giacomo Pregliasco sketched them in costume for Lefèvre's ballet "Issipile," created at La Scala in 1808. (Bibl Civica, Torino)

Costume sketch by R. Fleury for the last ballet created in Paris by Louis Henry: "L'Ile des Pirates" (1835), starring Fanny Elssler, at the Paris Opéra. (Bibl de l'Opéra)

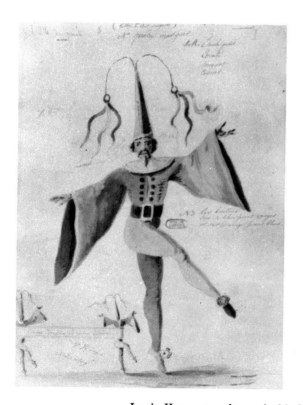

Louis Henry as a bonze in his ballet "Chao-Kang" at the Théâtre Nautique (1834). (Galerie Dramatique Martinet)

The plagiarisms of Philippe Taglioni from the works of Louis Henry and other of his contemporaries were common knowledge among his colleagues and balletophiles of Austria, Italy and France. The first of these two prints points out the resemblances between Taglioni's masked ball scene in the Opera "Gustave III" (Paris, 1831) with an explanatory text (see note 56) and Louis Henry's ballet "Le Bal Masqué" (created at La Scala in 1830), shown in the second Viennese print.

Stage sets for two of Louis Henry's ballets at La Scala: "Gengis Khan" (1828), a popular subject for melodramas and ballets, already developed by the choreographer Monticini in 1802; and "Le Amazoni" (1827), plagiarized by Philippe Taglioni for "La Révolte au Sérail" at the Paris Opéra (1833).

Mr *Mazurier, rôle de* Frisac *dans* Denise & André, *Ballet.*

lith. de L. Brunet à Lyon.

These prints constitute a Mazurier album, from his début in Lyon to his last performances in Paris. On the left: the first known portrait of Mazurier, a lithograph by Brunet of Lyon, circa 1822, in a "happy villagers" ballet, "Denise et André," at the Grand Théâtre, Lyon. Above, the first Parisian print of Mazurier in his first Parisian role, "Polichinelle Vampire." There are ten or more prints of Mazurier in this part (including one published in London), which feature the splits and other acrobatic dance tricks. His "Monsieur de Pourceaugnac" gets its belly laughs from the same repertoire of gags as the fairground "parades." Alexandre Valentin, who worked in France and England, drew a series of plates showing Mazurier in his various parts: below, in "The Gascon with Three Faces" and as the simpleton in "The Millers."

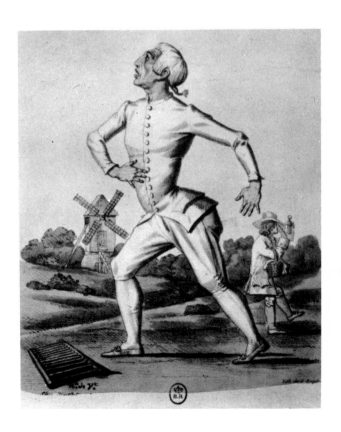

Mazurier as portrayed by Fauconnier, staff artist for the magazine "Le Diable boîteux," in his most famous part—Jocko—vis-à-vis Gobert as his master.

Greek folk dance with Mazurier at the head of a male corps de ballet in "A Visit to Bedlam." (Galerie Martinet-Hautecoeur)

The German acrobat-contortionist Klischnigg made Jocko a career; after years as a "human frog" he became a "man-monkey" travelling all over Europe and America. He was launched in his simian career by a Viennese farce, Nestroy's "Der Posse, der Affe und der Brautigam." These two Viennese prints give some idea of his presentation—the monkey has overtones of the frog. (Vienna, 1836)

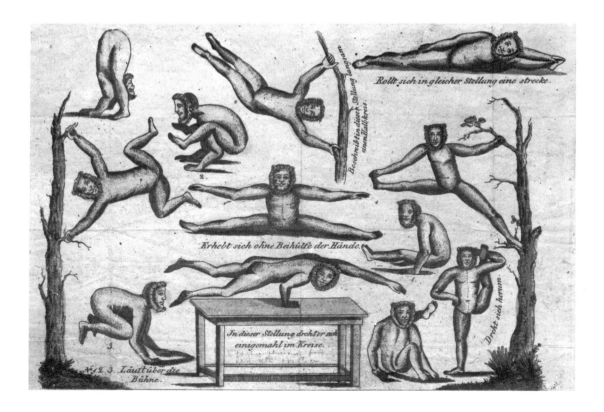

MR CORBY.

"MR. CORBY THE AMERICAN COMIC DANCER, DANS LE CARACTERS DE FRISAC" Corby made his debut at the Park Theatre with the Bartholomin-Monplaisir Ballet Company, billed as "Mons. Corby, First Comic Dancer of the Grand Theatre of Bordeaux." He created the role of Quasimodo in the Monplaisirs' production of Perrot's "Esméralda." Corby remained in America and joined forces with the Rousset Sisters in 1852. He filled all the Mazurier roles such as Frisac which may have been in the ballet "Denise et André" of 1821, or, more likely, Jean Petipa's "Frisac ou la Double Noce" of 1825. The barber Frisac retained his characteristics from one ballet to another.

Gabriel

Jerome Ravel.　3. Francois Ravel.　4. Antoine Ravel.　5. Mr. C. Lehmannn.　6. Mr. Blondin.　7. Mr. Marzetti.　8. Mad. Marzetti.　9. Mad. Axel.　10. Mad. J. Ravel.　11. Mr. A

TABLEAU FORMED BY THE RAVEL FAMILY IN THE BALLET OF JEANNETTE AND JEANNOT.

THE RAVEL FAMILY IN THE BALLET "JEANNETTE AND JEANNOT" This action scene has gathered together performers from several of the great fairground dynasties. The four Ravel brothers, Gabriel, Jerome, Francois and Antoine, joined Marzettis, Axels, Lehmanns and Blondin. This type of acrobatic ballet-pantomime is no longer performed except in the Chinese opera.

MENAGE AS CHAMPANZEE (1801) An English predecessor of Mazurier (probably also of French origin) in one of the innumerable London pantomimes of La Peyrouse.

The Performances of the famous MᴿMADDOX at Sadler's Wells

1ˢᵗ He ballances seven Pipes in one another on his Chin, and walks up and down on the Wire 2 A Chair topsiturvy on his Chin which he performs on one of the reverse Corners
3 A Coach Wheel which he likewise ballances on his Chin 4 beating a Drum 5 His Performance on the Violin. 6 Blowing the trumpet 7 Ballancing a Sword on y Edge of a Wineglass
8 Ballancing several Glasses full of Liquor. 9 The Ballance of two Pipes crossway, on a Hoop 10 His Exhibition of the Balls, where he keeps half a Dozen successively tossing without dropping one
11 Ballancing the Hat on his Nose & Standing on his Head while the Wire is in full swing, without touching it with his Hands, all which Exhibitions he performs on the Wire, with or without Pole
according to the Nature of the Ballance. The grand front figure is an exact Representation of his ballancing a Straw as he stands on the Stage, which he tosses from his Foot to his Forehead, working
d from thence to his Nose, Eye or Cheek and, sticking it to his Shoulder keeps it there in a Ballance for some time, when he tosses it back again to his Foot & stands with it as in the Posture described
He likewise ballances a Straw on the Wire tho' in a different manner, with several other extraordinary Feats in Equilibrio.—
Printed for Jˢ. Jackson at Tembianets Head in Fleet Street.
Publisht according to Act of Parliament July 1ˢᵗ 1752. Price

(Above) A print of the famous English rope dancer Mr. Maddox, published in 1752; and—(below) a later performance at the same theatre. Prints by T. Major, London, circa 1825.

CHAPTER VIII

The Choreographers

❧ JEAN AUMER ❧

JEAN Aumer was born in Paris in 1776. He was a protégé of Dauberval who taught him Noverre's principles and launched him at the Paris Opéra. Aumer subsequently rejoined his master in Bordeaux as a dancer at the Grand Théâtre.

In about 1801 he returned to Paris and entered the Opéra "empire," where he distinguished himself by standing up to its chief. Since no opportunity for showing his choreographic ability presented itself, he joined the Porte-Saint-Martin as ballet-master; in 1802, while still at the Opéra, he began his career as a choreographer with melodrama-ballets.

According to the *Repertoire* of the Porte-Saint-Martin, Aumer's first ballet was performed during *Ecbert, premier Roi d'Angleterre ou La Fin de l'heptarchie (Egbert, First King of England, or the End of the Heptarchy)*, a melodrama by Plancher-Valcour, on November 2nd, 1802. Between this first production and his departure at the end of July 1806, when he entered into battle with the Opéra, he produced a prodigious amount of work. Among others, he created ballets for the melodramas *Clodomire ou La Prêtresse d'Irmainsul (Clodomire, or The Priestess of Irmainsul), Les Français en Alger (The French in Algiers), Les Hussites ou Le Siège de Naumberg (The Hussites, or The Siege of Naumburg), Stanislas, Roi de Pologne (Stanislas, King of Poland), La Fausse Marquise (The Sham Marquise)* and *le Solitaire de la Roche-Noire (The Recluse of Black Rock)*. The words "Ballet and *mise en scène* by Aumer" also appear on the title pages of *Tippo-Saeb ou La Prise de Seringanatam (Tippoo Sahib, or The Capture of Seringanatam), Le Désastre de Lisbonne (The Lisbon Disaster), Caroline et Dorville ou La Bataille des Dunes (Caroline and Dorville, or The Battle of the Dunes), Frédéric de Spandau ou Le Libellé (Frederick of Spandau, or The Decree)* and *Gonzale de Cordoue ou Le Siège de Grenade (Gonzalvo of Cordoba, or The Siege of Grenada)*.

Aumer started at the Porte-Saint-Martin with a rash gesture, in reviving the great ballets of his teacher Dauberval: *Les Jeux d'Eglé (The Games of Aglaë)* in 1802, *Le Déserteur (The Deserter)* in 1803, *Annette et Lubin* and *La Fille mal gardée (The Ill Guarded Maiden)* in 1804 and *Le Page inconstant (The*

Fickle Page) in 1805. Gardel could not endure these triumphs by a master he himself had banished from Paris. But Aumer was to go even further!

At a time when Pixérécourt was doing so well for the Porte-Saint-Martin, the young choreographer was sure of a welcome if he could first satisfy the exigent author. He quickly made his mark with his ballets in *La Forteresse du Danube (The Danube Fortress)* (1805), in which the ballerina Mme Quériau made her first appearance in Paris as an actress. In his introduction to this play in the *Théâtre Complet de Pixérécourt* the critic Geoffroy remarks: "The play ends with a pretty ballet, very well designed; it is another proof of the talent of M. Aumer, artiste of the Académie Impériale de Musique who is responsible for the ballets at the Porte-Saint-Martin theatre."

Although they were staged by Aumer, the ballet scenes in *La Forteresse du Danube* were designed by Pixérécourt. Mme Quériau, in the role of Célestine, is disguised as a Savoyard, with a case in the shape of a magic lantern on "his" back and a box containing a marmot in front. As mountains were more or less inaccessible in stage coach days they constituted a sort of indigenous exotic setting, and the young Savoyard with his marmot aroused great interest in the theatre and on the street for a long time. The special elements of suspense and emotional contrasts in the third act ballet would not have been out of place in an 1840 scenario. Célestine is at a fête which takes place before a great chateau, awaiting news of her father. She keeps stopping to see if a messenger has arrived. Although her partners continue drawing her into the dance her anxiety finally communicates itself, so that each time she stops to listen the other dancers do likewise, and at each pause there is absolute silence as the groups stand frozen in position. Finally the old retainer rushes precipitately on stage— bringing unhappy tidings. Realistic details of "local color" which recur in Aumer's melodrama ballets were to culminate in his ensembles for *La Muette de Portici (The Dumb Girl of Portici*, premiere 1828).

However, the success of *La Forteresse du Danube* was eclipsed by that of *Robinson Crusoe*, in which the dancing had progressed in authenticity since *Les Indes Galantes* and attempted to be "Caribbean." Grotesque and comic elements are incorporated because dramatic effects in ethnic dancing were already being sought.

An open clash with Gardel finally came in 1806. Aumer had just composed his second ballet, *Jenny ou le Mariage Secret (Jenny or the Secret Marriage)* [35] on a Scottish theme which, with the general enthusiasm for Sir Walter Scott, was a popular certainty. Folkloric, rustic and rather coy, it introduced no great novelties, despite its success. In turn, Gardel now wished to make an experiment, if not in pre-Romanticism, at least in the "sensitive" manner. The popularity of *Paul et Virginie* had not declined since its publication; the novel was clearly in the realm of the exotic. This was Gardel's choice for his new ballet. Three days after its opening on June 28th, 1806, Aumer presented *his* version of *Paul et Virginie*, titled *Les Deux Créoles (The Two Creoles)*, thus defying the most privileged of the privileged theatres.

The scene was laid in "a wild part of Ile-de-France" (Mauritius). The road is crossed by a broad stream, whose water seems very low at the beginning of the act. It is strewn with rocks whose tops are always above water; "they must be close enough to one another for it to be possible to cross dryshod by using the rocks as stepping stones." "The spot must provide a picturesque

138

prospect. A sugar cane plantation is visible. A date palm covered with fruit is on the spectators' right. . . ." Aumer seems to have wanted to break all the rules that were dear to Gardel; he pushed mime and massed movements to frenzied extremes. The two lovers—re-baptized Zoë and Théodore—are united at the final curtain. There is no separation, no drowning, no unhappy ending.

Even more sugary than Aumer's ballet, Gardel's also had a happy ending. Thus from the "tragic" and literary standpoint the Opéra was not superior to the Boulevard, and the reviewers were distinctly divided: half of them, at least, ventured to prefer Aumer. Next, defying Gardel at the Opéra itself, Aumer succeeded in staging his ballet *Antoine et Cléopâtre* on March 8th, 1808. Then he left for Lyon where he directed its first performance at the Grand Théâtre. Rallying his powerful friends in the government, Gardel submitted his complaints to the Emperor, and with the administrators of the other privileged theatres asked for the suppression of their prosperous Boulevard rivals. Napoleon, whose correspondence betrays the fact that he was vexed at Josephine's preference for the secondary theatres, willingly complied. Accordingly, on July 9th, 1807, an Imperial Decree restricted the ballet repertory of the secondary theatres and the pantomime repertory as well; the total number of theatres in Paris was reduced to nine. The Porte-Saint-Martin closed and a hundred employees were thrown out of work.

Aumer, like many of his colleagues, had to look for a job outside Paris, but Italy, Austria, England, Portugal, Germany and Sweden welcomed the itinerant choreographers. In 1815, Aumer attained the rank of ballet-master and choreographer at the Hofburgoperntheater in Vienna. That same year he created *Les Pages du duc de Vendôme (The Duke of Vendôme's Pages)*, one of the works to which he owes his place in the history of choreography; in it, the management of the ensembles and the importance of mime recalled his innovations at the Porte-Saint-Martin.

When Gardel's grip at last relaxed a bit, Aumer returned to Paris and ended his career as ballet-master at the Opéra, although holding his post at Vienna until 1821. He supervised the Paris premiere of *Les Pages du duc de Vendôme* on October 18th, 1820, and then settled for good in his native city where, loaded with honors, he witnessed his daughter Julie's début at the Opéra.

Aumer, in the vanguard with his pre-Romantic works, had prepared the public for Romantic ballet itself on the Opéra stage. Like his illustrious predecessor Noverre in 1783, he was to be reproached with having travelled the provinces and foreign countries, and his works were criticized for constantly recalling the habits and effects of the Boulevard theatre. A critic like Delaforest, while upholding a new school and a radical transformation in performances at the Opéra in opposition to Gardel found it difficult to accept Boulevard production as such. He could not realize that the shocking bad taste and the gaudy improbabilities of melodrama concealed a genuine and promising dramatic form, and that the promise of its refinement was masked by the very excesses of its newness.

The first work staged by Aumer after his official return to the Opéra in 1822 was *Alfred le Grand (Alfred the Great)*. The plot is based on the exploits of the Anglo-Saxon king; disguised as a peasant and followed by a faithful page he has gone into hiding to escape the invading Danes. In his humble costume, he wins the heart of Alswitha, daughter of a great lord, and then reveals his rank to the peasants and knights, who all rally to his banner. Then he defeats the Danes, recovers his crown and marries Alswitha. For the designer Cicéri the period (848-899) lent itself rather prematurely to the troubadour style, in what might be called an architectural forecast. There was a wealth of diorama effects, notably a gallery with stained glass windows and a perspective view of a guardroom.

According to Delaforest, the "first two acts deserve nothing but praise. Their action is rapid . . . but the third act is not above reproach: it is too much like all the inevitable melodrama finales. The brutalities of the Danish general are all too obviously akin to those theatrical effects whose sad exploitation should be left to the Boulevards." Indeed, as a lithograph in the *Théâtres de Paris* series shows, one scene might have been taken from the Porte-Saint-Martin or the Ambigu, and several of the techniques used had often been encountered on the Boulevard. The critic brought the same charge against *Aline, Reine de Golconde (Aline, Queen of Golconda* (Hyderabad)), "which, like all M. Aumer's ballets, reminds us of the productions of the Porte-Saint-Martin; this is M. Aumer's great defect, and if the Opéra does not look out, the Royal Academy of Music will soon be more like a branch of the Boulevard theatres." He thought the *pas de sept*, an example of the new exoticism, intolerable and as ridiculous as Gardel's garlands and ribbons, and said of the little mirrors with bells held by four ballerinas in the same *pas:* "It amounts to making success dependent upon grotesque methods which have nothing to do with art." However, the work was an undisputed success.

The contemporary accounts give only meager information about the choreography as such. Pictures of an action ballet "in action," with dancers, corps de ballet and *mise en scène* are extremely rare. Even a decade later, in the high tide of Romanticism, collections like *Le Ménestrel, Les Souvenirs dramatique, Le Charivari, L'Album de l'Opéra, Le Monde dramatique* and the illustrated music books, which sometimes show theatrical scenes in their illustrations, have few ensemble prints in comparison with the countless plates devoted to the performers and their costumes. A single series, *Les Théâtres de Paris*, which was very short-lived and, incidentally, intended for export to Italy, can be compared to the great Italian collections. So in order to imagine the steps, and especially the great *"ballabile,"* apart from the verbal information in the scenarios and the small number of scenic illustrations, we have only fragments of description such as the following, taken from the review of *Aline* in *Le Corsaire:* "Gosselin, who is a match in strength and agility for his admirable sister, distinguishes himself in a magnificent group in which he holds the prettiest members of the academy entwined in twelve bands of sky blue gauze; it is as if Apollo had left his chariot to sport with the Hours. . . ." There is a feeling in this of George Balanchine's *Apollon Musagète*.

Aumer went on with his innovations. His ballet *La Somnambule* (1827) preceded Bellini's famous opera by four years; its classic sleepwalking scene and its plot place it among the early Romantic ballets.

The more than competent and very conscientious Louis Milon opened the Opéra's gates to the new school with his ballet *Clari*; had Gardel permitted it, he could doubtless have developed his tendencies toward Romanticism. However, Jean Aumer and Louis Henry, with the advantages of greater audacity and a European reputation, ushered in the Romantic ballet.

140

Jean Coralli.

"If you wish to produce an impression with a fantastic plot, you must not approach it as a disbeliever; be convinced yourself and the public will have no trouble in believing you, for they are more than half persuaded already. You are plucking strings too taut for them not to respond immediately."

"Auriol most certainly merits the good will lavished on him by the public, for he is the wittiest and most charming clown imaginable." The protean Auriol—Gautier also called him "a dainty Hercules"—was clown, equilibrist, acrobat, equestrian, contortionist and mime. The vase photographed above is but one of literally hundreds of objects in his image: he appeared on stamp boxes, make-up boxes, toothpick holders, pipes, cavorted above ormolu clocks and faience tobacco pots . . . in short he outdistanced Mazurier in the number of prints and objects devoted to him (but his career was long). This Alsatian lithograph shows him as equilibrist. (Harvard Theatre Collection)

Lawrence and Redisha, the English acrobatic-contortionists, were also known as mimes. Gautier devoted pages to their numbers and thought they represented ". . . a Britannic conscience pushed to its ultimate limits." The Viennese artist composed this print in the manner of ancient popular woodcuts, combining several numbers of the two acrobats into one picture. ("Scene aus Wien," undated, probably c. 1840)

Professor Risley and his Sons in the "Ballet Aérien"—1844 and 1845. Drawn by Alexandre Lacauchie and J. Petit respectively. "It is often said of famous ballerinas that they could march on a daisy's head without disturbing the dewdrop, but these are figures of rhetoric taken seriously only by the addressees; applied to the little Risleys it is truth rising naked from her well; the eye can scarcely follow them and the silver spangles which shine about them tremble in perpetual motion like a rippling lake reflecting the moonlight."

"Giselle" is the most durable ballet exhibit in the Theatre of Marvels. Carlotta Grisi created the role in 1841, Nathalie Fitzjames and Auguste Mabille danced in the ballet some 10 years later, and in recent decades Markova, Ulanova, Alonso, Fonteyn, Kaye, or any great prima ballerina assoluta one can name have continued to match their talents against the demands of this role.

Tamara Toumanova in "Giselle," at the Ballets Russes de Monte-Carlo under the direction of Rene Blum. (Phot. Baron.)

THE CRACOVIENNE, DANCED BY

MAD.^{LLE} FANNY ELSSLER.

IN THE GRAND BALLET OF THE GIPSEY.

Pub. by N. Currier.

J. Spence, 8^t N.Y.

An American lithograph (N. Currier, in a version of Formentin's famous study) of Fanny Elssler in the type of folk-ballet dance such as Pixérécourt liked to insert in his melodramas. The print probably appeared shortly after her American début in 1840.

Louis Xavier Stanislas Henri Bonnachon, known as Henry, was born at Versailles on March 7th, 1784. In 1792, he chanced to enter the building which had been constructed for the Opéra and was occupied by it from 1781 to 1794. Sold in the Year VI as State property, it was to become the Porte-Saint-Martin. Gardel, who was rehearsing *Psyche,* noticed the enraptured child and chatted with him; the conversation resulted in Louis Henry's admission as a pupil in the Opéra ballet school at the age of eight. [36]

He made his Opéra debut on March 7th, 1803, in a *pas de deux* with Mlle Clotilde Mafleuroy. Both of them were tall and rather majestic. The *Journal de l'Empire* devoted a few admiring paragraphs to this sensational debut: "In an age when everything is great, this couple is of its age." A pack of cards decorated with "portraits of Actors and Actresses of the Paris Theatres," dated 1802, shows Henry, as well as Duport, Mlle Clotilde and Mme Gardel, as "artists of the Opéra"; thus he must already have been a member of the Opéra company in 1802, and fairly well known.

When he wanted to obtain the post of choreographer, he encountered the normal intriguing of Gardel, who sensed a rival until, mollified by a scenario which was in conformity with all his prejudices, and by the eloquent pages which Henry dedicated to him in the preface, he consented to the staging of *L'Amour à Cythére (Cupid at Cythera).* This contained the old company of Games, Mirths, Pleasures, Winds, Nymphs and adult and child Cupids in a setting decorated with perfume burners, baskets of flowers and Cupid's darts. After his success—which was due more to freshness of choreographic invention than to a rather routine scenario—Henry, then twenty-two, received an offer from the Porte-Saint-Martin, where his colleague Aumer was choreographer and Eugène Hus director and choreographer. [37]

Henry hesitated about leaving the Opéra. However, in the very year of his first ballet, he irretrievably offended his old patron. Not knowing that Gardel had decided to make *Paul et Virginie* an exceptional experiment in the new style, he submitted to him a scenario based on the same novel. Although he withdrew it at once and had the outline of another ballet printed at his own expense, with pages of apology for his temerity and flattery of Gardel, he had to leave the Opéra. As for the substitute pantomime-ballet based on Voltaire, *Ce qui plaît aux dames (Ladies' Delight),* a mixture of Troubadour and Anacreontic pastoral, it was never produced. Henry then replaced Aumer as choreographer at the Porte-Saint-Martin.

He began by creating a ballet on the standard theme of *Deux Petits Savoyards (Two Little Savoyards)* (1807), in which he tried for the first time to reproduce on the stage a fairground scene complete with magicians, clowns, hawkers, coconut sellers and delighted bystanders. This scene was the great success of the ballet and Henry repeated it many times in his other works.

His most important ballet of this period, *Les Sauvages de la Floride (The Florida Savages),* is distinguished by ethnographic documentation which had become increasingly characteristic of the exotic style. The old formula of "the Noble Savage" was replaced by a story in which the hero, the villain and *all* the characters are natives. The series of ceremonial dances which comprise this pantomime-ballet contain both a semblance of truth and an interpretation on the lines of contemporary aesthetic conventions. Henry also took a few details from *L'Histoire de la Nouvelle France* by Charlevoix, a work much sought after by those interested in the development of the art of mime.

These two works were pronounced successes and the management of the Opéra, in order to put a stop to the rivalry with the Porte-Saint-Martin, asked Henry to choose one theatre or the other. He preferred to remain at the Porte-Saint-Martin, but it was closed shortly thereafter by the latest Decree. Fearing some chicanery from the Opéra, he left secretly for Milan disguised as a wine merchant.

There he found Noverre's two great Italian disciples, the choreographers Gaetono Gioja and Salvatore Viganò, and through them, the entire Noverre tradition. At that time the French choreographers Pierre Hus and Jean Briol and the Italians Salvatore Taglioni, Giovanni Galzerani, Armand Vestris, Villa and others quite as competent, were all working in Italy, although they were not as highly regarded as the Gioja-Vigano-Henry triumvirate.

Henry was soon dividing his time between Naples, Milan and Vienna. Mme Quériau, his favorite interpreter, joined him. This Boulevard celebrity, who always remained aloof from the Opéra, had a personal influence upon the development of mime which is attested by contemporary critics. Henry, who had been working with her since 1807, married her in about 1820 after she was widowed.

When the Porte-Saint-Martin reopened in 1814 with a license to produce ballet, the distinguished couple returned for a short season to show the Parisians the *azione mimiche* which they had created in Italy. The words "distinguished couple" seem fully justified on reading the published collection of libretti which Henry had created for the San Carlo of Naples alone. His prodigious inventiveness and his authority in dealing with his peers as well as those whom he far outclassed are evident throughout these texts. He was drawn to "noble" subjects, and the Italian influence is evident in the large number of tragic endings at a time when French ballet avoided them. His scenarios for *La Gerusalemme liberata (Jerusalem Liberated), Fitz-Henry, Armida et Rinaldo, Hamlet, Guillaume Tell* and *Don Giovanni Tenorio (Don Juan* with Mozart's music) demanded an even more accentuated mime than that of the Boulevard du Temple. However, this was not the only characteristic that links Louis Henry and the Theatre of Marvels so closely.

He particularly enriched the repertory of folkloric and exotic dances essential to every 19th-century choreographer with a series of *pas seuls* and *pas de deux* as well as the *grand ensembles* for the corps de ballet *(ballabile)*, in which a hundred or so participants of all trades and all countries, joined by elves, sylphs, demons, sprites and ghosts were whirled across the stage in a dazzling round. These were the elements from which he was to create the famous *Bal Masqué*, plagiarized by Philippe Taglioni for the ballroom scene in *Gustave III ou Le Bal Masqué (Gustave III, or The Masked Ball)*, when Duponchel staged it for the Opéra in 1833.

From the end of January to the end of October 1816, the Henry-Quériau partnership was all the rage in Paris: their repertory included *Hamlet, Le Rosier (The Rose Bush), Le Château infernal (The Infernal Castle), Samson* and *Le Mariage rompu (The Broken Marriage)*.

Hamlet, "tragic pantomime interspersed with dancing," which Henry extracted from Shakespeare's tragedy, was a sensational success, earning him more than 36,000 francs in royalties within a few months. The substitution in the French text of a happy ending for that of Shakespeare's is significant. Henry's *azione tragica* had to submit to the law imposed by the French conventions of melodrama: that vice would be punished and virtue rewarded.

On the title page of the text, which will remain one of the unlikeliest "adaptations" of *Hamlet*, Louis Henry gave prominence to the following sentence, which he thought adapted to his work: "Overwhelmed by so cruel a sorrow, my soul had only strength to feel it; love's murmurs were stifled by the anguished cry of Nature. *(La Nouvelle Héloïse)*."

The pantomime boasted a score by "the Count de Gallenberg, Knight of the Order of the Two Sicilies and Ballet Music Composer to the Royal Theatre of San Carlo, Naples." Its date—1816—explains the absence from this text of the essential features of Shakespeare's tragedy: some ten years were to pass before English actors performed in Paris (1827), and even in 1829, the indignant public's demonstrations when Baron Taylor produced *Othello, or The Moor of Venice* translated by Alfred de Vigny at the Théâtre Français, exceeded the bounds of decency.

At the time, this *Hamlet* seemed overwhelming to a public which would not accept anything stronger; they accepted even this much only because the tragedy had been reduced to a mimed melodrama in the supernatural style.

It was succeeded in April 1816, by *Le Château infernal (The Infernal Castle)*, pantomime-frolic and curious pot-pourri of all the styles and effects beloved by the public, on the lines of Martainville's parody of melodrama. Henry notes in the scenario: "I may be forgiven for having inserted at this point the Village fair scene which I have already presented to the public in *Les Petits Savoyards* in 1807: an author should be allowed to plagiarize himself on occasion." Indeed, his fairground scenes were only equalled in audience favor by his ballroom scenes. In *Le Château infernal* the charlatan, juggler, cavalier, magician, clown, old fogey and scheming valet, peasants, villagers, coconut vendor and a young fop with his lady mingle in dancing, swinging and seesaw contests and conjuring turns.

Samson, with an augmented corps de ballet for exotic dances by the Philistines, nevertheless ended with the collapse of the Temple, for the Porte-Saint-Martin could not alter Holy Writ (and would not have wanted to with so melodramatic a setting). Delilah's repentence for her treachery knew no bounds in this libretto. The success of *Samson* led to other Biblical ballets and pantomimes, such as *Suzanne et les Vieillards (Susanna and the Elders)* in 1817, *Daniel ou La Fosse aux Lions (Daniel, or The Lion's Den)* in the same year, and *David et Goliath* in 1838. Inasmuch as the Old Testament was a new source of exotic themes, there was every reason why an *Histoire Pittoresque des Religions* could and did appear shortly afterward.

Henry's season at the Porte-Saint-Martin in 1816 revived the prestige it had long enjoyed on account of its pantomimes and ballets. In return for these affronts, and while biding their time, the high command of the Opéra contented themselves with keeping him away from the privileged stage. So Henry went back to Italy, where his activity and research were increasingly directed toward mime. Garrick, Noverre's friend and patron who died in 1779, was discovered by Henry through Noverre's *Letters* and various English publications. Garrick influenced him considerably in his ballet scenarios and in little scenes of mime and dance which he described as *"imitata dal celebre Garrick attore inglese."*

In 1822, having been given a short holiday by Signor Barbaglia, manager of the royal theatres in Naples, Henry and Mme Quériau-Henry accepted an offer from the Porte-Saint-Martin to give some performances there during the height of the season. Despite bitter complaints by Gardel, who clung tenaciously to his power, Aumer's choreography had recently been imposed upon the Opéra personnel. Since Henry had no one to support him, Gardel had no intention of taking a second affront by leaving him a clear course. Censorship had been reintroduced in 1820 after the murder of the Duke of Berry, and the Royal Academy called in an ally who, on principle, was against anybody and anything. Accordingly Henry, subjected to a double inquisition, had certain of his compositions prohibited.

Their first performance was *Le Sacrifice indien ou La Veuve de Malabar (The Indian Sacrifice, or The Widow of Malabar)*, from Henry's Neapolitan repertory. This three-act pantomime-ballet had one of those exotic plots which had been rather popular for a long time, to be revived by Jules Verne: the rescue by a noble-minded European of an Indian widow about to be immolated on her husband's funeral pyre; the liberator was supposed to be a Portuguese general. Henry received a warm welcome from critics and public. "This first effort, although it did not provide a continuous or interesting plot, showed Henry to advantage. For his general stagecraft, his manner of directing groups and individuals, and finally for his art in imparting the necessary pantomime to his cast, I can think of few to rival him in France," wrote Chaalons d'Argé, one of the most influential contemporary critics, who must have been a thorn in Gardel's side. [38]

Their second pantomime-ballet, based on a melodrama, was titled *Agnès et Fitz-Henry*. The censorship slashed furiously at the representation of Fitz-Henry's madness: ". . . In the second act, not believing in the reality of what was going on about him, Fitz-Henry ordered a footman to bite his finger in order to be certain that he was not asleep. The censors expressly ordered the deletion of this business! The footman was only allowed to pinch his master's finger" (Chaalons d'Argé).

Before he left Paris, Henry was to achieve a spectacular triumph with a highly successful ballet, *La Fortune vient en dormant (Fortune Favors the Sleeper)*. The Opéra still opposed the performance of the works which had been submitted to it for examination, and the Porte-Saint-Martin did not have the money to stage Henry's new dramatic pantomime, *Romeo et Juliette*, so he abandoned his large-scale mimed ballet-pantomimes and lavished a series of divertissements that revealed his talent for "pure" dance on a story outline so fragile that he himself paid it little attention. As a good director he took an interest in theatrical machinery from which he got unexpected effects, invented some himself, and used combinations of dance and machinery to set off his subject. Dancing and fencing lessons, a broadsword combat, hunting and horse-riding scenes and a masked ball—all these were presented to the enthusiastic audience, while a golden sphere that moved across the entire width of the theatre seemed to support a ballerina representing Fortune, poised on the point of her right foot. Finally, there was a shower of gold—such were the ingredients of this "marvelous" tableau.

The season had ended with a resounding success, and Henry—whose contracts in Italy and Vienna had long since been signed—left Paris. He was recognized as one of the leading choreographers in the whole of Europe. His creations, if not his name, were known in America, where M. and Mme Ronzi-Vestris, after performing a considerable number of character dances under his direction, took them on tour. In Vienna he was choreographer for Marie Taglioni, then at the beginning of her career, and in Italy he created *Selico* (Naples, 1826) for Fanny Elssler, the first full-scale *ballet d'action* composed expressly for her.

Once again he was summoned to Paris, for the opening of the Théâtre Nautique. This was built around a stretch of water on the Seine; its life was short because the water was stagnant and its stench soon made the place unbearable. However, between 10 June and the end of November 1834, Louis Henry's creations achieved celebrity in Paris, to which the reviews, Martinet's drawings and the popular prints all testify.

The opening of the Théâtre Nautique gave him the opportunity for an "*à-propos*" curtain-raiser, a "nautical pantomime tableau" called *Les Ondines (The Sea Sprites)*, accompanied by *Guillaume Tell*, a historical pantomime created for La Scala of Milan in 1833. These pieces shared honors during four months. Although sometimes disconcerted by the long mimed scenes beloved of the Italians, the Paris public thronged to see them, for Romanticism had gradually conditioned the audience to the new complexities of mime.

The ballet *Chao-Kang*, created at Naples in 1820, put the seal on Henry's reputation in Paris. The French text is much longer than the Italian original, because it includes twelve leading parts and whole troops of dancers, *coryphées* and *figurants*. The author writes in a short introduction entitled "To the Public": "I have ventured to introduce a few scenes extraneous to the subject in order to render it more dramatic or gayer, for interest and contrast should be the mainsprings of drama."

With its "historical" plot thus tricked out, the ballet seen by the Paris public is one of the masterpieces of the exotic style, and also of Italian production techniques. This almost-expatriate Frenchman, who was honored twenty years after his death as one of the glories of French choreography, introduced his country to the Italian innovations that had been advocated by Stendhal some fifteen years before. These innovations were due to Noverre's disciples: the wheel had come full circle at last.

The company for the Paris production of *Chao-Kang* consisted of a somewhat curious assortment of performers, a sort of Franco-Italian medley from the leading and secondary theatres. Henry brought from Italy the famous dancer Gustave Carey and his wife, his own son, his nephew Achille Henry, Xavier Hus and Elisa Saxoni; at the Opéra he recruited the excellent and well known Gosselin, as well as Mmes Courtois, Mazilier, Coulon and Célarius and MM. Hazard, Gredelu and Laurent; and he added some famous Boulevard names, those of MM. Laurençon, the elder and younger Ahns and Télémaque, as well as Mlle Tigée. The leading roles were distributed between the three groups without the slightest partiality.

The plot, an ingenious and allegedly historical story, is a thread on which Henry strings his choreographic pearls. Accompanied by his faithful page, Chao-Kang, Emperor of China (the Henrys, father and son), travels over his kingdom disguised as a Bonze (priest). It was really only the peg for ethnographic research of the utmost imaginativeness: even the colors of the costumes were laid down by the choreographer in order to insure the maximum effectiveness in the arrangement of his squadrons of dancers. The *Recueil-Abrégé de l'Histoire Générale*, by Laharpe and Delpuech de Comeiras, was his source book for the costumes, properties and attitudes of his Literary Mandarin, Emperor and Bonzes, and for the Chinese dances, acting and funeral ceremonies. The five engravings that Martinet devoted to the ballet in its *Galerie Théâtrale* resemble its illustrations. Henry even went so far as to attempt—probably for the first time on a Western stage—the classical Chinese dance with a man impersonating a woman; the Chinese general, the "woman" and an "Emperor from the early history of China" who appear in it, use the stylized makeup and properties which are genuinely proper to the Chinese theatre. Henry also reincarnated in China the fairground scene from *Deux Petits Savoyards* and *Le Château infernal*: after a "general medley of tumblers and a popular dance, a tumbler in a boat and a singing nostrum peddler appear. A Parasol Dance by sixteen women in pink costumes and six men in green costumes with gold stripes," was followed by a great Bell Dance, the delights of which were described as follows in a review by Alfred Desessarts: "Nothing could be more charmingly droll than the women running with ribbons thirty feet long or than the Dance of the Parasols, which, when whirled around, make fast-turning wheels. Nothing could be more grotesque than the rising and falling scale represented by seven Chinese. The head of each of them responds to a particular note. As the notes rise, the noses rise to graduated heights, and similarly are lowered when the notes fall. The most astonishing thing in the ballet is the Epilogue, the Festival of Lanterns. An immense bridge lit by a thousand lanterns is reflected in the pool, which is genuine indeed. In the background glows Peking, crowned with countless lights, while in front of you speeds an indefatigable gallop, its dancers carrying mobile, brilliant, transparent lanterns: the effect must certainly be very beautiful, for everyone with eyes in his head is flocking to admire it."

Lovy, on the other hand, regarded the ethnographic dancing of *Chao-Kang* as a "formal manifesto against the classical pirouette . . . The entire ballet moved by leaps and bounds. It was as if the hands were dancing." The Martinets and the print-sellers of the Rue Saint-Jacques were not slow to publish plates that further document the splendors of this production. As to the Opéra, it no longer tried to ignore Henry, and inasmuch as Gardel's grip had relaxed thanks to Dr. Véron, it asked him to do a ballet for Fanny Elssler.

The production of *L'Ile des Pirates (The Pirates' Island)* in 1835, occurred in the very month in which Dr. Véron left the administration of the Opéra. In view of Henry's habitual success, neither he nor his admirers could claim that this ballet was one of the Opéra's great triumphs, though it was not the failure that some of his rivals hoped for either. At that time, twenty to forty performances of a new ballet were considered a very honorable result: *L'Ile des Pirates* had twenty-five. Coralli and Mazilier, Taglioni and even Aumer produced works which did not have more than six performances.

When Arthur Saint-Léon published his *Sténochorégraphie* (1852), with "biographies and portraits of the most famous ancient and modern ballet-masters of the French and Italian schools," he was first ballet-master at the Opéra; as he was more familiar than anyone with the intrigues of "the first house in

150

Europe," he must have known what he was talking about when he blamed the management of the theatre for Henry's difficulties.

The ballet seems to have been put on as a display piece for the entire repertory of folk and exotic character dances which Henry had assembled in his thirty-five-year career. That old reliable plot of the Italian Comedians, of Audinot and Nicolet, and all the Boulevard theatres—the pirate and his misdeeds—served as framework for this "international exposition of the dance." There was a further reason for the popularity of pirates and bandits with choreographers of the Romantic period. The supremacy of the ballerina, established for tactical reasons by Gardel and confirmed by the artistic triumph of Marie Taglioni, seldom left the male dancers an opportunity for distinguishing themselves. Folk dances and the dances of brigands and pirates remained among the few occasions for producing male ensembles. In *L'Ile des Pirates* the various nationalities of the pirates and their harem are the pretext for folk dances by Russian, Spanish and English sailors, Dutch cabin boys, sailors from the Barbary and Levant coasts, Lipari and Albania, a peasant woman from Fondi, a Spanish woman and an English woman, an Odalisque and "women of different countries distinguished by their costume."

The casting of this ballet reveals the extent of the exchanges of personnel between Boulevard and Opéra, and the influence which these two backgrounds had upon the theatre abroad, even as far as America. The principal ballerina was Fanny Elssler, an international star whose realm extended from New York to St. Petersburg and who fulfilled contracts for a certain number of performances at the Paris Opéra. Mazilier, the hero, former star dancer of the Porte-Saint-Martin, had filled the same post at the Opéra from 1830. Montjoie, the villain, had been strutting across the Opéra stage since his childhood.

Certain names had appeared in Boulevard casts: Mesdames Célarius, Laurent, Pierson, Saxoni; MM. Albert, Bégrand, Brillant, Célarius, Châtillon, Coralli *fils*, Gredelue, Laurent, Lefèvre, Mazilier, Mérante, Millot, Petit, Quériau and Ragaine; others on the London stages, and often in Vienna, Milan, St. Petersburg and other great European cities: Mesdames Beaupré, Bellon, Besnard, Brocard, Desvarennes, Dumilâtre, Alexis Dupont, Elssler, Fitzjames, Forster, Leroux, Noblet, Montessu, Pierson, Pérès, Saxoni, Stéphan; MM. Albert, Barré, Brillant, Coralli *fils*, Lefèvre, Mabille, Mazilier, Mérante, Petit, Ragaine, Saxoni and Simon; others also appear on American programs: Mesdames Desjardins, Elssler, N. Fitzjames; MM. Brilliant and Gredelue. Certain names in the cast of *L'Ile des Pirates*—Paul Brillant, Lucien Petipa and Mesdames Proche, Blangy and Ducy-Barré—even appear in all four categories: the Paris Opéra and Boulevard, the European opera houses and court theatres, and the American theatres. The fact that ballets of Dauberval, Aumer, Coralli, Mazilier, Marius Petipa and Perrot, as well as excerpts taken from Henry, Blache *père* and Lefèvre, appeared in the repertories of Europe and America until the 1860s gives an idea of the French influence, and particularly the Boulevard influence, on all productions which included ballet as well as on world ballet itself.

This, then, was the last work in France of a Frenchman who had spent more than half of his life abroad but who had a perceptible influence on his native theatre throughout the 19th century. His contributions to the Theatre of Marvels generally, and the Romantic ballet particularly, should restore him to that place of honor in current dance histories that he so fully merits, and receives only from the Italians.

Invited to Naples in 1836 for a brilliant engagement, Henry then left for Milan where La Scala awaited him. He was stricken by cholera on his arrival and died on November 4th, 1836.

﹌ MAZURIER AND HIS SCHOOL ﹌

While Louis Henry designed pantomime-ballets in which many performers were to find their style of interpretation, Mazurier, performer of genius, imposed on pantomime-ballet—and consequently on its ancillary spectacles—a personal imprint which was to engender a style. He created this style during his five-year reign at the Porte-Saint-Martin, using the works of Blache, Coralli, Duport and Petipa; he signed only one scenario, and that as member of a team. [39]

His career was brief: he was born at Lyon in 1793 and died in Paris on February 4th, 1828. His success in France and England was spectacular. Although he never went to America the name of the "celebrated Mazurier" was well known, and the Hungarian Kiralfy troupe were still playing his repertory at the Columbian Exposition of 1893 in Chicago. His London appearance influenced the English acrobatic mimes, for the Prices, Omers and Hanlon-Lees retained the techniques which Mazurier had initiated, and all of his "sight-gags," until the end of the century.

In 1820-1821 he was already an established star at the Grand Théâtre of Lyon, where the *premiers danseurs* Labottière and Quériau and the *première danseuse* Célina Feltis came from families famous on the provincial and Boulevard stages, and even in the Opéra casts. In its programs, Mazurier is called a "comic dancer," a category sometimes included in that of "character dancer": this was an accepted compound term in classical ballet terminology which perfectly suited Mazurier, whatever his influence on the tradition of clowning may have been.

It was thanks to him that the mask of Polichinelle, which had been somewhat neglected in France since the heyday of the Italian Comedy, became fashionable again. The Opéra's comic dancer, Elie, could never compete with Mazurier in this role, in which he too had specialized. Mazurier's humped Polichinelle was physically very much like the English Punch, and both were descendants of the Neapolitain Pulcinella. But apart from his greediness and his farcical activity, the French Polichinelle lacks a certain brutality in laying on with his cudgel which is characteristic of Punch, and in him Pulcinella's malice is only high-spirited mischievousness. Indeed, Mazurier's Polichinelle had a very French humor—gay, sparkling and without the macabre English irony.

His fame preceded him to Paris: the Porte-Saint-Martin, in whose company he remained a member until his death, commissioned a ballet—pantomime from Blache *fils* in order to show the Parisians the feats which they knew of by hearsay only. His partner was Louise Pierson, a pupil of Coulon *père*, one of the second generation of Piersons directed by Blaches, whose parents were stars of the Porte-Saint-Martin ballets in 1815-1820. More royalist than the king, the censors saw allusions to princely follies in the dialogue prologue which Blache published by way of introduction; whereupon the theatre had to revise the hierarchy of characters completely and delete the more satirical remarks.

The spoken piece was badly received, possibly because the prologue to this truncated version was incomprehensible, possibly because the audience was impatient to see Mazurier himself; at any rate, a disturbance compelled the actors to withdraw, and the curtain rose on *Polichinelle Vampire* amid a riot.

Polichinelle, friend of Juliano, has to bring some documents required by the father of Leontina before he will consent to her marriage with the *jeune premier*. A rival suitor, Dandini, engages the second class valet-magician Merlin to foil the mission of Polichinelle. Merlin tells the credulous peasantry that a vampire is devastating the region, shows them a picture of Polichinelle, and warns them to kill him on sight. The plot does not succeed.

But—Polichinelle arrives in a balloon, jumps from treetop to treetop on being pursued, dances a *"pas de caractère* with grace" and a dance on stilts, made from branches of a tree, with daring.

This "pantomime-ballet with burlesque sketches," perfectly adapted to the Commedia dell'Arte atmosphere referred to by Blache in his libretto, opened the series of Mazurier's triumphs in Paris, which ended only with his death five years later.

Jocko was one of the most discussed works of its period; however, it is hard to ascertain the exact sources of its notion of a "Noble Monkey," which competed with the idealistic conception of a "Noble Savage." Was it originated by Mazurier himself, who then commissioned a scenario based on his new numbers, or by Messrs. Gabriel and Rochefort, whose names adorn the title pages of a large number of forgotten libretti? Can it be a recollection of the Italian Comedians who contributed so greatly to the Theatre of Marvels? In *L'Homme à Bonne Fortune (The Fortunate Man)* [40] (1696), Harlequin opens a cabinet full of pictures by "Téniers," represented by motionless actors: "A moment later all the figures have left the pictures, singing, dancing and playing divers instruments. Among them, Pascariel, as a monkey, performs several somersaults, grimaces, seizes a guitar and starts accompanying an air sung by Mezzetin, dressed as a Fleming . . ." Is it an echo of the fantastic "historical Tableaux" known as *Lapeyrouse ou le Voyageur autour du monde (Lapeyrouse or The Globetrotter)* with its desert islands and troupes of performing monkeys?

Unlike Fréderick Lemaître's *Robert Macaire*, which despite many revivals had no successors, *Jocko* founded a school. The series of copies, plagiarisms and adaptations had a success worthy of the original production, although Mazurier's interpretation would seem to have put his rivals' and successors' interpretations in the shade. Despite negligible alterations made to avoid legal proceedings, the various texts remain true to the basic work: the scenario of dreams come true, of the unbelievable presented without fear of ridicule.

The scenario is titled: "*Jocko ou Le Singe de Brésil (Jocko, or the Brazilian Monkey)*. Spectacular Drama in Two Acts, with Music, Dancing and Pantomime. By Messrs. Gabriel and Rochefort. Performed for the first time in Paris on March 16th, 1825." The music was by Alexandre Piccini, the ballets by Blache *fils* and the decorations by Cicéri.

"The scene is laid in Brazil, near Para," and Cicéri was responsible for producing "a fair colonial prospect." Act I shows the entrance to a forest of bamboo; toward center stage there is a big tamarisk tree, with branches which bend down toward the ground; a large net is stretched to the middle of the tree; in the foreground, a bell hangs from a post; and in the background, there is a rice field. In the second act, the scenic instructions mention the new panorama technique under one of its many aliases: "The stage presents the appearance of a beautiful diorama."

The sad fate of the amiable monkey, killed by mistake at the moment when it had saved its master's young son after having saved his fortune, was extremely affecting, but most of the plagiarized versions did not end so tragically. They usually preferred a finale with a troupe of little monkeys, natives and star dancers followed by a *tableau vivant* for the curtain. However, the "character" of Jocko, his good behaviour and courtesy, fitted in with the "human" creations of Mazurier to form a new model of comic performer; just as producers in their casting requirements would list an *"emploi de Dugazon"* (i.e. someone who could play the sort of parts in which Dugazon had excelled), so henceforth they listed *"l'emploi de Mazurier."*

His dancing and mime were so closely linked to acrobatics that within a few weeks after the opening "Jockos" sprang up in fairgrounds, at the circus, on the provincial stages and the length of the Boulevard du Temple. The good servant, the good savage and the good monkey lasted through the 19th century, but only the acrobatic monkey has persisted into the 20th. [41]

As soon as *Jocko* was an established hit at the Porte-Saint-Martin, the Gaîté put on its monkey drama, *Sapajou*, with Jules Perrot, *its* prodigy from Lyon. The only remarkable thing about this script from the normal standpoint of the French theatre is a contempt for the natives which is occasionally cruel. However, the monkey is kindly treated and, unlike the agreeable Jocko, Sapajou lives to join in a closing frolic of negro slaves, monkeys, a Polichinelle and a dancer impersonating the famous trained bear Martin. *Sapajou* brought in appreciable receipts for the Gaîté and added to Perrot's laurels, but it remained a plagiarism— a successful one—of the master work.

This success was facilitated by Mazurier's departure in 1825 for London, where he carried the whole town along in a transport of enthusiasm and everyone—just as in Paris—wept over Jocko's fate. Yet Mazurier, though feted, acclaimed and sought after by portraitists, did not wish to abandon Paris any longer, and a year later he returned to the Porte-Saint-Martin.

Jocko had more competitors than Perrot's redoubtable *Sapajou*. At the Funambules it was *Jack l'Orang-Outang*, with Laurent *ainé* as the monkey vis-a-vis Deburau's Pierrot; at the Acrobates Madame Saqui herself rehearsed the role of *Pongo ou Le Singe Libérateur (Pongo, or Freed by a Monkey)*; Jean Petipa, ballet-master of the Royal Theatre in Brussels in 1826, produced a pantomime openly "imitated from Messrs. Gabriel and Rochefort's drama," called *Jocko ou Le Singe de Brésil* [42] with scenic descriptions and plot taken faithfully from the original script. The ballet was still in the Brussels repertory in 1828, with one of Mazurier's best-known imitators, Girel. That same year Girel was engaged by M. Belfort, manager of the Nouveau Théâtre Olympique at Nîmes, to reproduce the entire repertory of Mazurier's ballets. In 1827, Philippe Taglioni created *Danina ou Le Singe de Brésil* at the Stuttgart Opera, with the French dancer Briol playing in a monkey mask and suit obtained from Paris. The ballet was a success, and Briol continued his career touring Italy as a monkey. In 1835 the choreographer Antonio Monticini composed a *Jocko ossia il Secreto matrimonio* for Milan.

From their American début in 1832 the Ravels toured the appealing monkey for some forty years; he was equally at home in England, with French or English interpreters. The acrobats of every country put on the skilful grimacer's hide and mask. At the circus or in pantomimes, Jocko remained the fundamental "Mazurier" part.

Mazurier, having refurbished and virtually recreated the Polichinelle of the fairground parades, revived a ballet markedly French in spirit from the 1815 repertory: *Les Six Ingénus* (*The Six Innocents*). Its author was the Opéra dancer Duport, whose choreographic experiments had been so frustrated by Gardel; the plot was taken from a light comedy, *La Famille des Innocents ou Comme l'Amour vient* (*The Family of Simpletons or How Love Comes*), which Martinet's charming series of engravings shows us to have been particularly amusing. This pantomime, which was crammed with divertissements—a *pas de six* by the three couples, a *pas de huit* in which they were joined by their elders, and a *grand ensemble* with all the villagers—has definite affinities with the old acrobatic gags of *Les Forces de l'Amour et de la Magie*. There was a scene in which one of the three suitors starts by kissing the hand of his beloved and continues up the arm, when her Mother arrives and puts her head between to receive the kiss meant for her daughter. There is a scene where the suitor decides to hang himself, and the branch on which he ties himself breaks. There is a scene where the three tall simpletons all try to sit on their father's lap. These comic marvels were ingredients of the early French cinema.

Another scenario characteristic of Mazurier's type of pantomime-ballet was *La Neige* (*The Snow*), produced at the Porte-Saint-Martin on December 6th, 1827. Like all the "Mazuriads" it travelled America too, thanks to the Ravel company. It opened in the same year that Marie Taglioni made her Paris Opéra début—or the year that some consider the official opening date of Romantic Ballet.

The action takes place in Hungary at an unspecified date, but its picturesque costumes are troubadour in style, prettied up with additions of folk dress. Mazurier, aided by a master choreographer—Coralli—danced with an exceptionally fine company which included Mazilier, Madame Zelie-Paul and Mademoiselle Mimi-Dupuis, in a set designed by the gifted Lefebvre. The widely imitated "trick effects" in this ballet occurred in the skating scene. The setting represented an iced-over lake surrounded by snow-covered trees and mountains in the background. Mazurier arrived sliding in on stage and falling on his face. Then he began to attempt skating, at first unable to stand up or move, finally performing like a virtuoso. A sleigh ride, a skaters' *pas de quatre*, various games and races followed. A perfect illusion was produced by the "skaters" wearing two small perpendicular wheels attached to the soles of each shoe, skilfully masked by false blades; a shining white cloth covered the stage to represent ice. This "skating" scene had been originated at the Porte-Saint-Martin some ten years earlier by Blache *père* in his ballet *La Laitière Polonaise*. Coralli developed the sleighing festivities and skaters' quadrilles which revolved around Mazurier. Paul Taglioni some twenty-two years later recalled this effect, which had already been incorporated by Scribe into his libretto for Meyerbeer's *Le Prophète*, in *Les Plaisirs d'Hiver ou les Patineurs* (*Winter Pleasures, or The Skaters*). Produced in 1849 at Her Majesty's Theatre in London, it was a long divertissement, its idea was taken from Blache *père* and its execution from the Coralli-Mazurier *La Neige*. In order to defend himself against the charge that

155

THE MAJILTON FAMILY—CHARLES, MARIE AND FRANK
Charles Majilton, juggler and acrobatic dancer, trained his brother
and sister, and created their pantomimes. These London artistes
starred in Europe and America, and carried the Ravels' type of
acrobatic pantomime to even more fantastic heights.

The Black Crook Unveiled—The Majilton family and the Pas de Demon

THE GREAT KIRALFY'S

THE BROTHERS IMRE, BOLOSSY AND ARNOLD KIRALFY left their native Hungary, toured all over Europe, and came to the United States in 1868. They produced elaborate versions of the Mazurier ballets and branched out later into giant productions such as Jules Verne's "Around the World in 80 Days," and brought Manzotti's "Excelsior" from Paris with the Eden Theatre Ballet. Imre returned to Europe and ran theatres at the great international expositions in Brussels, Paris and London. There was also a Kiralfy theatre at the Columbian Exposition.

THE MAJILTONS in "Spectresheim," at the Royal Alhambra Theatre, London.

he had imitated the scene in Meyerbeer's opera—which actually made the same borrowings as he had—Taglioni claimed to have invented this scene for the Berlin stage in 1840. The Ravels also borrowed elements of *La Neige* for their pantomime *The Skaters of Vilno,* with echos from the older ballet of Blache *père* in the plot. As usual, local color combined with spectacular trickery proved irresistible.

At the period of *La Neige* there was a continual exchange of clowns, dancers and various categories of itinerant performers between France and England. English influence is evident in this ballet, particularly in the moments of "knock-about" farce: a fall midst pastry trays, another into the prompter's box, etc. A burlesque sequence of military pantomime drills in the first act was frequently imitated and turns up eventually in American minstrel shows half a century and more later. Coralli and Mazurier did not invent this drill—it had developed after the Revolution and was perfected by Blache *père* in *La Fille Soldat (Girl with the Colors)* and other ballets—but like all the comic dances embellished by Mazurier it became durably popular.

Mazurier's pantomime and ballet-pantomime formula, although it included certain elements of melodrama and fairy tale, introduced a type of fantasy which originated in the particular genius of the performer—a sort of likeableness and good humor, the creation of a type that might be grotesque but was always appealing.

When the Ravels took over his repertory it became overloaded, more pretentious and less subtle. As the Ravel family continued to ply their former profession of rope-dancers, that too was incorporated in their "Mazuriads"; then, as transportation methods improved, the quantity of "stunts" and transformation scenes increased; as interludes were necessary between changes of scenery, the ensemble element of ballet became more prominent. After Mazurier, the mixture of acrobatic and grotesque dancing with fantastic scenery became ever more spectacular, and what the Ravels had started the Majiltons and Kiralfys completed.

During the approximately forty years that the Ravels toured America with *Jocko, Godenski, The Magic Trumpet, Mazulme, or the Night Owl, Asphodel* and numerous other "French pantomimes" they never had to withdraw any of the productions which had figured on their first programs in 1832; they simply kept on presenting "Mazuriads" with a dash more of the supernatural melodrama and an expanded Romantic ballet.

In spite of his premature death, one can hazard the guess that Mazurier's style was fullfledged and probably would not have taken any other direction had he lived. He was the foremost comic dancer of his century.

JEAN CORALLI

Jean Coralli, son of a Bolognese actor, was born in Paris on January 15th, 1779. He was trained at the Opéra dancing school, and when quite young left for Vienna where he started his career as a dancer and then as a choreographer. The titles of the works that marked his stay in Vienna are a sample of the repertory of the leading operas in Europe (apart from Paris) and of the theatres of the Boulevard du Temple: *Paul et Rosette* (the "happy villagers"), *Le Calife*

Jules Perrot.

"Polichinelle Swallowed by a Whale" owed
its success to the brilliant début of the
thirteen-year old Perrot. This setting shows
the mines of the magician Cormoran; Perrot
flitted in and out between the columns. (Plate
from "Les Théâtres de Paris," Bibl de l'Opéra)

Fanny Elssler, always on the lookout for new "vehicles" took "An Artist's Dream" (variously known as "Le Délire d'un Peintre" and "Le Rêve d'un Peintre") from London to Moscow by way of Vienna. It is one of the first ballets of the type known as—and called—"divertissement."

In the series of folio prints "Le Musée de Moeurs en Action" (its duration was roughly that of the Second Empire), the lithograph of a "scene at the Cirque-Olympique (the Lady-jugglers)" from a drawing by Morlon, shows a typical spectacular circus ballet. (Printed by Lemercier, Paris, c. 1860)

A self-portrait by Ducrow, "Foremost Equestrian of London," in his number "The Gladiators" at the Franconi's Cirque-Olympique. A Paris print by Badoureau (circa 1819).
"During this season of overcoats and raincoats, is not a theatre in which splendid uniforms ablaze with gold braid, horses in rich trappings, magnificent decorations and pleasingly arranged groups greet the eye saddened by so much ugliness elsewhere, a magnet, a need, and indispensable?"

Poster for the only performances of Perrot's "Esmeralda" in Paris (1856). His name does not even appear, nor those of the stars: Mmes Scolti and Comba and Monsieur Paul.

The Marius Petipa and Lev Ivanov version of Tchaikovsky's ballet "Swan Lake" was first produced in St. Petersburg in 1895. It is one of the most brilliant examples of the Romantic ballet. In the above photo (by Baron) the Sadler's Wells Ballet is seen in the ballet's presentation at the Covent Garden, London.

"THE FAIRIE'S HOME" A large easel lithograph published by Currier & Ives, New York City, 1868. This is obviously one of the numerous reprints which followed on the success of "The Black Crook."

An untitled American lithograph of approximately the same period as "The Fairie's Home," with a ballerina who would seem to be a self-satisfied fairy queen.

RONZANI'S GRAND BALLET TROUPE

RONZANI'S GRAND BALLET TROUPE
Domenico Ronzani (1800-1868), was one of Italy's greatest dancer-mimes, and for many years a star of Milan's La Scala. He was a gifted "Maître de Ballet" and had performed in companies which included Jules Perrott and Fanny Elssler. His American debut, with a full ballet company, in Perott's "Faust," took place in 1857 at Philadelphia and coincided with a financial crisis which was disasterous to his presentations. He returned to Milan only to re-embark for America in 1859. He presented Perott's "Esméralda" and Mazilier's "Le Corsaire." It remains a mystery why Ronzani, dogged by ill-luck, elected to stay in America until his death in 1868. The center group in this lithograph poster was lifted from the "Illustrated London News'" woodcut of Perrott's ballet, "Le Jugement de Paris" (1846).

THE FOUR ROUSSET SISTERS, CAROLINE, CLEMENTINE, ADELAIDE & TERESINE,
well thought of dancers in the French provinces, made their debut in New York City in 1851, and for many years were a fixture on the American stage from coast to coast. This print of Caroline and Adelaide (in "travesti") dancing "La Marola" is typical of a period which consigned the male dancer to oblivion.

généreux (*The Generous Caliph*) (a Turkish drama), *Hélène et Pâris* ("Anacreontic"), and two major *ballets d'action, Les Incas* and *Les Abencérages,* using the historical events dear to the Italians and the French melodrama writers.

The wandering pupil returned to Paris with a trunk full of ballets. He made his debut at the Opéra in 1802, but was not granted the privilege of choreography, and his name does not appear among the Opéra personnel recorded by the *Almanach des Spectacles* for 1803. He visited Milan and Lisbon, and next spent a short time in France but did not visit the capital; he then returned to Vienna, to find a warm and rewarding welcome.

Again back in Paris, where he had been engaged by "the people's Opera" (the Porte-Saint-Martin), he succeeded Blache *fils* as ballet-master and director for a number of productions. According to the theatre's repertory, he was responsible for the overall direction and composition of ballets for fourteen plays—dramas, farces and comedies, melodramas and fairy plays—and ten ballets between June 7th, 1825, when his name first appears on the register, and July 30th, 1829, the date of his last creation for this theatre.

His position as director put Coralli in touch with hacks such as Chandezon, Boirie, Decomberousse and Poujol; with the witty Brazier; with Ferdinand Laloue, the producer at the Cirque-Olympique; with Merle, Anicet-Bourgeois and Carmouche, whose fairy plays are much above average; and with Charles Nodier and Casimir Delavigne. Alexandre Piccini, who wrote scores for the Opéra and the Porte-Saint-Martin, was his musical collaborator. The performers placed at his disposal were first class: Mazurier, Mazilier and Jules Perrot among the men; Mimi-Dupuis—star of the Vienna and London Operas, second role at the Paris Opéra—and Louise Pierson, who was to leave the Boulevard to star in the Vienna Hofburgoper ballet company, among the women.

Coralli made his choreographic debut with a topical little piece for the coronation of Charles X. In 1825 he produced a three-act pantomime with dances, *Lisbelle ou La Nouvelle Claudine (Lisbelle, or the New Claudine),* the all too-familiar story of a young girl abandoned by the philandering nobleman who had sworn to marry her. It was interpreted by Mazilier (the nobleman), Mazurier (a simpleton), Madame Zélie-Molard (the innocent victim) and Mademoiselle Louise Pierson (the gracious lady).

That same year Coralli also produced a ballet on Iberian themes, *Les Ruses Espagnoles (Spanish Trickery),* followed in 1826 by a comic ballet in two acts, *Monsieur de Pourceaugnac (Mr. Porker),* "with Lully's interludes, adapted from Molière's play by Corally . . ." for Mazurier. In this the Boulevard anticipated a return to 17th and 18th century subjects inaugurated at the Opéra around 1830. Its success was largely due to those passages in which Molière's humor was broad and basic. Another 1826 ballet for Mazurier, *Gulliver,* transformed Swift's fierce satire into a sort of fairy pantomime, probably for the first, but certainly not for the last time.

In 1828 Mazurier's death deprived the Porte-Saint-Martin and the Paris public of an irreplaceable star. Perrot, his most gifted imitator, was engaged by the Porte-Saint-Martin, on his own terms as *demi-caractère* dancer. Mazilier continued as *premier danseur* and mime, and Coralli's subsequent ballets feature him as such.

The trite plot of *Léocadie ou Cinq ans après (Leocadia, or Five Years Later)* does not account for its success. It is another tale of the village maiden led astray by a handsome soldier, "the regimental seducer," involved with a case of mistaken identity; five years later, the unmarried mother meets him again. In short, an Opéra-Comique plot. There were some village dances, Perrot appeared in a *pas de trois*, and there were general wedding festivities for the final curtain.

Léocadie was atoned for in 1829 by a really charming pantomime ballet, *Les Artistes*; it revived the touching atmosphere of "*genre* painting," the Romantic painters' first attempt at realism. Indeed, Coralli himself described the scenery as follows: "The stage represents a studio in which a painter, a musician and a choreographer are working simultaneously"; and a note adds "See the engraving of a painter's studio by M. Horace Vernet." The characters are "The Comte de Saint-Elme, an art lover; Jules, a painter; Gustave, a musician; Armand, a choreographer; César, nicknamed Sans-Quartier, an old Grenadier used as a model; Lucile, his daughter, the artistes' servant; Ducros, the landlord; and a bailiff." The mixture of *genre* scenes, realistic details, comic byplay going back to the fairground theatres and a most improbable *deus ex machina*, gives this ballet a very attractive flavor.

Of the fourteen pieces he directed, Coralli in his biographical notes mentions four, three of which are real steps toward Romantic drama: *Trente Ans ou La Vie d'un jouer (Thirty Years, or A Gambler's Life)* in 1827, *Faust* in 1828 and *Marino Faliero* in 1829; the fourth, *Mandrin* (1827), is referred to in contemporary memoirs and reviews because of its scenery.

In *Mandrin*, Coralli had to work with hallowed subject matter and re-animate the melodrama with brigands, aided by the scene designer Lefebvre. The "underground" scene was most impressive. "The setting, entirely in the foreground, represents differently colored stratifications of rock from floor to ceiling. A dried-out well and a hollowed-out cave are the only features which break the monotony of parallel zones of rock, clay and virgin soil." While retaining the commonplaces of Boulevard rhetoric, this melodrama has a somewhat Teutonic flavor, inasmuch as the hero Mandrin is a generous brigand-villain who inspires "his people" with boundless loyalty and who refuses to betray his comrades. He cherishes a hopeless passion for Isaure, daughter of a great noble, behind which looms a purely Germanic sense of fatality.

Mandrin's dream on the eve of his execution consists of three tableaux, one of them as curious as it is typical of the period urge for keeping company with the *beaux-arts*. Inserted between a scene in which Mandrin sees Isaure for the first time and declares his love, and a tableau of Hell with a burning wheel and pitiless demons, there is a great ball scene in the setting of the first act. The Comte de Montbrisan brings in his daughter Isaure to unite her to Mandrin, disguised as a Marquis. "Justice and Vengeance (as in the painting by Prudhon)," says the scenario, "appear and hover over the assembly. Vengeance extends her sword, on which is written in letters of fire the name MANDRIN. The entire company utters a cry of horror." [43]

The success of *Mandrin* furnished another argument in favor of transferring the fine arts to the stage through reproducing paintings of well-known artists.

In *Trente Ans ou La Vie d'un jouer*, the Theatre of Marvels was offered a most complete breach in the unity of time and the most extreme attempts at realism: familiar sights, views of the Seine, vistas of Paris, the boulevards with their lighted shop-fronts and a passing omnibus; markets, death-trap alleys, monuments, attics and cellars, and the Rue du Temple—faithfully reproduced—alternated with rajahs' palaces, Scottish castles, Inca temples and all the classic sites in the local color repertory. The iconography consecrated to this one melodrama vastly exceeds that devoted to other theatrical scenes in the collections published by *La Pandore, L'Artiste, La Silhouette,* etc. As for translations and plagiarized versions of the text and pictures, they would run to a small volume.

Faust, which was only a sort of fairy melodrama from which Goethe's philosophical problems had been eliminated, was predictably a great success, with its settings by Lefebvre and machinery by Griffe; the *valse infernale* was danced by Frédérick Lemaître and Mme Zélie-Paul. Hell with its fireworks and the Apotheosis were staged simultaneously (the vogue for a theatre divided horizontally in two, in order to enact two scenes at once, continued: *Le Cheval du Diable (The Devil's Horse)* and *Marco Spada* are two examples). Coralli's production must have impressed the young Perrot, who appeared in it as *premier danseur.* Twenty years later, as a renowned choreographer, he put on his own version, first in Milan, then in Saint-Petersburg and Vienna. (Although it was never presented in France, there was an 1857 production in New Orleans!) Whatever the relationship of the Perrot *Faust* to the melodrama by Beraud, Merle and Nodier, there is a distinct similarity between his Italian libretto and their French text for the great "Walpurgis Night" scene in the Harz Mountains.

The melodrama is not sparing of horrors. "Mothers holding their slaughtered children in their arms" flee from bands of murderers; men hold their severed heads in their arms; there are executioners with a corrupt judge, as well as ghosts and devils, dancing an infernal round. In one scene of Perrot's choreography, as terrifying as the one in the melodrama, *"streghi, maghi e demoni"* accompany countless historical characters.

The melodrama *Faust* contains a choreographic episode of great interest in the history of the Romantic ballet, and especially "white ballet": the 'Sylphides' Ballet" in the second scene of Act II, is a perfect illustration of the evolution which the Boulevard had long been accomplishing. Summoned by Mephistopheles, the Sylphides form a group which is supposed to charm the aged Faust and also establish the supernatural atmosphere. In theme and staging, *Le Ballet des Nonnes (The Nuns' Ballet), La Sylphide* and *Giselle* recall Coralli's *Faust* ballet.

Marino Faliero, a Romantic verse tragedy by Casimir Delavigne, had 130 consecutive performances on the Boulevard. In a preface to the edition of his play, the author himself was the first to thank its director. From the choreographer's point of view, it had been no longer a routine matter of melodramatic situations but of a noble tragedy which had to be embellished with all the glamor normally lavished upon spectacles in which only visual poetry was involved.

At the Porte-Saint-Martin, Coralli presided over the last moments of the pre-Romantic period and the beginnings of Romanticism in all branches of the theatre. Although the Theatre of Marvels normally manages very well without poetry, and exists on visual and kinetic prestige, its masterpieces are those in which poetry also has a place. Indeed, Coralli's subsequent masterpieces confine themselves to themes of Le Sage, Heine, H. de Saint-Georges and Théophile Gautier; all the materials which he had moulded so skilfully in order to strike hard, later enabled him to strike true.

In 1826, *Le Magicien et le Monstre* was an example of how to make the most of supernatural effects. Although it was a great success, Coralli does not mention this play in his notes, perhaps because its methods were too crude. In fact, an English machinist, one Tompkins, was engaged for this fairy melodrama with novel "stunts," and he appeared on the program as co-designer with Lefebvre. The iconography of *Le Magicien* can give us information about some of his marvels. The illustration in Martinet's *Costumes* only shows the contrast between the gentle Mme Dorval and Cook, the English mime who performed the monster and whose "savage" appearance is more amusing than terrifying; it is an inaccurate interpretation, in which the Martinets were unable to render the character. A lithograph published by Genty of the Rue Saint-Jacques, drawn by H. Platel, transmits the simple horror of the character. Another series of eight little vignettes, published by E. Jourdan as candybox tops, shows the various melodramatic incidents more effectively than the portraits of performers.

The management of the Opéra with Dr. Véron at its head in 1831 at last shook off the last vestiges of Gardel's aesthetics and policy. Despite criticism of his taste for lavish spectacle, the door was opened to new talent. Aumer, the pioneer, weary of the intrigues of his old and implacable opponents at the Opéra, had retired in 1830. Dr. Véron did not hesitate to secure the new ballet-master of the Boulevard and Coralli accordingly entered the Royal Academy in 1831.

His Opéra career was marked by three works; two of them dominated ballet repertory and iconography in the nineteenth century, and the third is a living classic. Gautier's reviews and the vast iconography of these three ballets, *Le Diable boîteux*, *Giselle* and *La Péri*, insured them immortality. That they were performed in Europe and America, that their interpreters and scenes from them were a source of "souvenirs" for the French lithographers and illustrated music-titles which were lucrative exports, do not alone justify their claim to fame: they are among the rare ballets which inspired plays, light comedies, "*burlettas*" and operettas, as well as the usual parodies.

In 1836 the Opéra needed a new ballet as suitable for Fanny Elssler as *La Sylphide* had been for Marie Taglioni. The plot of *Le Diable boîteux*, based upon Le Sage's celebrated novel, was written by Edmond Burat de Gurgy, a young author whose talents Gautier praised when he lamented his premature death. [44] Le Sage's novel has all the attractions to be found in his *Theatre de la Foire*: local color, magic, a "breeches part," transformation scenes, characters similar to the "masks" of the Italian Comedy, and violent contrasts of settings. There is an Alchemist's laboratory, which goes back to Barbastal and even earlier, to the Italian Comedy, with its setting of a study full of "Téniers."

The new realism of the Marvelous appeared in *Le Diable boîteux* in a ballet scene at the Madrid Opera, seen from behind the curtain. The stage manager signaling "Curtain!" and the corps de ballet dancing with their backs to the audience, gave the spectator the impression that he was backstage. The backcloth, which rose to reveal a painted auditorium full of spectators, is a "realistic" technique if ever there was one, and was forecast by Pixérécourt when he mixed real and painted "supers" in *La Fille de l'Exilé* (The Exile's Daughter).

The scene in which Asmodeus, the limping devil, engages a troop of servants, each with an animal's head, recalls the contemporary drawings of Grandville, but it goes back to 16th century woodcuts such as "The Good Servant" with his "Ass's ears" and "Stag's feet." The desire to "humanize" animals is found in Disney's films, but the English pantomimes, adapted on the Boulevard du

Temple by practioners such as Laurent *ainé*, had long been using the world of histrionic animals. Boulevard fairy plays like *Les Petites Danaïdes* in 1819, in which the inimitable Potier has a set-to with an aggressive ostrich, or *La Biche au Bois* in 1845 with its Kingdom of Fishes, *Les Sept Châteaux du Diable*, with polka-dancing bears, *Le Sylphe d'Or (The Golden Sylph)* and its ballet of rabbits, or *Les Pilules du Diable*, in which the amazing dancing acrobats Lawrence and Redisha leaped out of a pond in frog costume—are but some examples of the "humanization" of animals.

Two other scenes in *Le Diable boîteux* are in the tradition of grand spectacle: a fancy dress ball at the Opéra with dominos and fantastic disguises; and a Spanish festival, in which local color could not be carried to greater lengths. In his deployment of groups of peasants, merchants, fairground hucksters and gamblers, as well as his leading artists, Coralli equalled the two great masters of local color—Louis Henry and Jean Aumer.

Coralli's second masterpiece, *Giselle ou Les Wilis*, the most successful and lasting creation in the history of the Theatre of Marvels, is strictly speaking a joint masterpiece of Coralli and Perrot. Although Coralli's name appeared alone on the bills of the first performance (for perfectly normal reasons to do with the Opéra administration) Perrot's contribution to the choreography of *Giselle*— that is to say, all the dances in which Giselle appeared, was an open secret. Unfortunately, the oblivion in which Perrot's name was long shrouded resulted in Coralli alone being credited with the choreography. As early as 1844 Gautier mentions only Coralli in this capacity. However, the *pas seul*, like all the scenes in which Giselle dances, were due to Perrot and so greatly contribute to his glory that it would seem fair to include his name on the programs for modern performances. On the other hand, the dances for Myrtha and her *wilis* and for the other ensembles, demonstrate Coralli's genuine merit from beginning to end and attest to a completely successful choreographic collaboration. [45]

So June 1841 saw the birth of this ballet, inspired by Heinrich Heine, outlined by Gautier, made into a scenario by H. V. de Saint-Georges, set to music by Adolphe Adam and produced by two choreographers from the Boulevard du Temple. What are the reasons for its longevity?

Gautier over-modestly thought he had created a pretty ballet for Carlotta Grisi: "The role is now impossible for any other dancer, and the name of Carlotta has become inseparable from that of Giselle." The iconography and contemporary reviews are indeed a guarantee that the creator of the role will not be forgotten. However, *Giselle* has become the consecrated test for every outstanding ballerina—a test in which she must reveal herself as both dancer and mime—in the same way that the part of Albrecht is a touchstone of the *premier danseur étoile*. Its entire choreography is most demanding. Thus one of the main reasons for its popularity may be due to a rebirth of interest in "pure dance," analagous to an interest in abstract art. In this domain it recalls the enthusiasm aroused by revivals of certain *pas de deux* such as *L'Oiseau bleu* and *Le Cygne noir* by Marius Petipa (who greatly contributed to the present version of *Giselle*), as well as Georges Balanchine's so-called "abstract" ballets which are distinguished by their technical requirements and visual poetry. Yet, this alone does not explain the success of *Giselle*.

The village on the Rhine, the forest beside the hamlet and the hunting scene in troubadour style are even more exotic now than they were in 1841;

but the modern public cannot be held by attempted exoticism, or by the attractions of a supernatural world which is no longer felt to be just beyond its confines and which was actually just as far from the materialism of the Restoration and the Second Empire as from that of the 20th century.

The combination of techniques from the popular theatre and a poetic idea made *Giselle* a masterpiece which, like all highly-charged works of quality, conceals an eternal vitality, so that its picturesqueness and fantasy have never ceased to delight even the most disenchanted eyes.

There was no choreographic collaborator in Coralli's last important ballet, *La Péri*, performed in February 1843.

In a description written by Gautier in a letter to his friend Gérard de Nerval, author of the scenario, after amusing himself with the idea that all the Romantic celebrities had a particular exotic milieu which corresponded to their characters, he specified: "I am a Turk, not from Constantinople but from Egypt." Having determined his own specific exotic milieu, he then outlined the ballet's story: Ahmed, a young eastern potentate whose harem of four hundred women contains beauties from all races and all countries, remains cold before this display of physical splendor. "Like all great voluptuaries, he is in love with the unattainable; he would fain speed away to ideal lands in search of beauty without a flaw . . ." A Péri observes this dreamer, so thirsty for spiritual beauty. "The earth, symbolized by Ahmed, raises its arms to heaven," and the Péri approaches him in his dream world. Of all the dances which follow, the "Dream Dance" is the most interesting. In the first place, it ends in an acrobatic bound in which the Péri leaps down from a cloud into Ahmed's arms, recalling the feats of such Boulevard dancers as Mazurier. Secondly, the recollection of this leap a year later, when the American acrobat Risley and his sons were dazzling the Parisians with their "aerial ballet," impelled Gautier to write his outline of a new type of ballet, which has been never more than partially realized.

"While watching them catapulted so far, falling from so high, we thought to what degree the training as dancers of the Opéra is incomplete and backward.—One day, we spoke to Perrot of the superiority of his dance; he made us this profound reply: 'I was three years Polichinelle and two years Monkey,' meaning thus to say that he had filled the roles of Mazurier. In reality, the exercises of equilibrists and acrobats, as gymnastic, as dynamic, are very differently understood than those of the dancing-class; they give an extraordinary suppleness, agility, strength and assurance. What could not an imaginative choreographer attempt, with such gay creatures as Auriol, Lawrence and Redisha, Ducrow, Risley and his sons? A ballerina who would be at the same time a ropedancer should realize marvelous effects in a fantastic ballet. Use of the springboard would help obtain prodigies of elevation, and equilibrium would give groups and turnings a completely new effect. The famous jump of Carlotta, in *la Péri*, shows to what good account these means might be turned—and, with a well trained ballerina, it would be simple to invent things of even more striking and daring grace. . . ."[46]

Although Perrot was definitely in favor of acrobatic training according to descriptions of his rehearsals with Carlotta, the idea of the famous leap was probably not his inspiration, as Serge Lifar believes. Indeed, Lifar's excessive severity toward Coralli is perhaps the only reservation concerning his excellent study of *Giselle*, especially when he suggests that Coralli made no innovations

170

in dancing, but used those of his own period "several years late." Coralli was an innovator. His "Sylphides" ballet in *Faust*, and the ensembles in *Giselle*—which some rather testy critics noted at the time—were like the "white" ensembles at which he was already a past master. If it was desired to belittle the actual originality of the poetic scenario of *Giselle*, one could mention *La Fille de l'Air (The Daughter of Air)*, a fairy play by the Cogniard brothers and Raymond, a sort of parody of *La Sylphide*, in which the *Wilis* are characterized in the dialogue just as they are described in the scenario of *Giselle*. Moreover, the choreographic reworking by Marius Petipa in Saint Petersburg, whence comes our *Giselle*, also counts, so that it seems fair to divide the laurels into three crowns.

While the contributions of acrobatics are evident in Perrot's choreography, it must be conceded that before he arrived at the Porte-Saint-Martin, Coralli had already worked with the great Mazurier, who served as model for the young Perrot; the use to which acrobatic effects could be put was obvious in *La Neige, Une visite à Bedlam* and other ballets created by Coralli. It is to be expected of the man whom Gautier characterized as "still our youngest choreographer" in 1844 when he was aged 65, that the end of his career should achieve distinction with a ballet linked to his old creations on the Boulevard.

While not of the caliber of Jules Perrot, Coralli remains one of the great masters of ballet in the Romantic period. He left the Opéra after the revolution of 1848, and died in Paris on May 1st, 1854. His son Eugène was well known as a dancer, a mime and a distinguished teacher. [47]

JULES PERROT

In 1823, the Théâtre de la Gaîté discovered in Jules Perrot the dancer who could compete with Mazurier, if not equal him. His career on the boulevards at this time is particularly interesting, not on account of the virtually non-existent novelties in performance but because of the horizons that opened before him.

Born in 1810 in Lyon, birthplace of Mazurier, son of the chief machinist of its theatres, he entered dancing school at the age of nine. "That was the heyday of Mazuriez (sic): Mazuriez, darling of the people of Lyon and joy of the silk weaver who, in his laborious semi-immobility, dreamt of the wonders of the somersault, Polichinelle's doubt splits and the miracle of the carp's leap. He conceived the bold project of learning the master's secrets; he watched him surreptitiously, observed him and studied him to such effect that he could soon exactly imitate Polichinelle's gestures, poses, movements, dances, feats, buffooneries and gait. He put on the costume of the double-humped Neapolitan and appeared at the Célestins Theatre in a play called *Le Petit Carnaval de Venise (The Little Venetian Carnival)*. His boldness was crowned with success." Such is the portrait of Perrot given, about 1842, by the *Galerie des Artistes Dramatiques*.

Mazurier had hardly settled in Paris when the youngster turned up at the Gaîté. With his arrival, six months after *Polichinelle Vampire, Polichinelle avalé par la Baleine (Polichinelle Swallowed by the Whale)* was on its program. The author and choreographer, Lefèvre, was a skilful Boulevard practitioner who never achieved the Blaches' reputation because he was content to copy an established success. Maurice's machinery and Gué's settings also played a large part in the success of this scenario, in which another aspect of the Marvelous appeared, and one which was to become increasingly important: the mimes.

Today, when mines are quite unpoetic and only appear in a sociological or economic context, it is hard to imagine them as ingredients in ballets and fairy plays; perhaps this was a development of the love of underground scenes already present in 18th-century pantomimes and melodramas. Abandoned mines were also the refuge of conspirators and brigands, and sometimes haunts of the supernatural. The situation in *Polichinelle avalé* is thus described in the scenario: "Zelia, an orphan on a desert island, is in the power of Cormoran, who owns mines in the Iron Mountain, is master of many slaves, and is protected by the infernal powers." [48]

As regards tradition, the Dream Scene with its apparitions might be a prototype of all the nocturnal fantasies which are scattered throughout 19th-century spectacles; its setting and the development of the dream point specifically to Ulrick's dream in *Le Cheval du Diable (The Devil's Horse)*. The contrast with *Polichinelle Vampire*, which manages entirely without *le noir* for its effects, and whose surprises are otherwise manoeuvred, is also notable: inevitably, "the stage represents a Gothic Hall in Cormoran's castle. Hideous heads, monsters and cabbalistic symbols are its only decoration; at the beginning, the stage is covered with clouds and thick vapors."

Later on, young Perrot performed the stilt dance of Mazurier with virtuosity. Finally, there was a "Chinese divertissement, in which Polichinelle dances. General tableau. Conclusion."

A thirteen-year old Perrot was obviously less suitable for a love story than a Mazurier of about twenty-five who was a good looking young man in spite of his comic makeup, according to contemporaries. It was not until the following year that the fourteen-year old Perrot was made a sort of comic *jeune premier* who married in the final tableau.

This was in another fairy pantomime by Lefevre, "imitated from the German": in 1824, *Le Rameau d'Or ou La Fée du Vieux Chêne (The Golden Bough, or The Fairy of the Old Oak Tree)* was packed with all the transformation scenes derived from English pantomime, as well as with supernatural visions of burlesque "gloom." The Cupids, genies and nymphs of the corps de ballet were not yet elves, sprites and sylphides, but they had a part to play in the action. The plot also contains the old legend of the talisman which becomes smaller with every wish (the Shagreen Skin, the Magic Bit, etc.,); this time it is the leaves of a golden bough which have the magic power: when they have all been plucked, the lovers are unprotected. The tradition that a number are wasted in frivolous wishes is respected, so that the fairy has to go on protecting the lovers after reproaching them for their improvidence.

The characters have German names—Fandler, Fridolin, Hermann and Crettle (sic); they include a jockey, Phlips, explained by Perrot's youth and lack of inches. The evil magician Horloribo could have erupted at the Funambules or Drury Lane; his train of birds and animals, his horse in the shape of a snail and the buffooneries of his demons recall certain aspects of court ballets under Louis XIII, scenes of the Italian Comedy or a popular version of *Freischutz*.

So Perrot played Mazurier's roles for four years in Paris, but his ambition led him to the Opéra, despite a body and appearance unsuitable for a noble or *demi-caractère* dancer. After his classes with Coulon *père*, which he considered valueless, he went to the aged Vestris, who transmitted to Perrot his impeccable technique and traditions which he had received from Noverre.

The question of the part played by acrobatics in his art will be debated for a long time to come. He himself never concealed his debt to the Boulevard; both as choreographer and as dancer; he prided himself on having played the 'Mazurier' parts. It is said that it was he who urged Dr. Véron to engage Deburau at the Opéra. Miming played a remarkable part in his work, because he used the "expressive body" techniques derived from the fairground players. But what he had learned on the Boulevard became polished, refined and elegant. The relationship between Perrot's *Faust* or *Esméralda* and the work of other distinguished Boulevard practitioners, who also became choreographers at the Opéra, is analogous to that between Pixérécourt's melodramas and the dramas of Victor Hugo.

In 1830, Perrot made his début at the Opéra shortly after that of Marie Taglioni. Meanwhile, he had won an enviable reputation in London. At this period, when the ballerina's reign was beginning, his triumph was all the more phenomenal.

After five years' delight for ballet lovers, who have left many accounts of the "aerial Perrot" and the Sylphide, he departed the Opéra. Rumor had it that La Taglioni was jealous and urged the management to offer him a derisory salary; this story seems unlikely, because they continued to meet in London, and their correspondence testifies to their friendly relations. It would be more realistic to attribute his departure to Duponchel, Dr. Véron's successor, who refused to increase his salary and gave the twenty-five year old dancer no definite hope of being a choreographer.

So Perrot left the Opéra, certain of his future. Indeed, profitable contracts awaited him all over Europe: England and Germany loaded him with honors; the Operas of Vienna and Milan competed for him; and at Vienna a hoped for event occurred—he choreographed his first full-length ballet, *Le Kobold (The Sprite)*.

In Italy he met Carlotta Grisi, who at seventeen was already an "infant prodigy"; he induced her to leave Naples for London in 1832 as his pupil and partner. On August 30th, 1836, en route to Vienna, they stopped in Paris and were part of a group of performers sent by the Opéra to a benefit performance given at the Comédie Française; that was the exact date on which Carlotta Grisi made her debut in Paris. The journal *Cancans de l'Opéra* was venomous about Perrot's defection, while praising Carlotta Grisi's "charming person and angelic features." The couple left at once for Vienna, and at Milan in 1838 they were called "*la Coppia Danzante dei Conjugi Carlotta et Giulio Perrot*" (the Dancing Couple, Carlotta and Jules Perrot). He was already entitled to use the title "First Dancer of the Paris Opéra" after his name.

In 1839 he returned to Paris briefly, simply fulfilled the terms of his expiring contract and then left again for Russia. However, he wanted Carlotta to become *première danseuse* at the Paris Opéra. The couple accordingly returned to the capital in 1840 and achieved a success even greater than they had hoped for, though at a secondary theatre, the Renaissance. *Le Zingaro (The Gypsy)* appears in Gautier's collection of reviews in which his celebrated prose portrait of Perrot occurs, and the Martinets devoted a plate to the dancers in the *Galerie Théâtrale*.

The Opéra already had three choreographers, of whom Coralli was the chief, and could not easily take on Perrot. Yet Léon Pillet, the new Administrator, was convinced that the time was ripe for introducing a new ballerina in the person of Carlotta Grisi, and that nobody could show her to better advantage than Perrot. Besides, a large number of season ticket-holders and critics were calling for the Perrots and talking about "injustice." So Carlotta was engaged, and by common accord it was decided that all her dances should be composed by Perrot. Now, as Serge Lifar has pointed out, inasmuch as custom requires the payment of royalties to the composer and choreographer whose names are credited on the printed scenario, the choreographer, who does not appear before the footlights like the dancers, is thus recompensed for the countless rehearsals necessitated by a performance at the Opéra. Coralli, who was responsible for the production, staging and everything to do with *Giselle* except Carlotta's dances and scenes, was therefore considered as within his rights when he had his name printed alone on the scenario and later on the posters and programs.

The reviews of the first performance very carefully noted Perrot's contribution to the ballet; but later on, partisans of the Opéra such as M. Charles de Boigne, who did not forgive Perrot for earning his living outside Paris—six years in London and six in Russia—tended gradually to suppress his name. One certain fact is that apart from *La Filleule des Fées (The Fairies' Goddaughter)* in 1849, Perrot's ballets were never given at the Opéra under his own direction; his career was divided mainly between London and Saint Petersburg, and until 1859 he was indisputably the leading choreographer and dancer in Europe.

Yet, the Opéra administration, which was both miserly and vindictive, never forgave him his triumphs and ignored him when he came back to Paris in 1859. He did no more work in the theatre before his death in 1892. Great ballerinas came from all over to consult him about the interpretation of their roles in his ballets. Here and there, truncated versions of his ballets appeared on the Boulevard. Nevertheless, the great Perrot, most illustrious of all the nurslings of the Boulevard, faded into an oblivion from which he has only recently emerged.

174

CHAPTER IX

Performing Animals

SPECTACLES which featured performing animals did not continue into the 20th century, perhaps on account of the enormous expense involved. The cinema has occasionally had its animal stars and some vestiges still remain in the modern circus. Both are but pale reflections of a specialty which, from several points of view, was one of the highest manifestations of the Theatre of Marvels. [49]

Animal shows ranged from elaborate combinations of pantomime, ballet and melodrama to the simple turn of a performing dog, but never lost their relationship to the old fairground traditions. Prints and drawings devoted to performing animals are more numerous than those for all other aspects of the Theatre of Marvels combined.

If the Romantic ballet may have been the highest and most poetic expression of the Marvelous, trained animals were certainly the most universal. The basic animal act could do without music, scenery, even without a tent or a booth. The animal shows had a very special aesthetic and philosophy for many 19th-century writers, among them Balzac and Gautier. Because of the extensive iconography, the many reviews and articles consecrated to them and the numerous play texts which have survived, it is possible to recreate this unique form of escapist theatre in one's mind's eye.

There is nothing novel about performing animals in themselves, for rope-walking elephants have existed since the Pharaohs and Romans. In France, during the reign of Louis XI, gypsies and poor strolling players entering Paris "were discharged from all taxes provided they made their monkeys cut some capers before the tollkeepers," whence the expression: "*payer en monnaie de singe*" (literally, "To pay in monkey money.") [50]

The idea of showing a group of trained animals performing within the framework of a scenario appeared some fifty years before the modern circus emerged. From November 4th to 8th, 1722, the Duke of Bourbon offered Louis XV a sumptuous celebration on the occasion of his coronation, and the acrobat Anthony de Sceaux was summoned to Chantilly with his troupe from the Foire Saint-Germain. Disguised as bears, lions, tigers and other exotic beasts, the acrobats constituted a menagerie. In turn, "by magic art," Orpheus appeared in the center of a grotto adorned with rose-laurel and orange trees, and the animals became motionless at the sound of his violin (Orpheus was played by a violinist from the Opéra). Suddenly hunting horns and barking were heard, and "the bear climbs to the treetops, springs on to a tightrope and performs a score of feats of agility and equilibrium. The others make prodigious leaps and bounds, but always so that they keep within the spirit of their roles and the characters of the animals they are to enact."

In 1774, Philip Astley, the Englishman who created the modern circus, arrived in France to give equestrian performances. A former Sergeant Major of Dragoons, his entertainment reflected a taste for military trappings. He was the first to introduce acrobats, rope dancers and short mimed or dialogued scenes into what had been purely equestrian spectacles.

In 1782, he built the first permanent circus in Paris and broadened the scope of his comic interludes; towards 1787, he imported from England: *The Tailor of Brentford*, source of the classic French interlude *Rognolet et Passe-Carreau* at the Cirque-Olympique. For the French as for the English, and for the Americans a little later, the buffoon was a military tailor, whose appearance is thus described in a little book for children: "His hair is curled and powdered white, after the fashion in which Gascons are represented on the stage. He has several rolls of cloth over his shoulder; they are samples which he keeps ready to show his customers." Poor Rognolet, after a thousand misadventures with his servant Passe-Carreau, is thrown by his horse. When he tries to take refuge in his house (a little square setpiece made of paper), the horse chases him and comes in through the window. In this case the horse obviously becomes an actor.

Between 1782 and 1792, the equestrian "mimodramas" *Marlborough, Don Quichotte (Don Quixote)*, *Montauciel, L'Arrivée de Nicodème dans la Lune (Nicodemus Arrives on the Moon)*, *Frédégonde, Robert le Diable* and *Geneviève de Brabant* appeared in the repertory of the Amphithéâtre Astley, with numerous trained animal acts. The encroaching Reign of Terror induced Astley to sell his Paris circus to that picturesque adventurer Antonio Franconi, founder of the great dynasty.

Born in Italy on August 5th, 1737, Antonio Franconi killed a young nobleman in a duel and took refuge in France. He had to join a fairground menagerie and attempted some experiments in lion-taming; then he showed some performing canaries, toured throughout France and Spain, put on a "battle of bulls" and was at the Amphithéâtre Astley with his birds in 1783. Thenceforth he concerned himself with horses. During his years on the road, he married a compatriot by whom he had two sons, Laurent and Henri. He became Astley's associate, replaced him during his journeys to England and took over his Amphithéâtre on March 21, 1793. It was known as the Amphithéâtre Franconi and later, in 1810, as the Cirque-Olympique.

It was at the Cirque-Olympique, during the Restoration, that Cuvelier, in addition to his historical pieces and fairy plays, paid homage to Napoleon with *La Mort de Kléber ou Les Français en Egypte (The Death of Kleber, or The French in Egypt)* in 1819, and, despite the censorship, *La Prise de la Flotte ou La Charge de Cavalerie (The Capture of the Fleet, or The Cavalry Charge)* in 1822, and other plays full of nostalgia for the Napoleonic epic. At the same time,

MR. HICKS, AS ROBERT MACAIRE.

London. Pub by J. REDINGTON. 208. Hoxton Old Town & sold by J.WEBB. 78. Brick Lane St. Luke.

Mr. Hicks in "Robert Macaire," another adaptation of a routine melodrama, "L'Auberge des Adrets," which Fréderick Lemaître had transformed into ". . . a triumph of revolutionary art which followed the July (1830) Revolution" and "pitiless Gallic raillery." The English version, to judge by this "tuppence coloured," reverted to melodrama and its typical postures.

"The Incomparable Stag of the North, named Azor, or a New Ascension never before accomplished Compared to those of our most famous Rope Dancers. Latest Masterpiece of Monsieur Franconi "père," to which he consecrated 2 Years and 1/2 of work, not only for the actual training, but moreover to find the means of constructing a Tower which might be raised and lowered at Will, and to arrive at connecting a little Plank five inches wide with its Buttresses, which is placed on two ropes. The Stag, by means of a Runway, will lead a figure of Fame which will serve him as a Parachute: it sometimes happens that his great vivacity causes him to plunge when he is 20 or 25 feet high; this fact alone will give some idea of all the Efforts and pains which Monsieur Franconi "père" of necessity had to take in order to train it in this manner. "Vide et Crede."

The "Polka of the Bears" in "Les Sept Chateaux du Diable" (The Seven Castles of the Devil), a "féerie" of MM. Dennery and Clairville. "The polka wants to be danced and to be talked about, that's all. It will make a tour of all the theatres and probably a tour of the world. Yesterday at the Palais-Royal, today at the Variétés, tomorrow at the Opéra—one keeps finding it everywhere."

The equestrian Gustave Price, member of a dynasty whose descendants are still active in the theatre and circus. This print is by Kiersdorff of Ghent, who edited some of the handsomest circus souvenir prints. (C. 1835)

This provincial lithograph (Légé of Bordeaux) shows the child star in a trilogy of scenes. The "demi-fine" provincial prints are often closely related to the medieval popular woodcuts, which often used this type of presentation. It is amusing to realize that the Savoyards and their marmots were exotics at a period when the railroads had not yet brought the mountains within everyone's reach. (C. 1839)

Die Sylphiden
Gruppe aus dem Cirque olympique

"... It's rumoured that it is always the same white horse which goes round and round with a man standing on its back, poised on one foot. Maybe so, but just the same one's eyes are always fixed on the horse and his rider, posed like a Zephyr." A Cirque-Olympique group seen by a German artist in a Munich print which rather transforms the Sylphides into Valkyrie.

in 1821 he wrote *Le Berceau ou Les Trois Ages d'Henri IV* (*The Cradle, or The Three Ages of Henri IV*), and some topical pieces on "*L'Heureux Accouchement de S.A.R. la Duchesse de Berry*" (*H.R.H. the Duchess of Berry's Happy Event*) in 1817. These equestrian shows were first given in the Amphithéâtre on the Faubourg du Temple, fitted up in 1809 by the architect Dubois to resemble Astley's Amphitheatre in London, that is to say, provided with a ring and a stage for pantomime. This building, destroyed by fire in 1826, was rebuilt the following year on the Boulevard du Temple, according to plans of the architect Bourla (or Bourlat).

Since the beginning of the 19th century, the Cirque-Olympique and its regular authors had been making use of more exotic animals than their familiar horses: the stags Coco and Azor and the elephants Baba and Kiouny appear in the prints, children's books and memoirs of the period. They can be seen on china plates from Choisy-le-Roi, Gien and Paris. Baba, in the form of a white opaline bottle, was as popular as the famous giraffe in the Jardin des Plantes which was reproduced on snuffboxes and *bonbonnières*.

Later on, when the menageries of the great animal tamers appeared—those of Henri Martin, Huguet de Massilia, Van Amburgh and Carter for example—the team of scenario writers for four-footed stars adapted themselves just as easily to tigers, lions and panthers. They were, besides Cuvelier and Franconi *jeune*, Augustin Hapdé, Frédéric (Dupetitmaré), Nicholas Brazier (the author of the *Chroniques des Petits Théâtres de Paris*), Léopold Chandezon, P. Villiers, Henri Blanchard, Louis Ponet, Fabrice Labrousse, Théodore Nézel, Henri Ville-mot, V. de Saint-Hilaire, Ferdinand Laloue and Anicet-Bourgeois.

Summaries of the dramas staged by Franconi, even the unlikeliest and most ridiculous of them, show a complete mastery of arranging exotic settings in time, space or the supernatural. As regards the titles, texts and visual elements, their links to the popular and *demi-fine* prints of the Rue Saint-Jacques are also close.

"Equestrian pantomimes representing the Age of Chivalry," "imitated from the novel by Tressan" composed the spectacle *Gérard de Nevers ou la Belle Euriante* (February, 1810), in the words of its authors Cuvelier and Franconi *jeune*. "The stag Coco, pursued by hounds and riders, runs over the winding mountain and forest tracks represented by the scenery; he arrives at the edge of a precipice; the hounds are about to overtake him; he does not hesitate, but leaps out of their reach. The hounds draw back shuddering from the obstacle (a chasm?) which separates them from their prey."

The work had a lively score by d'Haussy, full of hunting horns, trumpets and fanfares. The scene painters and machinists had to wait a year for the well-merited honor of having their names on the program. The entertainment was revived several times.

In the same year, one of the Circus's greatest successes, *Martial et Angélique ou Le Cheval accusateur* (*Martial and Angélique, or The Accusing Horse*)—the sub-title was sometimes given as: *Ou Le Témoin irrécusable* (*Or the Unimpeachable Witness*), by Cuvelier, was immortalized in the Paris prints. The old technique of showing a triptych of scenes on a single large plate was happily adopted here; the intelligent horse is shown presenting a piece of the culprit's coat to Laurent Franconi. The actor was turned out in a jacket with resplendent epaulets and froggings, skintight breeches and riding boots, with a ring-master's whip resting lightly against his right shoulder. Underneath the triptych, in which the horse appears without a saddle, is Laurent's head in a medallion portrait, garlanded and crowned. (51)

A fanatical Bonapartist, Cuvelier already foreshadowed the epoch of Louis-Philippe, in which the Napoleonic Legend flourished. He patrolled the Boulevard in a semi-military frogged greatcoat, always followed by his mistress, the pretty dancing mime Mme Dumouchel, similarly togged out. The action of his *Martial et Angélique* takes place toward the middle of the reign of Louis XV. A certain Colonel Saint-Amar, the libertine Lord of the Manor, importunes a pretty village girl—Angélique—beloved of the young farmer Martial; a clairvoyant horse saves its master, unmasks two assassins, recognizes one of them as the murderer and prevents an innocent man from being executed. At the finale the intelligent horse is made much of and draped with garlands. Dialogue is reduced to the minimum, and ample time and opportunity given for the mimed scenes.

Hunting, with the sumptuous costumes of earlier centuries or the classical tunics which were fashionable under the Empire, became one of the *raisons d'etre* of pantomime: *Acteon changé en cerf ou La Vengeance de Diane (Actaeon Changed to a Stag, or Diana's Vengeance)* by A. Hapde (1811), *Le Pont infernal ou Le Cerf intrepide (The Devil's Bridge, or The Courageous Stag)* by Franconi *jeune* (1812), and that great and most often revived success, *Saint Hubert ou Le Cerf miraculeux (St. Hubert, or The Miraculous Stag)* by the master hand, Cuvelier (1815), are full of hunts. The scenario of *Saint Hubert* shows that it was a highly spectacular piece, with music arranged by MM. Vanderburck and d'Haussy and ballet music composed by M. Alexandre (Piccini); the scenery is attributed to M. Isidore, one of the deans of the profession in Paris.

Cuvelier, who tailored the piece for the star and his special talents, turned the story of primitive Christianity to surprising account. Azor, the flying stag, had been so well-trained by Franconi *père* that he could withstand ascensions in the basket of a faked balloon, surrounded by torches and Bengal fire. The pantomime ended with a final apotheosis in which he could display his talents. After a festival and ballet, followed by a number of brilliant episodes featuring Druidic rites; a chase by a mad wolf; a hunt in a raging thunderstorm; a swan bearing a golden key and finally the appearance of the stag rising from the clouds with a luminous cross between its antlers; Hubert abandons his perfidious mistress. Thanks to the sacred stag, he finds his wife and two children, whom he had abandoned in the forest. "The crags in the background open up and the miraculous stag appears and rises into the clouds, flashing the heavenly sign which adorns his head." Everyone falls to his knees, a heavenly voice intones a blessing, and the script ends with these words: "The bloody cult of the Druids was abolished in the Ardennes, and France had no more idolaters."

When the animal required by the plot, like that of *L'Ours et l'Enfant ou la Ville Bavière (The Bear and The Child or the Bavarian Town,* 1819) was too dangerous to be left at liberty on the stage or in the ring, a cardboard head made by Hallé, specialist in theatrical properties, and an animal skin enabled an actor to replace it. When pursuing wolves were at the heroine's heels, Hallé supplied properly ferocious-looking cardboard heads to fit on well-trained dog actors. Versatile dogs from generation to generation played the lead in Pixérécourt's *Le Chien de Montargis ou la Forêt de Bondy* (translated as *The Forest of Bondy or the Dog of Montargis* and presented at Covent Garden in 1814—the same year as its Parisian premiere). *Le Chien de Terre-Neuve ou Le Farouche*

Indien (The Newfoundland Dog, or The Wild Indian, 1819) by Henri Blanchard
was produced in the year when Byron's *Mazeppa* was published, which leads
us to horse-operas of loftier inspiration.

The adventures of Mazeppa, who was strapped half-naked to the back of
a wild horse and sent careering across the Ukraine, and then elected hetman
of Cossacks during the reign of Peter the Great, captivated the poetic imagination of Victor Hugo and the popular imagination as well. Half a century after
his first appearance, Mazeppa magnetized the crowds. It is difficult to find an
equivalent theatrical drawing card in modern times. The fiery steed with its
half-naked rider appeared in albums, popular prints and Salon paintings in
Europe and America. It was the famous vehicle of Adah Isaacs Menken. *Mazeppa
ou Le Cheval tartare* in 1825, "a mimodrama after Lord Byron," was practically
Cuvelier's last work and was produced posthumously.

The distinguished animal tamer Huguet de Massilia seems to have been
the first person to think of writing a play for an elephant—his "pupil" Miss
Djeck (or Dick)—sometime toward 1828. Adolphe Franconi, Henri's son, had
succeeded his father as collaborator and producer of pantomimes and other
circus plays. With F. Laloue and Léopold Chandezon, he created *L'Eléphant
du Roi de Siam (The King of Siam's Elephant)* at the Cirque-Olympique on
July 4th, 1829.

At the beginning of the Restoration, the elephants Baba and Kiouny had
already performed most of the feats incorporated into this melodrama. Dugourc's
illustrations in the children's book *Le Cirque-Olympique* show them playing the
hurdy-gurdy, hammering nails into a plank, uncorking bottles (the most popular
turn in these "Elephantiads"), catching apples, kneeling for their mahout to
mount them, and balancing on a stout wooden stool. It would have been hard
to find a more remote spot than Siam; surviving lithographs prove that a veritable
team of scene painters (Leroux, Dumay and Philastre) succeeded in reproducing it at the Circus. Bertotto, already successful on the boulevards, was responsible for the ballets. The score was by Sergent.

The authors ransacked travel memoirs and albums of costumes and landscapes. The ardor with which they worked is shown by the cast of characters:
Nadir-Siam, the young Crown Prince of Siam; his rival Temulkain, a Burmese
prince; Mutalib, High Priest of Samono-Kodom, Nadir's guardian and Prime
Minister; Taherbad, the head of the Talapoins, Siamese monks; Idamora, a
young princess betrothed to Nadir, and her servant Ziloe; two comic characters, Badur Bibi Khan, Superintendent of the Elephant Palace, and Tsi-Tchi,
the Elephant's groom. The list of "supers" is fairly heterogeneous: "Mandarins,
high officials, Talapoins, Fakirs, Slaves of the Elephant, Dancing Girls, Populace." "The action takes place in the kingdom of Siam," and the authors begin
with a description as detailed as a geography book: "A rustic spot amid a
thick forest on the banks of the Menam, the chief river in the States of Siam,
on its estuary in the gulf of the same name. The ramparts of Juthia, the capital
of the kingdom, are visible in the distance, and various buildings on both banks.
In the foreground, on one side of the stage, is a retreat inhabited by Talapoins,
Siamese hermits devoted to contemplation; it is built on rocks which contain
a number of caves at the bottom. Above there is a little pagoda under a projecting roof, rising to a height of several stories in pyramid shape." This highly
documented setting was by Dumay. As usual in these spectacles, its set pieces

were essential to the plot, which could not have progressed without the lattice-work, balustrades and bunches of flowers placed so as to motivate the skilful movements of the pachyderm's trunk.

The second act represents, in full detail, the underground temple in the Grand Pagoda of Samono-Kadom, "in gigantic and strange proportions, adorned with colossal statues of men and beasts with several heads and a multitude of arms"; it is the setting for a scene of Siamese manners and customs admirably designed for the amazement of stay-at-home Parisians. Then came a setting by Leroux, the Elephant's Pavilion, in which luncheon was served—a scene so popular that it was revived a few years later in *Les Eléphants de la Pagode (The Elephants of the Pagoda)*. The ladies of the court sat on folding stools and formed a magnificent honor guard on each side of the table at which the elephant gravely installed himself; guards were drawn up in line, and slaves brought two gilt ladders which were placed on each side of the elephant. Tsi-Tchi and a slave climbed up and fastened a napkin round their master's neck (an enormous Cashmere shawl). A huge bell was put on the table, and the elephant would ring it when he wanted something. However, the last part was the most dazzling, and seems to have exhausted the property vendor's stocks: "It is an immense temple resplendent with all the marvels of the arts and gleaming with all the richest, most lavish and most extraordinary devices of Asiatic invention: statues, columns, vases, draperies, paintings, etc." In the background there was a view of the gardens and an overall panorama of the Great Pagoda, with its countless domes and pyramids, its terraces and galleries full of people. The spectacle ended with a brilliant procession, in the middle of which the Royal Elephant—having saved all the situations from the beginning—proceeds triumphantly, bedecked with gold and precious stones.

In the following year, the Cirque-Olympique presented another novelty, *Les Lions de Mysore*, designed for Henri Martin, the remarkable animal tamer from Marseilles, and his menagerie.

A first class equestrian acrobat, he had become a lion and tiger tamer in order to win the hand of Gertrude van Aken, joint owner of a famous Dutch travelling menagerie. He toured Europe, received several animals from the Royal Menagerie of Frederick William III, and returned to France in 1829. Balzac, among other literary figures, regularly attended his performances. The great tamer (a term reserved for those who work with wild beasts as distinguished from trainers) seems, according to the scenario, to have "done it all by kindness." Adolphe Franconi's production, Sergent's music and Philastre and Cambon's settings again catered to the contemporary passion for Orientalia. Lithographs showing Martin and his animals are fairly plentiful and detailed; as there was an export trade in these prints between France and America, they may have influenced the future great American tamer, Isaac Van Amburgh.

In 1835, the dignified and faithful Kiouny appeared again in a three-act melodrama by Emile Vanderburck, *Kiouny ou L'Eléphant et le Page (Kiouny, or The Elephant and the Page)*, at the Théâtre du Panthéon—which made use of all the tricks already described. But it was the accommodation of an entire menagerie on stage, inaugurated by *Les Lions de Mysore* and Henri Martin, that produced the most spectacular developments.

After a visit to London, first for six months at Astley's Amphitheatre and then in a sketch called *Charlemagne* at Drury Lane, Van Amburgh opened in

184

Paris in *La Fille de l'Emir (The Emir's Daughter)* at the Porte-Saint-Martin, in 1838. ". . . No jaded man of the world," says Gautier's review, "no exhausted journalist, no sensitive woman will want to miss an evening performance in which one has the chance to see a lion eat a man. . . . By six o'clock the hall was full; the audience, piled up and crammed in the boxes, was aquiver with impatience; the tip-up seats in the aisle were hotly disputed; highly skilled urchins imitated a cock crowing, while others sang the *Marseillaise—*the *Marseillaise* calling for the lions: it was splendid."

After an uproarious wait, followed by the first scene, in which everyone was waiting for the beasts, ". . . some scene shifters appeared in front of the curtain with strings of oil lamps which they hung up on each side of the forestage. This procedure greatly excited our curiosity: footlights probably scare the wild beasts, and that is why they are illuminated from the side; the critics indulged in a thousand conjectures, each more mysterious than the last. However, it is unlikely that a row of smoky oil lamps would dazzle the lion's yellow eye or the tiger's green-hued iris which is used to the blinding African sun—indeed, now they are lifting the footlights away. . . . This time, it is the animals. Two cages placed side by side fill the entire width of the theatre, which represents a kind of circus; behind the bars, which look rather flimsy, the savage family frets and fumes."

These animals were not shown "in ferocity" (a technique used later on), and Gautier noted that as many could be seen at the Jardin des Plantes, but that it was already a feat to show those natural enemies, lions, panthers and tigers, in the same cage. Some spectators considered them almost too tame and supposed that they had been drugged. However, a few years later Van Amburgh was seriously wounded by his favorite tiger.

At last came the *dénouement*, and an Arab Chief, none other than Van Amburgh himself, enters the cage to rescue his little daughter. There follows a description of the masterly skill of the "phlegmatic American," braving the menagerie with a little switch; the animals' tenderness to him was almost excessive. Moreover, not satisfied with these marvels: "Van Amburgh threw down, amid all those claws and teeth, a delightful little lamb, very frightened, succulent and appetizing; the tiger snarled at it, fixing its green and shining eyes on Van Amburgh"; and the lamb sheltered in the lion's embrace. "The lamb is a substitute for little Aidie, for the scene of the child among the beasts, which was performed in England, was not allowed in France where, be it said, no mother would have been willing to lend her child for so terrible a performance: for this the composure of British motherhood was required. Van Amburgh reappears on the other side of the cage, holding the hand of the little girl who is supposed to have been rescued."

Gautier drew a fairly accurate conclusion from this spectacle: "This will seem cruel to many people; but these scenes at least inspired a noble contempt for life and were not without a certain wild grandeur. In our view, witless comedies which poke fun at everything and bring out the sordid side of things are far more barbarous, unhealthy and immoral than circus combats. Blood is cleaner than mud, and ferocity better than corruption."

A show of this kind given elsewhere than in a circus was an exception, and *La Fille de l'Emir* stimulated competition from the Cirque-Olympique. As Henri Martin had retired, an Englishman, James Carter (obviously another mute part),

185

was engaged with his beasts in the same year for *Le Lion du Désert (The Desert Lion)*.

The French campaigns in North Africa provided a less hackneyed scenario than the usual Far Eastern plots. How could a non-speaking part be found for Carter? Those two skilful practitioners Laloue and Labrousse decided that he must obviously be an Arab, but not just any Arab, because his tribe has cut out his tongue for helping two French officers to escape. For local color use was made of places given prominence in the daily papers, and descriptions of the settings were fairly well documented.

The first setting—a guardroom and its staff—which was frequently imitated, is thus explained by Henry Thétard: "It was a pretext for having the uniform-loving Parisians applaud the red trousers, then in the full glory of their novelty. Our splendid infantrymen, still hampered by the cumbersome Napoleonic equipment, marched briskly beneath the glaring African sun, represented by the circus's great chandelier."

Then a struggle between an Arab soldier and a tiger constituted one of the first experiments in the "ferocity" technique, which added new thrills; finally the beast was thrown to the ground, and even became a protective weapon for the Arab who had tamed it; later, it pulled his chariot when he made a triumphal entry into the town.

The next animal star was a dog—a dog that was given a more than five-page review by Gautier. *Le Chien des Pyrénées (The Dog from the Pyrenees)* showed "an innocent girl persecuted by a villain, with the inevitable accompaniment of Lover, Simpleton, Devoted Retainer and a babe in arms; there is a fire, an underground passage and a bridge over a torrent! Nothing is lacking." As for Emile, an Alsatian crossed with a griffon, he began with the classical exercise of the luncheon, searching for the knife, bottle of wine and plate; then, left to his own devices he became part of the story and, a dog prodigy, helped the hero to escape from a dungeon in which he was imprisoned with his faithful servant.

In 1845, *Les Eléphants de la Pagode*, a drama in three acts by V. de Saint-Hilaire and Anicet-Bourgeois, was devised to show off the talents of two interesting tuskers, Kiouny and our old friend Mlle Djeck. The scene is laid at Nagpur, India, in 1740—an India full of singular features, such as a Prime Minister called Missouri and a sacred elephant called Kelly. Somewhat curiously, French comedians are found there: Thomas a shoemaker and a former Paris urchin ("I was called the Cherubino of the Rue Tiquetonne. . . ."), has gone off with his wife, who hailed from the Rue Mouffetard, to seek his fortune as a slipper maker in the East; he has taken on as apprentice a young Indian who speaks pidgin French and is called Omichoud. This astute team helps the sacred elephants to thwart a plot mounted by a villainous Grand Brahmin against the legal heir to the Rajah's throne.

In his review, Gautier complains of a certain banality in the scenery, and mentions Danniell's illustrations and the abundant documentation available: "The English," he says, "have produced some splendid publications on India, which MM. Despléchin, Diéterle and Séchan might use as sources." However, such niggling reservations did not interfere with the success of the show.

The second act contains the famous comic luncheon scene illustrated in Martinet's *Galerie Dramatique*: the two elephants, caparisoned in red with headbands of the same color and gold braid over everything, sit opposite one another at table while Thomas, in Rajah's costume, occupies the central place, facing the audience; the servants have fastened enormous napkins around the elephant's necks. The scene is described as follows in the scenario: "One of the elephants rings. The servants offer several dishes in succession to Thomas, but each elephant, in turn, takes what is put before him just as he wants to taste it. Thomas is furious. As he holds out his cup and a slave brings the bottle up to it, one of the elephants snatches it away with his trunk and drinks. Thomas gets up in a rage."

In February 1846, *Le Cheval du Diable*, designed solely for horses and equestrian performers, was one of the great successes of the Cirque-Olympique. In his review, Gautier produced a document of the first importance as regards the criticism and aesthetics of the "spectacle for the eyes."

Villain de Saint-Hilaire had borrowed the plot from Balzac's *Le Peau de Chagrin*. The Circus staged the play with music by Francastel, ballets by Laurent *aîné*, machinery by Sacre and no less than four scenic artists: MM. Martin, Wagner, Derchy and Thierry. For the latter, a Salon painter, it was the beginning of a brilliant career in scene design. Its cast included some of the most aristocratic names in the circus world: Ducrow, Gauthier and Mathilde Monnet among others.

In spite of his remarks about the tedious length of the dialogue ("The circus is forgetting that it is primarily a spectacle for the eyes . . . that is what gives it originality, this opera for the eye"), Gautier admitted that the show contained elements capable of attracting the public for a long time. To begin with, there was Zisko, the diabolical horse which, like the dog Emile, could play complicated scenes on his own: "Zisko carries off a princess at a spanking rate, from the back of the arena to clear up to the footlights; unmasks a villainous knight, drags him with his teeth before the Court and kicks him to death; routs a pack of walruses and Polar bears by breathing fireworks at them from his nostrils; searches for the Emperor's child in a brigand's lair which can only be reached by crossing a bridge of iron chains overhanging a precipice; dances the tarbuka before the wonderstruck populace of Damascus, and hurls himself into Hell at an infernal gallop." "Zisko, without being a natural beauty, has elegance and distinction. . . . His coat, of a strange off-white, is dotted with brown marks and scored with black slashes like a panther's hide mixed with a tiger's. Are these peculiarities natural or produced by skillful makeup? We cannot be sure. The result is that Zisko, thus bedizoned looks reasonably satanic."

The knightly plot was Troubadour in period; there were countless Exotic settings, and the entire concept was based on acceptance of the Supernatural. Not one single time-tested effect was omitted from *Le Cheval du Diable*, and its success was predictacle.

The monstrous "hero" resembles several established models: the melodrama tyrant shuddering at his misdeeds as he finally meets his doom; the great Shakespearean villain as reworked by Cuvelier—more complicated because his conscience is tormented by remorse although he cannot resist committing his fore-ordained crimes—and the man who sells himself to the devil, a theme that goes back to the Middle Ages and may be used by a Goethe as well as a Cuvelier. [52]

Circus horses, artificial bears, living statues, a novelty in exotic settings—Iceland [53]—were all combined in a medley which would inevitably see its three-hundredth performance. The settings mentioned by Gautier included a vision of Hell, "swarming with all the grotesque, terrifying and monstrous creations of Callot and Téniers."

Full-length plays with animal stars in no way diminished the appeal of short *dressage* interludes. A typical example is a number by the elephant Baba, who danced to the strains of a hurdy-gurdy played by a little Savoyard. When the tune (*Vive Henri IV*) was finished, the child put down his instrument and walked away, whereupon Baba went over and turned the handle to recommence the serenade.

The stags Coco and Azor performed both in plays and interludes, just as the human members of the circus company were required to do. Coco leapt over eight men, then over four horses and finally through a series of flaming hoops, remained impassive when Laurent Franconi fired a pistol between his antlers, presented bouquets to the ladies and threatened their husbands with his antlers. Azor, rivaling the rope dancers Forioso and Ravel, made a vertical ascension on two tightropes, supported by a sort of parachute. *L'Histoire Dramatique* is studded with detailed accounts of stars such as the jumper Transylvain or the dogs and monkeys of Schneider, for Gautier considered their debuts worthy of those of most human artistes.

Although animal shows could be put on with the greatest splendor and detail in the circus arena, their origins were never so remote as to preclude performances on the sidewalk or any other convenient spot. For example, the old bandstand in the Turkish Garden sheltered a troupe of performing monkeys and dogs which, still according to Gautier, might have been that of M. Schneider which had aroused his enthusiasm a few years before at the Circus. [54] Now he was again delighted at the buffooneries, as well as amused by the "*naif*" setting: "When the curtain goes up, the stage represents an African landscape—pumpkin-colored sky, palm trees lifted from a druggist's window display, and aloes of the purest verdigris." "This parody of human life by animals," he added, "is profoundly comic—its monkey cooks, virtuosos, painters, and picture lovers are excellent caricatures, full of humor and philosophy. The Turkish Garden actors make terrible game of us, intentionally or not." The popularity of these interludes is reflected in contemporary pictures, toys and *objets d'art*; Charles Rivière's cut-out mechanical pictures are interesting because of their fidelity to the models.

It is nevertheless in the great, full-length pantomimes and mimodramas with their animal stars that the Theatre of Marvels furnished one of the greatest chapters in its history—whether at Astley's in London or Astley's in Paris, Drury Lane and the Royal Coburg in London, the Porte-Saint-Martin or Cirque-Olympique in Paris and the Broadway Theatre in New York.

Henri Martin and his Tiger, Atir. Lithograph by Engelmann, Paris, c. 1844.
". . . one finds the tiger a courtier like the cat . . ."

Van Amburgh in his number at Drury Lane (November 1838). ". . . One might say a father surrounded by his family: the tiger had his arm, the lion, his head; the panther, a leg; the lioness, finally, placed her paw amicably on his shoulder, like a mistress wishing to murmur some little confidence to her lover; nothing could have been more intimate and more cordial . . ."

This untitled lithograph (which might be called "The Courrier of Saint Petersburg," "The Postillion of Longjumeau" or "The English Post," to mention some of the classic titles for the number), presents an equestrian whose gigantic proportions in relation to his horses expresses a child's wonder at the feat itself. Nicétas Périaux of Rouen, publisher of this plate, belongs to a family of printmakers already well-established in the 16th century. One finds in the later lithographs the fantasy of children's drawings and a belief in the miraculous characteristic of the early woodcuts.

Lyon, the third city of France, possessed the second largest centre of popular printmakers and dealers after the rue Saint-Jacques in Paris: the "faubourg de la Guillotière." There is a series of eight oblong plates, without any information other than the editor's name: Pascal à la Guillotière, devoted to the circus. Seven show equestrian numbers and the eighth an acrobat as Jocko, style Mazurier. Thus the date must be some time after 1825—probably about 1840. The pointed index fingers of the "Chinese" equestrians was a typically fashionable exotic touch.

MR CONY AS LANDRI

Published Dec.r 4, 1843 by W.C.WEBB, 19, Cloth Fair, West Smithfield, London.

N.o 1 Horses

BARKHAM CONY, styled "The Dog Star" (Ely 1802—Chicago 1858), first appeared at the Cobourg Theatre, London (1828) in "Love Me, Love My Dog. He made his American debut in 1835 "with a number of well-trained dogs, who assisted in the evening's performance." This consisted of the "Forest of Bondy" (Pixérécourt's "Le Chien de Montargis," English adaptation by William Barrymore) and "The Cherokee Chief" (also titled "The Red Indian"). Two English theatrical portraits—on the left as Pattipaw in "The Red Indian," and on the right as Landri in the "Forest of Bondy," a print by W. C. Webb, London, 1843.

Scene from "The Black Crook," first presented in New York in 1866. It continued on tour almost uninterruptedly until 1909, taken to every part of the United States by road companies, and was revived in Hoboken, N.J. in the 1920s. The costumes and décors were from a Parisian revival of the "Biche au Bois" at the Porte-Saint-Martin in 1865.

MUSIC FROM THE BLACK CROOK.

ELMOTT, FORBRIGER & CO. LITH. CINCINNATI.

GOLDEN REALM
WALTZ.

FAIRY QUEEN MARCH.

GOLDEN REALM
POLKA.

6

7½

6

Published by J.L.PETERS & BRO., Cincinnati.

CINCINNATI.
J J Dobmeyer & Co.

ST LOUIS.
J.J. Dobmeyer & Co.

Entered according to Act of Congress in the year 1866 by J.L.Peters & Bro. in the Clerk's Office of the District Court for the Southern District of Ohio.

Conclusion

His incursion into the Theatre of Marvels in France from 1789 to the 1860s could be carried much farther. For example, does not Romantic drama owe at least as much to the melodramatic formulas of a Pixérécourt as to the masterpieces of Shakespeare? And may not Victor Hugo have written his *Preface to Cromwell* simply in order to liberate his Romantic coterie from the compromising sponsorship of an Arnould-Mussot or a Cuvelier de Trye? Again, without distorting the facts, it was certainly in the miscellaneous repertory of the Boulevard du Crime that the authors of *Monte Cristo* and *Capitaine Fracasse* found certain situations in their novels already assembled and ready for use.

If we have had to go at length into the origins of Romantic ballet and Noverre's influence, and into the feud of Gardel—defender of the chilly allegories inherited from classical mythology—with men like Aumer and Henry who were imbued with the spirit of the Boulevard, the reason is simply that an evolution was taking place at the Opéra identical to that which shook the Comédie Française at the time of *Hernani*.

The Theatre of Marvels was primarily responsible for the revolution in choreography that first appeared at the Porte-Saint-Martin, the Gaîté and the Ambigu. Similarly, it has served some purpose to make a foray into the domain of higher literary criticism in order to show that the Theatre of Marvels is the ancestor of those *féeries* which were once applauded at the Gaîté of the Square des Arts-et-Métiers, and which still delight the Châtelet audiences of today.

A single spirit animated the Theatre of Marvels in all its manifestations, whether melodrama, ballet, pantomime or even the circus or fairground plays whose chief actors were horses, dogs, elephants, monkeys or lions— a spirit which signified a desire to escape from everyday life. During the political and economic upheavals of the 19th century it constituted an art form in which the Western world exhibited a certain optimism, for the moral aspect of its manifestations should not be forgotten.

The great "super-spectacular" productions have often been criticized as lacking in poetry. Yet their special kind of poetry, that which appeals to the eye, inspired such writers as Victor Hugo, Alexandre Dumas and Théophile Gautier.

The latter appreciated the Theatre of Marvels with more perception than any other poet or critic and his reviews constitute a veritable history of what is called "opera for the eye."

The iconography devoted to these spectacles, most of it ephemeral, would be sufficient in itself to indicate their importance, for those thousands of pictures were published because thousands of people wished to keep a record of their rich hours of escapism.

Ever widening its search for contrasts, the Theatre of Marvels resorted to realistic scenes that were interspersed between the exotic locales. This was the beginning of the end: the realistic theatre had but little room for the old magnificence.

Although the influence of Italy, England and Germany on the Theatre of Marvels and its iconography was incontestable, the highly spectacular forms which were French exports throughout the 19th century retained their mark of origin. This is proved by the prints that were exported to the four corners of the globe to the greater glory of the Rue Saint-Jacques.

This visual, unliterary, moral and unrealistic theatre was international and constituted a fundamental source of pleasure for the most diverse classes of society during the first half of the 19th century. It was prolonged into the second half of the century by the splendors of music-hall and circus, and only declined in popularity as the cinema gradually took over its magic. Yet it can never be ousted completely as long as some part of the public prefers its splendors "live" rather than "canned."

The head of that team of designers, composers, machinists, choreographers, actors and dancers whose profession crystallized between 1789 and 1848 into the form as we know it today, carries on much in the original spirit of the period of his evolution. He is still "the Director" and his apotheosis has come with the cinema.

The great French contribution to this Theatre of Marvels was that Frenchmen, subtle artists, went beyond acrobatic feats and made the entire production a coordinated spectacle. Mazurier was admittedly a great acrobat, but above all a mime and a dancer. Similarly, the great performers in the Franconi troupe were not only wonderful horsemen—veritable Centaurs—and jumpers, but also expressive mimes and elegant dancers of a kind rare in the modern circus, for they had been formed in the special schools for circus children, such as those directed by the Chiarini.

But more than all that, the Theatre of Marvels, through the medium of some of its great performances by its best performers, was one of the elements in the immense influence exerted by the artistic capital of the world which was Paris between 1789 and 1860.

Notes

[1] We regret that we can no longer reply to MM. de Manne Ménétrier, who wondered whether the performer who was admired on all the pre-Revolutionary fairground and secondary theatres was the poor white-haired old man crawling along the Boulevard du Temple, nor to M. Péricaud, who confused him with his homonym, a pleasant but negligible character who appeared at the Funambules during the period of Deburau.

[2] It is dated April 26th, 1794. The text adds: "Originally at the Theatre in Paris" (Harvard Theatre Collection).

[3] Their leader was Gabriel Ravel, a rival of Mazurier and a famous rope dancer. In 1856, for its revival of *Le Monstre et Le Magicien (The Monster and the Magician)*, the Porte-Saint-Martin program introduced his brother François as "the celebrated American Mime."

[4] The scenic directions for the first tableau of his *Arcadius* (1852) are an example: "The abode of the Great Spirit of the Indians, a sort of gilt German Gothic hall, closed at the rear by silk curtains." In the same pantomime, which is set in America, he introduces "a chain of mountains, bathed by the Caspian sea." At a quite different level, Victor Hugo in *Mon Enfance (My Childhood)* (1823) refers to the poetry of the names of rivers, mountains and towns; *La Bande Noire* also made a point of accurate local color.

[5] We may mention *Le Juif Errant (The Wandering Jew)*, by Caignez (Théâtre de la Gaîté, 1812), the one by Merville and Mallian (Ambique-Comique, 1834) in which the apotheosis unites Marcus Aurelius, Franklin and Napoleon, and the one by Eugène Sue, based on his novel (Ambigu-Comique, 1849)—"rather a long way from the legend," according to Gautier, but with settings linked to the Marvelous (the Catacombs, the Albigensians, Hell, the Apotheosis, etc.).

[6] It is remarkable that the representation of the center of the earth should be no less fantastic than that of lunar landscapes. As real travels gradually dissipated "the mystery of new worlds and continents," Man inevitably sought escape from his little "prison cell of a world." Hence such experiments as *Nicodème dans la Lune (Nicodemus on the Moon)*, by Cousin Jacques (1790), and several *Arlequin dans la Lune* (Harlequin on the Moon) at the fairground theatres.

[7] The imagination and fantasy of these 18th-century ballet costumes link them to the medieval *Images du Monde*. Thus, for example, Noverre's description of a costume for *Geography* covered with inscriptions: "On the breast and near the heart, *Gallia*, on the belly, *Germania*, on one leg *Italia*, on the fundament *Terra Australia incognita*, on one arm *Hispania*," etc. He mentions the *Winds*, represented with "bellows in their hands, windmills on their heads and feather costumes

to indicate lightness." By Noverre's time, however, these accessories had become banal and standardized and were shortly outmoded. They reappeared in Second Empire costume designs with much of their former brilliance. In short, Rameau's collection of persons, from the four corners of the earth, sing, dance and dress *à la française*. Grétry was the great innovator who transformed the 18th-century exotic style into Romantic exoticism. In this connection mention may be made of his comic ballet *Zémire et Azor* in 1771 and his comic opera *Le Caravane du Caire (The Cairo Caravan)* in 1783.

[8] "The great landscape-architect" wrote Diderot, "has his special enthusiasm; it is a sort of sacred horror. His caves are dark and deep; torrents roar out of them breaking the august silence of his forests from afar. . . If I fix my gaze upon this mysterious imitation of Nature, I tremble." One can almost overhear Pixérécourt's stage directions for *Coelina!*

[9] Victor Hugo himself did not disdain this procedure, for he stated categorically: "Nature sometimes mingles her effects and spectacles and our actions with a kind of somber and intelligent aptness." From the technical point of view, the flashes of lightning during the encounter of Jean Valjean and Monsignor Bienvenue are exactly the same as those scattered broadside by Pixérécourt, Cuvelier, Henry, Aumer and their competitors in the Boulevard theatres.

[10] The definitive edition is that of 1787-89, *Oeuvres Choisies* in ten volumes, with drawings by Marillier which are a part of the pre-Romantic iconography.

[11] This study is not the place to consider the literary themes and psychological problems of nostalgia for "love in the good old days" whether in the feudal castle or the humble villager's cottage. In a mass of more or less indistinguishable scenarios this one is of interest because of its supernatural aspects and extensive decorative requirements.

[12] *L'Enlèvement ou la Caverne des Pyrénées* in 1792, *La Fête de l'Etre Suprème* in 1794, *Les Akansas* followed by *Les Espagnols dans la Floride (The Spaniards in Florida)*, *Le Génie Azouf et les Deux Coffrets (The Jinn Azouf and the Two Coffers)* in 1797, *Les Tentations ou Tous les Diables (Temptations, or All the Devils)* in 1796, etc. The Cité-Variétés theatre was built with the stones of the demolished church of St. Barthélémin.

[13] Thus the frontispiece shows the author wearing a broad-brimmed hat surmounted by an owl and draped in a great cloak from which he is never separated during his appearances in the succeeding illustrations. In some of them he hides his face by raising a cloaked arm to eye level, a classic gesture in melodramatic panto-

mime. The plate showing apprentice surgeons "body-snatching" has a "Gothick" background which resembles any number of Cicéri's stage sets.

[14] *The Castle of Otranto*, according to its author, is a translation of an Italian manuscript discovered in the library of "an old Catholic family in the north of England." This essentially literary artifice was hardly adaptable to the early pantomimes and melodramas, the documentation for which was based rather on archaeological material. In the case of expositions such as those in Pixérécourt, we are closer to the "travels" than to the "Gothick" novel. The stratagem of the "newly-discovered manuscript" is used in the "scientific" *féeries*, but not in an early one such as *Le Magicien et le Monstre* of 1827.

[15] Certain of Noverre's precepts concerning production and direction of crowd scenes are given in our remarks on the Hus family; here it may be said by way of example that he disapproved of the bands of apathetic "supers" at the Opéra who appeared as "warriors"—accoutered with the utmost care, but with hardly a sign of animation. Accustomed as we are to the entire range of realistic costume, the elegant stylizations of the 18th century seem particularly charming. To Noverre and his disciples they had—quite understandably—become flat cliches, often cumbersome and impeding development of the action.

[16] Noverre does not specify whether the pantomimes he mentions are "harlequinades," which incidentally are not in the majority "tasteless" and "uninteresting." He would seem intent on disassociating himself from the popular theatre at all costs.

[17] Noverre was crowned with laurels on the London stage in 1788. The English awarded this honor to only one other choreographer—Perrot, in 1845, after his celebrated *pas de quatre* for the ballerinas Grisi, Taglioni, Grahn and Cerrito.

[18] Daughter of the acrobat Sallé and niece of the celebrated Harlequin-acrobat Francisque, she had a fairground training and also learned much from the more natural style of the English actors observed during her youthful engagements in London. Noverre and Voltaire, among a host of famous men, admired her greatly. Dr. Artur Michel also makes a most convincing case for the Viennese choreographer Franz Hilverding (1710-1768) as a precursor of Noverre, who succeeded him at the Vienna Opera in 1767 and benefited from the Hilverding-trained performers placed at his disposal.

[19] The Franconis associated themselves at an early date with public festivities. At Longchamp, their procession was a veritable advertisement: "All the way along the dusty road, joyous fanfares ring out: it is the equestrian performer Franconi, who has assembled all the musicians of his spectacle in a vast gondola [on wheels], which is followed and preceded by his entire troupe on horseback." This item was taken by the Goncourts from the journal *Le Miroir* (Germinal, Year V). An illustration of the *Fête de la Fondation de la*

République (1st Vendémiaire, Year V), shows a chariot race similar to those which appear in the Franconis' programs.

[20] In an article by Marcel Astruc, Pixérécourt is regarded as a "forerunner of the cinema by virtue of the predominance of the settings and the introduction of crowd scenes on stage." And the author adds: "What a marvelous [film] director this man would no doubt have made!" We entirely agree, but when M. Astruc gives Pixérécourt the credit for having been the first to introduce "crowds of extras" on stage, or for "scenic discoveries which were his alone" it would seem but just to set aside a few garlands to the memory of Noverre and David, and for the secondary theatre generally.

[21] In the first act, the heroine and her father make an entry from a stormy sea in which their vessel is sinking. As early as 1683, *Arlequin Protée (Harlequin Proteus)* shows us Harlequin and Mezzetin coming out of the sea; and this genealogy may be supplemented by a few earlier shipwrecks, such as the one in *Arlequin, Roi de Serendib (Harlequin, King of Serendib)* by Le Sage, and those which occurred at the Tuileries in Servandoni's "mechanical" spectacles.

[22] *Le Chien de Montargis ou La Forêt de Bondy* was one of Pixérécourt's most popular translated works, known by its subtitle: *The Forest of Bondy*. Charles Nodier's account of it is a sympathetic and accurate description. The London production at Covent Garden followed the Paris premiere by a few months within the same year, and was staged by William Barrymore, the great English pantomime director who also worked at La Scala.

[23] Another worldwide success, which Maurice Albert considered as important in destroying Aristotle's unities as Mairet's *Sophonisbe* had been in imposing them. Never did an author put more energy into the scenic production of his work.

[24] *Ondine ou la Nymphe des Eaux* is interesting because of its date. It has so often been stated as historical fact that the ballet *La Sylphide* (Opéra, 1832) created the vogue for supernatural beings of German or Scottish origin—the Romantics set great store in the Nordic provenance of these pale phantoms—that many people have come to believe it. *La Sylphide* actually followed the current vogue for creatures living in elements which human beings could not inhabit. Gratifying this taste, the chief character in the plots of *féeries*, pantomimes and ballets was often a supernatural being tempted by an earthly love, or else a man struggling against hostile elements in pursuit of his non-earthly love. Thus *La Sylphide, La Fille du Danube, Giselle, La Péri, Ondine* (by Perrot in London), and *La Filleule des Fées* did not arrive by chance. J. B. Martin's costume design for "a sylphide" in 1760, and Garnerey's for "*la Sylphide*" in a ballet for *La Mort du Tasse* (opera with libretto by Cuvelier, 1821), are noteworthy. And sylphides had already appeared in Italian ballets, such as *la Silfide* of Arnaldo Cortesi, which preceded that of the Paris Opéra by several years.

[25]   The miniatures of Salome for St. Mark's Gospel, which are simply captioned "She danceth," show her doing a somersault before Herod (13th and 14th centuries). Towards 1788, although Nicolet's troupe consisted mainly of acrobats and rope dancers they were called *Les Grands Danseurs du Roi*.

[26]   In his letters, Stendhal tried vainly to arouse the enthusiasm of his influential friends for the Italian masterpieces. Our wandering choreographers did better. There is a whole volume waiting to be written on the French performers in Italy between 1796 and 1849. The Italian performers had long influenced the popular theatre in Europe, and a strong Italian influence was now felt on the Boulevard staging, due mainly to choreographers-in-exile such as Louis Henry. The early 19th century witnessed a veritable scenographic and choreographic renaissance in Italy. Alessandro Sanquirico and Luigi Basoli, artist-decorators in the great tradition of the Bibbienas and Parigis, collaborated with choreographers such as Salvatore Viganò and Gaetano Gioja.

[27]   Opened on September 27th, 1802; closed by Decree on August 15th, 1807; existed under the name "Jeux-Gymniques" from January 1st, 1810 until June 4th, 1812; closed until December 1814, when it reopened under its old name of Porte-Saint-Martin.

[28]   The Franconi circus built itself a new hall, opened on December 28th, 1827, under the name "Cirque-Olympique" after fire destroyed the old amphitheatre of the Faubourg du Temple.

[29]   He particularly approved of the Théâtre des Jeunes Artistes on the Boulevard du Temple (founded in 1794 in the former Théâtre Français Comique et Lyrique which had been closed by the Decree of 1807): "I saw *La Naissance d'Arelquin ou Arlequin dans un Oeuf (Harlequin's Birth, or Harlequin in an Egg)*, a fairy play enhanced with decorations, dances, singing, pantomime, music, etc., and so well done that even in the large cities of Germany such a play, so produced, would have attracted many people."

[30]   Arnould-Mussot died in 1795, two years before the enormous vogue for Robertson and the Supernatural in general.

[31]   Auguste Hus II (Turin 1769—Paris 1829), called "the buffoon of the age," first obtained the post of dancer at the Court of Turin, previously held by his father. In 1792 he arrived in France as a fanatical revolutionary, gave up dancing and devoted himself to the production of countless political pamphlets of all complexions, for he later changed politics several times. Pierre Hus was well known in Italy, where his name appeared on the scenarios of ballets staged in Naples between 1811 and 1827. Auguste Hus III, probably Pierre's son, formed the triumvirate of choreographers at the *carnevale e quaresima* in Milan in 1848 with Jules Perrot and Andrea Palladini. In 1852-3, "Signor Augusto Hus" was "*Maestro de perfezionamento e dirigente de la Scuola di Ballo*" at Milan. They were an Italianized French family which played a fairly important part in cultural relations between the two countries.

[32]   Although *Estelle et Némorin* "a pastoral melodrama interspersed with dances," by Gabiot de Salina (Ambigu-Comique, 1788), was one of the first plays described as melodramas.

[33]   From December 1st onwards, the *Moniteur Universel* advertised "Shortly, a Ballet by M. Perrot, *La Esméralda*, for the First Performance of Mmes Scolti and Comba and of M. Paul." In this review Gautier noted one of the reasons for development of the full-length fairy play to fill an evening at the theatre, instead of the *ballet d'action* presented as a supplement to melodramas.

[34]   A technique which she soon mastered herself. Mlle Brugnoli was an Italian-trained ballerina who was already celebrated at Naples and Milan. She became more widely known after she had married the choreographer Samengo.

[35]   Hitherto, historians of ballet such as Mr. C. W. Beaumont have stated that *Jenny ou Le Mariage Secret* was Aumer's first *ballet d'action* as contrasted with the *divertissement* ballets created for melodramas. However, on March 6th, 1805, *Rosina et Lorenzo ou Les Gondoliers Vénitiens (Rosina and Lorenzo, or The Venetian Gondoliers)*, a one-act pantomime-ballet with music by Darondeau, seems to have had that honor. We mention it simply for the record, as the scenario has not come down to us. *Jenny ou Le Mariage Secret*, presented at the Porte-Saint-Martin on March 20th, 1806, was revived most successfully at the Panorama-Dramatique in 1823.

[36]   The name is written alternatively "Henri," and "Henry," but the latter spelling appears on most of the scenarios and documents; we shall therefore write "Henry," in accordance with normal usage, except for quotations in which the other form appears.

[37]   And others as well: Richard, ballet-master at the Cité-Variétés in 1796-1797, according to the *Indicateur dramatique*, whose début at the Opéra brought him nothing but trouble, became ballet-master at the Ambigu-Comique; he engaged Mérante (pupil of that Borda who was a *figurant* at the Opéra and former Boulevard ballet-master) as *premier danseur*. Aumer happened to attend a performance of the melodrama *Le Grand Chasseur ou L'Ile des Palmiers (The Great Hunter, or The Isle of Palms)*, with ballets by Richard, saw the young Mérante and was impressed. Aumer engaged him to star in his first ballet at the Porte-Saint-Martin. The Opéra now cast covetous glances at Mérante but to no avail. It is obvious how envenomed the situation had become; revolt was brewing against the potentate of the Opéra, and a dazzling and speedy revenge was to be expected.

[38]   He was the founder of the *Journal des Comédiens* (1829-43) and the *Moniteur des Théâtres* (1836-42).

[39] *Jean-Jean ou Les Bonnes d'Enfants (Jean-Jean, or The Nursemaids)*, a two-act pantomime-ballet by Blache and Mazurier (together with Léopold Chandezon and Hector Boirie). First performed at the Porte-Saint-Martin on August 13th, 1824.

[40] A comedy by Régnard, in Gherardi's *Théâtre Italien*. Similarly, Frère Ménétrier in his *Traité des Ballets Anciens et Modernes* (1682), refers to the solemnities of the beatification of St Ignatius Loyola. On the second day (February 1st, 1610) the ceremonies were enlivened by a ballet of young children disguised as male and female monkeys and parrots.

[41] Circus historians claim that Mazurier, like Grimaldi, was an acrobatic clown (neither ever appeared in the ring). References to him will be found in Thétard, Rémy, etc. Actually, his creation *Jocko* was revived in the circus by Auriol and Klischnigg from 1840 on, and by lesser figures from the time of its first appearance.

[42] In the cast we find the Bartholomins and Hypolite (Monplaisir), who made a triumphal tour of America in 1847; Benoni also went to America, and Ragaine was ballet-master at the Porte-Saint-Martin during the same period.

[43] The supposition that good will triumph over evil is always upheld in the popular arts; this same *tableau vivant: La Justice et la Vengeance Poursuivant le Crime (Justice and Vengeance Pursuing Crime)* appears in *Mandrin* (1827) and in a film by Méliès in 1908, *La Civilisation à Travers les Ages (Civilization Through the Ages)*.

[44] We regret that we cannot reproduce Gautier's summaries in full and that they are only referred to here. In order to follow the development which was completed in the important works falling between 1830 and 1850, scenarios of *Les Chevaliers du Soleil, Le Château Infernal, Le Petit Poucet*, etc., had to be mentioned at some length—they were less inspired, but are indispensable to the Theatre of Marvels.

[45] Around 1937, the historians Y. Slonimsky in Russia, C. W. Beaumont in England and G. Chaffee in America, independently of one another, started studies designed to rehabilitate Perrot. In *Giselle, Apothéose du Ballet Romantique*, Serge Lifar has made the soundest study of the ballet itself.

[46] The Risleys, as well as certain acrobatic troupes such as the Rappos, Zanfrettas, Chiarinis and Ravels, produced this type of hybrid ballet, especially in Italy, England and America.

[47] In his *Histoire du Ballet Russe* (Nagel, Paris, 1950), Serge Lifar alleges that "Perrot seems to have had a great deal to do with" the choreography of *La Tarentule (The Tarantula)*, "attributed to Coralli when it was created at the Opéra." The fact that this ballet was first performed in June 1839, when Perrot was in London, and long before his triumphant return in *Le Zingaro*, seems to prove that he was not concerned in its creation. Lifar undeviatingly duplicates Slonimsky's efforts to enhance Perrot's reputation at the expense of his colleagues. He assigns sole authorship of the ballet *Marco-Bomba* (St. Petersburg, 1854) to Perrot, although Jean Petipa had already composed a ballet of the same title and subject matter in 1839 which was presented on his American tour after try-outs in Brussels.

[48] "*Mines* are the great topical item in our current theatre; on the Boulevards people talk of nothing but *The Polish Mines* (of Pixérécourt); *The Mines of Coberbergt* at the Marais; and *The Mines of Dalécarlie;* whoever delivers the most terrifying, most picturesque underground scene is the sure winner." (*Le Courrier des Spectacles*, 25 Thermidor An XI)

[49] In 1935 Mr. Billy Rose attempted to revive performances of this sort. His first—and last—experiment, *Jumbo*, was a brilliant success, with an elephant star, and all the trimmings of dancing, acrobatics, song, scenery and staging. Although there were full houses at the New York Hippodrome, the cost of maintaining a menagerie, horses and riders, a tremendous cast, scene shifters and the rest of the backstage personnel, did not permit him to make both ends meet. Transportation costs prevented taking the show on the road, and Mr. Rose had to close it with a deficit. Those privileged to have seen *Jumbo* on stage will always cherish the memory. (A disappointing film of the same title, based on the stage production, was shown a few years ago.)

Between 1914 and 1925, the French tamer, Georges Marck, produced two or three mimodramas in which his lions performed.

[50] This reconciliation and submission of beast to man was something which fascinated writers such as Balzac, Banville and above all Théophile Gautier, who expounds a theory both amusing and fantastical: ". . . . For it is every animal's dream to become Man's partner, and we are a source of astonishment and concern to them; our cities, ships and machines leave them in a state of admiring stupefaction; the light of thought which shines in our eyes fascinates and dazzles them; they would like to enter into communication with us and ask us to supplement their instinct. They find the idea of a higher existence vaguely disquieting, and they wish to attain it. We produce the same effect on them as the gods would produce on us should they come down to earth."

[51] In Cuvelier's "equestrian prose," as his contemporaries called it, there are a bombast of style and a naivete of sentiment analogous to the texts which told a tale in four parts for the popular prints from the rue Saint-Jacques (each subject was issued in a series of four plates).

[52] Cf. Cuvelier's *C'est le Diable ou la Bohémienne*. There is also a connection with the "*Schicksal-tragodien*" and certain English novels in which the "nemesis which will punish the guilty is suspended like the sword of Damocles during the entire action." *Le Moine* by Camille Saint-Aubin (Théâtre de l'Emulation, Decem-

ber 27th, 1797, revived in 1802 at the Gaîté) had a scene in Hell very similar to that of *Le Cheval du Diable.*

[53] In the "scientific" fantasies *à la* Jules Verne, the North Pole would figure in the scenic repertory.

[54] It was actually the Théâtre des Singes of Jacopo Corvi (1815-1890), father of the Ferdinand Corvi whose booth was one of the great attractions of Paris fairgrounds between 1872 and 1914.

[55] In *Le Pays d'Or* (1892) for example, the beautiful Mlle Cassive, then at the beginning of her career, crossed Niagara on a tightrope in imitation of the famous Blondin.

[56] This curious text appears under the print of Louis Henry's ballet: "Some scenes from *le Bal Masqué,* a ballet by M. L. Henry performed for the first time in Milan during the 1830 Carneval. This is an exact copy of a print which was published in Milan in 1830,

right after the first performances of M. Henry's ballet. One can instantly see that M. Taglioni has taken over this work and inserted it in *Gustave III;* he hasn't overlooked the Allemande, the Follies, and the double masquerade of the Minuet and Savoyard which formed part of M. Henry's ballet. M. Taglioni, who has followed the same practice with the creations of many other choreographers, passed himself off as the author. We are informed that M. Taglioni has in hand a new work comprising: (1) Part of *La Belle Arsène,* a ballet by M. Henry performed at Naples in 1818 and Vienna in 1823, in which M. Taglioni himself danced and his daughter played the part of "The Prude"; (2) the Revolt and the warrior dances from *The Amazons,* a ballet by M. Henry performed in Vienna during 1823, in which Mlle Taglioni danced; and (3) a rifle drill performed by women, scene from the 3rd act of the *Ballet des Grecs (Ballet of the Greeks* (vs the Turks)) by M. Blache *fils,* performed at Bordeaux, in which Mlle Taglioni danced at a special performance in 1829. . . . Time will reveal many other thefts. (1 November 1833, Paris, at the Print Dealers)"

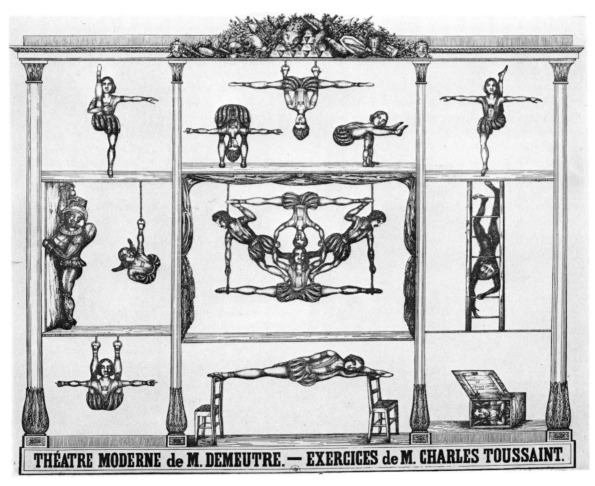

THÉÂTRE MODERNE de M. DEMEUTRE. — EXERCICES de M. CHARLES TOUSSAINT.

Bibliography

ABBEVILLE (Claude d').—*Histoire de la Mission des Pères Capuchins.* Huby, Paris, 1614.

ALBERT (Maurice).—*Les Théâtres de la Foire* (1660-1789). Hachette, Paris, 1900. *Les Théâtres des Boulevards* (1789-1868). Société française d'Imprimerie, Paris, 1902.

ALLEVY (M. A.).—*La Mise en scène en France dans la première moitié du XIXᵉ siècle.* Droz, Paris, 1938.

ASTRUC (Marcel).—*Guilbert de Pixérécourt ou Le Mélodrame.* In Vogue, Paris, May, 1950.

ATKINSON (G.).—*The Extraordinary Voyage in French Literature from 1700-1750.* Champion, Paris, 1922.

B . . . nee de V . . . (Mme).—*Le Cirque-Olympique ou Les Exercices des chevaux de MM. Franconi, du Cerf Coco et du Cerf Azor, de l'Eléphant Baba, etc.* . . . Nepveu, Paris, 1817.

BACULARD D'ARNAUD (F. T. M.).—*Oeuvres dramatiques.* Amsterdam, 1782. Two volumes.

BANVILLE (Théodore de).—*Préface aux Mémoires des Hanlon-Lees.* Paris.

BAPST (Germain).—*Essai sur l'Histoire des Panoramas et des Dioramas.* Masson, Paris, 1891.

BARBA (J. N.).—*Souvenirs.* Ledoyen et Giret, Paris, 1846.

BEAULIEU (Henri).—*Les Théâtres du Boulevard du Crime* (1752-1862). Daragon, Paris, 1904.

BEAUMONT (C. W.).—*The Complete Book of Ballets.* London, Beaumont, 1937. *The Ballet called Giselle.* London, Beaumont, 1941.

BERTARELLI (A.) and ARRIGONI (P.)—*Rittrati di Musicisti ed artisti di Theatro conservati nella Raccolta delle Stampe.* Catalogo descrittivo. Typo. del Popolo d'Italia, 1934, in-8°
Biographie des Ecuyers et Ecuyeres du Théâtre National du Cirque-Olympique, par un flâneur. Ancienne maison Barba, Paris, 1846.

BOUCHOT (Henri).—*Le Luxe français: l'Empire.* A la Librairie illustrée, Paris, n.d. *Le Luxe français: la Restauration.* Bibliothèque Illustrée, Paris, 1893. *Cabinet des Estampes: Guide des collections,* etc. Dentu, Paris, 1895. *Catalogue des dessins relatifs à l'histoire du théâtre.* B.N. Cabinet des Estampes. E. Bouillon, Paris, 1896.

BRAZIER (Nicolas).—*Chronique des petits théâtres de Paris.* Republiée avec notice, variantes et notes par Georges d'Heylli. Rouveyre, Paris, 1883. Two volumes.

CAMBIASI (P).—*La Scala* (1778-1889). Note storiche e statistiche. Milan, G. Riccordi.

CAMPARDON (Emile)—*Les Spectacles de la Foire.* Berger-Levrault, Paris, 1877. Two volumes.

CASTIL-BLAZE.—*L'Académie Impériale de Musique.* Castil-Blaze, Paris, 1855. Two volumes.
Catalogue des oeuvres dramatiques et lyriques faisant partie du répertoire de la Société des Auteurs. A. Guyot, Paris, 1863.

CHAALONS D'ARGE.—*Histoire critique des Théâtres de Paris pendant 1821-1822.* Lelong, Delannay, Paris,

1822. Two volumes.

CHAFFEE (George).—*Three or Four Graces, a centerary Salvo with Catalogue of the French Souvenir Lithographs (and varia) of the Romantic Ballet.* In Dance Index, vol. III, nos. 9, 10, 11, New York, 1944.

CHALLAMEL (A.).—*Album de l'Opéra.* Paris, Challamel, 1844.

CHASLES (P.), ed.—*Les Beautés de l'Opéra.* Soulié, Paris, 1845. (With articles by Th. Gautier and J. Janin. This book, published in installments during the year 1844 and bound for the day of the Year, etc., has an equally fantastic pagination.)

CHINARD (Gilbert).—*L'Amérique et le Rêve exotique.* Hachette, Paris, 1913.

COLAS (R.).—*Bibliographie générale du costume et de la mode.* R. Colas, Paris, 1933. Two volumes.

COURTIRAS (Gabrielle-Anne, called comtesse DASH). —*Mémoires des Autres.* Lib. III, Paris, 1895. Six volumes.

DAGUERRE.—*Historique et Description des procédés du Daguerreotype et du Diorama.* Susse, Paris, 1839.

DELAFOREST (M. A.).—*Théâtre moderne; cours de Littérature dramatique* (1822-1836). Allardin, Paris, 1836. Two volumes.

DEPPING (G. W.).—*Merveilles de la Force et de l'Adresse.* Hatchette, Paris, 1871.

DIDEROT (Denis).—*Oeuvres.* Garnier, Paris, 1875.

DOUAI (G.).—*Répertoire général de toutes les pièces représentées sur les théâtres de Paris.* (General repertory of all the plays represented on the Paris stage). Manuscript. Fonds Rondel, Arsenal.

DOWD (J. L.)—*David, Pageant Master of the French Revolution.* Univ. of Nebraska Studies, no. 3, June, 1948.

DUBECH (L.) and HORN-MONVAL (M.).—*Histoire générale du théâtre.* Plon, Paris, 1931-1934. Five volumes.

DUCHARTRE (P.-L.) and SAULNIER (R.).—*L'Imaégrie parisienne.* Gründ, Paris, 1944.

EINSTEIN (A.).—*Music in the Romantic Era.* Holt, New York, 1947.

ENGEL (J. J.).—*Idées sur le geste et l'action théâtrale.* Translated from the German (Ideen zu einer Mimik.) With 34 plates. Jansen, Paris, An III. Two volumes.

ESTREE (Paul d')—*Le Théâtre sous la Terreur* (1739-1794). Emile-Paul frères, Paris, 1913.

FILIPPI (J. de).—*Essai d'une bibliographie générale du Théâtre* (an extension of the celebrated Soleinne Catalogue). Tresse, Paris, 1861.

FISCHER (Carlos)—*Les Costumes de l'Opéra.* Librairie de France, Paris, 1931.

FOURNEL (V.).—*Le Vieux Paris: Fêtes, Jeux et Spectacles.* Mame, Tours, 1887.
Galérie Biographique des Artistes dramatiques des Théâtres royaux.—Première livraison. L'Académie Royale de Musique. Ponthieu, Paris, 1826.

GAUTIER (Théophile).—*Histoire de l'Art dramatique en France depuis vingt-cinq ans.* Hetzel, Bruxelles, 1858-1859. Six volumes.

MSS. GENTIL —*Les Cancans de l'Opéra en 1836.* (Mss note describes this as "Extracts from the diary of a wardrobe mistress concerning matters which came to her attention during the year 1836" (until 1838, actually). Opéra Réserve 658:1-5.

GEOFFROY (J. L.).—*Cours de Littérature dramatique.* Blanchard, Paris, 1819-1820. Five volumes.

GEREON (L.).—*La Rampe et les Coulisses.* Marchands de Nouveautés, Paris, 1832.

GINISTY (Paul)—*Le Mélodrame.* Michaud, Paris, 1910. *La Féerie.* Michaud, Paris, 1910. *Le Théâtre de la rue.* Morance, Paris, 1925.

GOEDEKE.—*Grundriss zur Geschichte der deutschen Dichtung.* Elfter Band. Drama und Theater von 1815 bis 1830. Verlag Ehlermann, Düsseldorf (1952-1953). 2 Halband. Lief. 1 (Bogen 108). 2 Auflage.

GOIZET (M.).—*Table générale du catalogue de la bibliothèque dramatique de M. de Soleinne.* Adm. de l'Alliance des Arts, Paris, 1845.

GONCOURT (E. and J. de).—*Histoire de la Société française pendant le Directoire.* Nouv. Ed. G. Charpentier, Paris, 1880.

GOT (Edmond).—*Journal.* Édité par Médéric Got. Plon-Nourrit. Paris, 1910.

Grand Dictionnaire du XIXᵉ siecle. Ed. P. Larousse, 1866-1876, Paris, fifteen volumes.

GRILLE (J. F.).—*Les Théâtres.* Aymery et Delaunay, Paris, 1817.

GRIMM (F. M.) and others—*Correspondance littéraire.* Ed. Tourneux, Paris, 1872. Sixteen volumes.

HALL (L. A.).—*Catalogue of Dramatic Portraits in the Theatre Collection,* Harvard College Library. Harvard University Press, Cambridge, Mass, 1930-1934. Four volumes.

HAREL (F. A.).—*Dictionnaire théâtral ou 1233 vérités.* Barba, Paris, 1824.

HARTOG (W.).—*Guilbert de Pixérécourt.* Champion, Paris, 1914.

HENRY-LECOMTE (L.).—*Histoire des Théâtres de Paris. Les Jeux-Gymniques (1810-1812). Le Panorama Dramatique (1821-1823).* Daragon, Paris, 1908.

HILLEMACHER (F.).—*Le Cirque-Olympique.* Perrin et Marinet, Lyon, 1875.

Indicateur dramatique ou Almanach des Théâtres de Paris. Lefort. Malherbes (sic.), An VII, Paris.

Indicateur général des Spectacles de Paris. Par A. . . . et D. . . . Troisième année. Marchands de Nouveautés, Paris, 1822.

JACOUBET (H.).—*Le Genre Troubadour et les Origines françaises du Romantisme.* "Les Belles Lettres," Paris, 1929.

JANIN (Jules).—*Histoire de la Littérature dramatique.* Lévy, Paris, 1853-1858. Six volumes.

KOTZEBUE (A.).—*Souvenirs de Paris en 1804.* Barba, Paris, 1805.

LACROIX (P. L.).—called the *Bibliophile Jacob. Bibliothéque dramatique de M. de Soleinne.* Adm. de l'Alliance des Arts, Paris, 1843-1844. Five volumes.

LAFITAU (Pere)—*Moeurs des Sauvages américains comparées aux moeurs des Premiers Temps.* Paris, 1724.

LANSON (R.).—*Le gout du moyen age en France au XVIIIᵉ siècle.* Paris. Bruxelles. G. Van-Oest, 1926.

LAVEDAN (P.).—*L'Architecture française.* Larousse, Paris, 1944.

LE SAGE (Rene) and DORNEVAL.—*Le Théâtre de la Foire.* Gandouin, Paris, 1737. Nine volumes.

LEVINSON (A.).—*Le Ballet romantique.* Ed. Trianon, Paris, 1931. *Préface aux Lettres de Jean-Georges Noverre.* Paris, 1927.

LIFAR (Serge).—*Carlotta Grisi.* Albin Michel, Paris, n.d. (1941). *Giselle, apothéose du ballet romantique.* Albin Michel, Paris, 1942. *Notes,* in *Le Ballet et la Danse a l'époque romantique (1800-1850).* Musée des Arts Decoratifs, Paris, 1942.

LYONNET (H.).—*Dictionnaire des Comédiens français (Ceux d'Hier). Biographie, bibliographie et iconographie.* E. Jorel, Paris, n.d. (1904). Two volumes.

MAINDRON (E.).—*Le Champ de Mars (1751-1889).* Baschet, Lille; Danel, Paris, 1889.

DE MANNE and MENETRIER.—*Galerie historique des Comédiens de la Troupe de Nicolet.* N. Scheuring, Lyon, M D CCC LXIX. Two volumes.

MAURICE (C.).—*Histoire anecdotique du théâtre, de la littérature, etc.* Principaux libraries, Paris, 1856. Two volumes.

Melpomène et Thalie vengées ou Nouvelle Critique impartiale et raisonnée, tant des différents théâtres de Paris que des pièces qui y ont été représentées. Deuxième année. Marchand, An VII, Paris.

Mémoires secrets. De Bachaumont and others. London, 1777-1789.

MICHAUT (Pierre).—*Histoire du ballet.* Presses Universitaires de France, Paris, 1948.

MONGLAND (Andre).—*La France révolutionnaire et impériale. Annales de Bibliographie méthodique et Descriptions des Livres illustrés.* Ed. B. Arthaud, Grenoble, 1930 (and ff.). Six volumes.

MORNET (Daniel).—*Le Romantisme en France au XVIIIᵉ siècle.* Hachette, Paris, 1912.

MOYNET (M. J.).—*L'Envers du Theatre.* Hachette, Paris, 1875.

NODIER (Charles).—In *La Revue de Paris,* T. XIX, no. 1, July, 1835.

NOVERRE (Jean-Georges).—*Lettres sur la danse.* Stuttgart, 1760.

ODELL (G.).—*Annals of the New York Stage.* Columbia University Press. N.Y.

PERCHEVAL (Maurice).—*La Tradition gothique dans l'imagerie populaire.* Olliver, Cayeux-sur-Mer, 1908.

PERICAUD (Louis).—*Le Théâtre des Funambules.* Sapin, Paris, 1897.

PILLET (Fabien) and others.—*La Nouvelle Lorgnette des Spectacles.* Barba, Paris. An IX.

PIXERECOURT (G. de).—*Théâtre choisi.* (Preface by Charles Nodier). Chez l'Auteur. Nancy, 1841. Four volumes.

PRUNIERES (Henry).—*Salvatore Vigano,* in *La Revue Musicale.* December, 1921.

QUERARD (M.) and others.—*Supercheries littéraires.* Daffis, Paris, 1869. Two volumes.

REMY (Tristan).—*Les Clowns.* Grasset, Paris, 1945.
ROBERT-HOUDIN.—*Magie et Physique amusantes.* Calmann-Levy, Paris, 1898.
ROBERTSON (E. G.).—*Mémoires récréatifs, scientifiques et anecdotiques de Physicien-aéronaute.* Paris, chez l'Auteur, 1831. Two volumes.
RONDEL (A.).—*Catalogue analytique sommaire de la collection théâtrale Rondel.* Berger-Levrault, Paris, 1932.
ROSENTHAL (L.).—*Du Romantisme au Réalisme.* Laurens, Paris, 1914.

SAINT-LEON (Arthur).—*La Sténochorégraphie ou Art d'écrire promptement la danse . . . Avec la biographie et le portrait des plus célèbres maîtres de ballets anciens et modernes de l'école française et italienne.* Paris, chez l'Auteur, rue des Martyrs, 58, 1852. Two volumes.
SAPIN (Léon).—*Catalogue de la bibliothèque théâtrale de Léon Sapin.* A Voisin, Paris, 1877.
SIMOND (Charles).—*La Vie parisienne au XIXe siècle.* Paris, 1901-1903. Three volumes.
SLONIMSKY (Y.).—*Jules Perrot.* Trans. by A. Chujoy, in *Dance Index*, T. IV, no. 12, 1945.
STENDHAL.—*Correspondance* (1800-1842). Paris. (Préface by Maurice Barrès), 1908. Five volumes.

THETARD (Henry).—*Les Dompteurs.* Gallimard, Paris, 1928. *La Merveilleuse Histoire du Cirque.* Prisma, Paris, 1947. Three volumes.

VAILLAT (Léandre).—*Marie Taglioni.* Albin Michel, Paris, 1942.
VAN BELLEN (E. C.).—*Les Origines du mélodrame.* Utrecht, n.d. n.p. Paris, Nizet et Bastard, 1933.
VERON (L.).—*Mémoires d'un Bourgeois de Paris.* Gonet, Paris, 1866 (T. III).
VIGNIE (Pierre).—*La Couleur locale au théâtre classique et romantique,* in the *Mercure de France,* Volume 199, Paris, 1927.

WINTER (M. H.).—*American Theatrical Dancing* (1750-1800), in *Musical Quarterly,* vol. XXIV, no. 1, January 1938, New York. *Theatre of Marvels,* in *Dance Index,* vol. VII, No. 1, 2, 1948, New York. *Le Théâtre du Merveilleux,* in *Opéra, Ballet Music-Hall,* no. 1, 1952, Oliver Perrin, Paris.

FILES in the FONDS RONDEL, *Bibliothèque de l'Arsenal, Paris*
  Le Théâtre de la Porte Saint-Martin
  Le Théâtre de la Gaîté
  Le Théâtre de l'Ambigu-Comique
  Le Panorama-Dramatique
  Le Cirque-Olympique
  Le Théâtre Nautique (or Théâtre Ventadour).

NEWSPAPERS AND MAGAZINES
  L'Album, 1e serie: 1821-1823, 2e serie: 1828-1829
  L'Album des Théâtres, 1836-1837
  L'Artiste, 1re serie: 1831-1841, 2e serie: 1842-1855
  Le Charivari, 1832-1850
  Le Corsaire, 1822-1852
  Le Coureur des Spectacles, 1842-1849
  Le Diable boiteux, 1823-1825
  L'Entracte lyonnais
  La Gazette des Théâtres, 1831
  L'Illustration, 1843
  Le Journal des Modes
  Le Journal des Théâtres, 1821-1829
  La Lorgnette, 1824-1826
  Le Ménestral (journal de Musique)
  Le Miroir des Spectacles, 1821-1823
  La Mode
  Le Monde dramatique, 1835-1841
  Le Moniteur des Théâtres, 1836-1842
  La Pandore, 1823-1830
  La Revue du Théâtre, 1834-1838
  La Silhouette, 1830-1850
  L'Union des Arts

ICONOGRAPHY
(A Selection of Series)

Album de l'Opéra (1st), published by Gault de Saint-Germain, Laederich et Senez, Paris, 1832.
Album de l'Opéra (2nd) ("Principal scenes and most outstanding settings of the best works performed at the Academy of Music"). Published by Challamel. Drawn by MM. Alophe, Challamel, Celestin Deshays, A. Deveria, Français, Lepaulle, Mouilleron and Célestin Nanteuil. Paris. Edited by Challamel circa 1844.
Les Annales de l'Opéra or "Collection of the premières danseuses." Lithographs by Desmaisons after Guerard Paris. Bulla et Delarue. Printed by Lemercier (twelve plates, 1844).
Besondere Bilderbeilage zur Theaterzeitung 1836. Zu haben in Wien im Bureau der Theaterzeitung, Wollzeil no. 780, Vienna.

Bild zur Wiener Allegemeinen Zeitung. Im Bureau der Wiener Allegemeinen Zeitung, 926, Rauhensteingasse. Vienna, circa 1848.
Cirque National des Champs-Elysées (6 plates). *Hippodrome National* (6 plates). *Hippodrome National-Camp du Drap d'Or* (6 plates). These 18 plates, all by Victor Adam, are in the great series on horsemanship which he drew for Jeannin who published them from 1842 through 1847. Lemercier, Benard & Cie. were the lithographers.
Collection de portraits des Artistes des Théâtres de Paris. ("Drawn and lithographed from life by Colin.") Paris, Francisque Noël, 1823-1825 (Folio)
Costume Bilder zur Theaterzeitung (These plates were given to subscribers to the magazine "Allegemeine Thea-

terzeitung und Originalblatt für Kunst, Literatur, Musik, Mode und geselliges Leben"—first number appeared on January 1, 1835). Bureau der Theaterzeitung Rauhensteingasse No. 926. Vienna.

Galerie des Artistes dramatiques. ("Composed of eighty portraits and biographical notices"). Paris. Marchan, n.d. (about 1842). Two volumes.

Galerie dramatique: Costumes des théâtres de Paris, by MM. Dollet, Lacauchie and L. Lasalle. Paris, Maison Martinet-Hautecoeur, frères. Imp. J. Rigo et Cie, 1844-1870. Ten volumes.

Gallerie Drolliger Scenen (also appears under titles: *Gallerie drolliger und interessanten Scenen* and *Gallerie interessanten und drolliger Scenen*). 1826-1833. Vienna.

Galerie Théâtrale or ("Collection of full-length portraits of the principal actors of the first three theatres of the capital"). Paris, chez Bance, 1812-1834. Three volumes.

Les Gloires de l'Opéra: Poses et Portraits des Principales Danseuses de Paris et de Londres. Paris, Aubert et Cie, ed. Journal des Modes, Paris. Imp. d'Aubert et Cie, 1845-1846 (Album demi-folio).

L'Hippodrome au Coin du Feu. (Series of sixteen lithographs) by Victor Adam. Aubert et Cie. 1847.

Loisirs. By V. Adam. Paris. Published by Jeannin, printed by Lemercier, Bernard et Cie, 1837-1840. Series of four plates of the "Cirque des Champs-Elysées."

Petite Galerie dramatique ou Receuil des différents costumes d'acteurs des Théâtres de la Capitale . . . Paris. Martinet (later Martinet-Hautecoeur), rue du Coq No. 15. First series (1796-1843). Sixteen Volumes.

Prämien Bilder Zur Theaterzeitung. Vienna. 1830. (Specialized in scenes from melodramas).

Recueil des costumes de tous les ouvrages dramatiques répresentés avec succès sur les grands théâtres de Paris. Ed. Augustin Vizentini, à Paris, chez Martinet, libraire, 1819-1827.

Scenen aus Wien. Zu haben in Wien im Bureau der Theaterzeitung, Rauhensteingasse no. 906 (sic. 926?), circa 1840.

Theatralische Bilder-Gallerie. Vienna, 1834-1836. (For the greater part reproduces plates from the series *Gallerie Drolliger Scenen.*)

The following libraries have been consulted: Paris: the Bibliothèque Nationale (Cabinet des Estampes), the Opéra, the Musée des Arts Décoratifs, the Musée Carnavalet, the Fonds Rondel of the Arsenal; Vienna: Osterreichische National Bibliotek; Turin: Biblioteca Civica; Parma: Biblioteca Palatina; Milan: Biblioteca Teatrale Livia Simoni alla Scala, and Coll. Bertarelli, Castello Sforzesco; Harvard Theatre Collection, Cambridge, Mass.; London: Enthoven Collection, Victoria and Albert Museum; New York: Dance Division, NY Public Library.

Index to Names

Index of Ballets and Plays